X-mAs 1991

D0392613

# Bud Wilkinson

## *An Intimate Portrait of an American Legend*

**Jay Wilkinson**
with
**Gretchen Hirsch**

SAGAMORE PUBLISHING
Champaign, IL

Production Manager: Susan M. McKinney
Cover design: Michelle R. Dressen and Amy L. Todd
Insert design: Amy L. Todd
Proofreader: Phyllis L. Bannon


ISBN: 1-57167-001-7
Library of Congress Catalog Card Number: 94-67277

Every effort has been made to trace the ownership of copyrighted photos. If we have failed to give adequate credit, we will be pleased to make changes in future printings.

Printed in the United States.

*To Rita*

*and to*

*Kirsten, Holly, P.J. and Julie*

---

# Contents

# Acknowledgments

When I first started this book, I was naive about the amount of time required to complete such an enormous project. In the early stages, before I began the intense drafting and interviews, a few people gave me the confidence, encouragement and motivation to commit to the completion of the project. I thank Terry Kahn, Chris Schenkel, Bill Myles, Bill Welter, Walter Hailey and Steve Bull for their support prior to and during the embryonic stages of the book.

The members of my immediate family—my mother, Mary; my brother, Pat; my wife, Rita; my daughters, Kirsten and Holly; and Donna Wilkinson also lent encouragement as well as considerable background material.

Special thanks to Ned Hockman for his recollections and for many of the pictures that appear in the book. Thanks also to Mike Treps, former Sports Information Director at the University of Oklahoma, who allowed me to quote extensively from interviews he conducted with Dad.

I am grateful to Bill Carmack and Dick Snider, not only for background information, but also for their editorial suggestions as the project took shape.

I want to thank all those whose comments appear in the book. Their enthusiastic response to my requests for interviews was overwhelming. Their contributions give the book much greater dimension and depth. I also appreciate the time and interest of those whose comments were not included.

I thank my assistant, Cathy Baker, who not only lent encouragement and support, but also spent countless hours typing and retyping drafts and interviews.

Finally, I commend my collaborator and friend, Gretchen Hirsch, who was recommended to me by our priest, Michael Jupin. Terry Kahn told me early in the project, "Jay, you don't want to write the book at all unless it's going to be a good book." It never could have been completed in its present form without Gretchen's professional skills, for which I remain most grateful.

# Preface

For several years, I encouraged my Dad to share all the diverse aspects of his life in an autobiography. Although he was well known as a football coach, his accomplishments and interests ranged far beyond sports, and I thought many Americans would be interested in a whole-life perspective on this outstanding man—what made him "tick" and how he became such a success in so many different fields of endeavor, from sports to politics to broadcasting to business.

When I realized his health was such that the autobiography would never be written, I decided to tell the story myself, from my vantage point as Bud's son. The book is not a scholarly treatise on Dad's career, but an affectionate and, I hope, a balanced picture of the man as I knew him.

My plan was to complete the book, if possible, prior to Dad's death. That didn't happen. However, the project was well underway before his final illness, and I am glad I was able to read many of the chapters to him. He was emotionally moved by the memories contained in the various stories, and that in itself made the entire project worthwhile.

Jay Wilkinson
Columbus, Ohio
April 15, 1994

# Foreword

Forty-seven straight victories.

For all the contributions Bud Wilkinson made to college football—and he made plenty, in particular the class way he represented himself and the University of Oklahoma—none will be better remembered than the record forty-seven-game winning streak compiled by his Sooners in the '50s.

I'll never forget where I was when it ended.

Notre Dame played Oklahoma in Norman on November 16, 1957. I was in Kalamazoo, Michigan, that day, playing for Kent State against a Western Michigan team that beat us in what turned out to be my last football game. I was stepping onto the bus when someone told us Notre Dame had beaten Oklahoma 7-0. I had knee surgery that next spring and never played football again, so I've always remembered that date.

Trevor Wilson was head coach at Kent State when I played there, and he visited Wilkinson at Oklahoma to get some different ideas from him. When Wilson came back from the visit, we started to play offense and defense just like the Sooners did. Wilson's reasoning was simple: "Because that's the way Oklahoma does it."

What's notable about Wilson's trip was that we started to use the 5-4 defense at Kent, just like they did at Oklahoma. That defense was innovative and new, and many teams still use it today. It's commonly known as the "Okie" defense.

I never thought that much about the forty-seven game streak back then, although we all knew it was the longest streak in college football history. Nearly forty years later, the record still stands for Wilkinson and Oklahoma. It didn't take many years of coaching for me to understand what that record meant.

Once I became a head coach, I understood a lot more about what the job entailed at that level, and that made me appreciate Bud Wilkinson even more. What was most impressive was the class way he handled everything, and particularly the way he handled winning. Amazingly, that's difficult for some coaches to deal with, but Bud was as gracious in victory as anyone I've ever seen. I don't know a coach who enjoys losing, but I've also never seen a coach create as little animosity as Bud did in winning so many games.

I had the opportunity to speak with Bud at a number of clinics and came to know him well. He had an air about him, and it was obvious he was someone special. I can't think of anyone in coaching who was more highly regarded than he was during his years at Oklahoma. Yet I don't think I realized at the time the impact he had on our profession.

Bud was always willing to help younger coaches and also made a great color commentator on television. I think it is a compliment to a man as both a person and a coach when a son decides to write a book about his father.

Little did I know, when I was playing for Kent State at the age of twenty, what meaning the name Bud Wilkinson would hold for anyone involved with college football. In a game played by amateurs, he came to stand for what professionalism was all about.

Lou Holtz, head coach
University of Notre Dame
Notre Dame, Indiana
June 14, 1994

# 1

## The Genesis of Success

&

*"The childhood shows the man ..."*
—*Milton*

For as long as I can remember, my father was famous. Whenever we walked through a restaurant, a grocery store, or an airport, I'd hear people whispering, "That's Bud Wilkinson." They knew him—from football, from television, from politics and from business—and they considered him a friend. Often when we were together, someone would walk up, look Dad square in the eye and say, "Bud, I'll bet you don't remember me, do you?" Dad would always respond, "Well, you look familiar, but ..." He might then discover that the questioner had spoken to him for thirty seconds at a convention ten years previously, to which Dad would reply, "Oh, now I remember."

Of course, he probably didn't remember, since he met thousands of people over the course of his life, but because he was such a warm, charming, and charismatic person, he never seemed like a distant, remote "celebrity." To people in all walks of life, from presidents of the United States to stadium ushers, he was just Bud, and they felt comfortable approaching him wherever he was.

Not every person handles fame—or life—as graciously as Dad did. As his vigor waned in recent years, and I saw him coping with some of the exigencies poor health can bring, I was struck by the fact that his warmth and dignity never deserted him, even in his last days. I began to wonder what the source of his great personal power was. What had made him such a success in so many areas of endeavor?

I think Dad was a unique combination of good genes and a sound environment. Clearly his upbringing provided a basic moral framework on which he built his entire life, but he was a highly sensitive, talented person from the moment he first made his appearance in the family.

Dad was born in Minneapolis on Easter Sunday, April 23, 1916, and his early life was safe, stable and secure. His mother, Edith, her sister Florence, and their brother were born in the United States shortly after their parents emigrated from Sweden. Blonde, blue-eyed Edith was the soloist in the church choir and played the piano. It was directly from his mother and father that Dad inherited his fondness for music. All the family sang, seemingly all the time and everywhere—school songs, popular music and show tunes. My mother says, "They would hardly even say hello; they would just start harmonizing." This passion for singing would pop out, sometimes in unlikely places, throughout Dad's entire life and career.

Dad's father, Charles Patton, known as C.P., was the greatest influence in Dad's early life. A successful mortgage broker who believed in neatness, order and self-discipline, he taught Dad life was tough and a positive outlook was essential for overcoming disappointments and disillusionments. He told Dad, "If you ever see a man over fifty years of age who has a smile on his face, take off your hat and bow," for that man surely had the right attitude.

C.P. had a hot temper, which he apparently passed on to Dad's older brother, Bill. Bill and C.P. were often at loggerheads, and Dad, who was much more even tempered, said he developed his own quiet demeanor in reaction to watching his brother and father argue. At an early age he learned it was more expedient not to get into emotional disagreements. He also related, "Any speed I had in athletics, I picked up running away from Bill." They fought as most brothers close in age do, but they also enjoyed one another's company and spent a great deal of time together.

Dad's extended family lived in three adjacent houses. C.P.'s mother occupied one house. The middle house was C.P.

and Edith's, and in the house on the other side lived Edith's sister, Florence, her husband, Al, and their children. This large, loving, cross-generational mix was to become increasingly important to Dad's life, for around the corner a tragedy was waiting that would affect the entire family.

On Saturday afternoon, August 12, 1922, a Soo Line passenger train carrying Dad, Bill, Edith, Uncle Al, and several of the cousins struck an oil delivery truck just southeast of the town of Annandale, Minnesota. The impact of the crash threw the oil truck against a switch that then derailed several passenger cars of the train. Those cars collided with the engine of a freight train that was waiting to pull out from the siding.

The baggage car of the passenger train was destroyed; the wreckage of the smoker car caught fire immediately. Most of the thirty-two people who were killed or injured were riding in that car. Directly behind them was the car carrying Dad's family. Many years later Dad would describe the scene as his six-year-old eyes perceived it. He saw passengers strewn about, dead, dying, or bleeding, some pinned in the wreckage. He remembered being dropped from the car and someone catching him before he hit the ground. He recalled smoke and terror.

In newspaper accounts of the tragedy, Dad's family is not listed among the injured, but his mother did require a day or two of hospitalization. She became a semi-invalid, and a year later she died of heart and liver ailments believed to be crash-related.

At the age of seven, then, Dad was motherless. It was a difficult and terrible time for him, but, as he did in later life, he looked forward, not back, and tried not to dwell on the sadness of his situation.

It was at this time that C.P. showed another side of his nature. Not long after Edith's death, one of the neighborhood children died in a house fire down the block. Not surprisingly, Dad's witnessing the carnage of the train wreck and losing a childhood acquaintance in a short period of time had some unsettling effects. Chief among them was that he became afraid to go to sleep at night. So, for many nights, C.P. picked him up and held him in his arms until Dad drifted off. Only then would his father put him to bed. Dad says it was from these experiences with his father that he learned the importance of touching, holding and expressing affection.

C.P. had dinner with Dad every Wednesday evening at the Minneapolis Athletic Club before C.P. bowled in the Kiwanis league. Dad would sometimes watch the bowling, but more often, he spent the time shooting baskets. It was also at the Athletic Club that Dad and his father would listen to the wire reports of the football games, especially those of the fierce Minnesota-Michigan rivalry. Together they would watch the ball moving on the game chart, and Dad was always thrilled to know almost up to the minute where the ball was, what down was being played and what distance needed to be covered to gain the next first down.

In spite of his tenderness, though, C.P. was no easy touch. If Dad wanted to skip school because he didn't feel well, C.P. always said, "You go to school. If you are so sick you can't stay there, call me." Dad missed very few days and he internalized the habits of discipline and responsibility, habits C.P. strongly reinforced.

It might have been easier for C.P to turn over his sons' upbringing to the women of the family who lived so close by, and many men of his era would have done so. C.P., however, chose to rear his boys himself, and he did his best to provide Dad and Bill with both fathering and mothering.

Nonetheless, the rest of the extended family was critical to Dad's development. When C.P. was away on business, Dad lived with his grandmother or with his aunt, uncle and cousins. In addition, Dad and Bill spent their summers with Florence and Al and their children at their summer cottage in western Minnesota. Though there were chores, there was also a relaxed family atmosphere. Florence, a warm and loving surrogate mother, always felt a special responsibility to care for her sister's children; they were not left to drift, but were always supported by a strong and affectionate family.

They also received support from their friends. One of Dad's closest childhood pals was Patty Berg, who, of course, grew up to become one of the world's greatest golfers. "Bud lived seven or eight doors from me," Berg says. "We played football, hockey, baseball—all kind of sports together, with Bill and my brother, Herman, the Greathouse brothers and [four or five other boys]."

Patty Berg was the quarterback of the 50th Street Tigers. "Bud was the guard, the tackle, the captain and the coach. The reason I was the quarterback was I was the only one who could remember the signals. We had one signal, 22, where everybody ran whichever way they wanted. We didn't have any offense at all. We just used a single wing. I was the only one back. We didn't have any tight ends or wide ends. We just had a lot of loose ends. We never lost a game. Just teeth. I have a picture, and everybody in the line has their teeth out.

"After a while, Bud told me, 'You ought to quit this football. You're too small, too slow, and there isn't any future in it for you.' My mother was happy because I was having one black eye after another, one bad knee after another, clothes torn and everything. She said that was the best statement Bud ever made."

Years later, when Berg was playing an exhibition in Norman, Oklahoma, where Dad was coaching, "Bud said, 'Come on over and see my practice. We're going to have a little practice and then go to Notre Dame.' I went over, and just before they were leaving, he said, 'Boys, this is the lady who taught me to play football.' "

Besides their common interest in sports, Dad and Berg also had fathers who instilled in them a drive for perfection. "I learned if I worked hard," Berg says, "I could always go home, whether I won or lost, and put my head down on my pillow and say, 'Well, I did my very best.' I would then fall asleep. Now, if I didn't do my best, it didn't go unchallenged. The next day I was out there working twice as hard."

Dad had been taught the same things, in virtually identical words, and he responded in the same way. "He had all the characteristics of a champion," says Berg. "You could tell that because he was always captain of our team . . . . A lot of people have the wish to win, but champions have the will to win. That's what Bud had. He always strived for perfection. He was a good athlete, but more than that, too. He was a great leader.

"[He carried that with him into coaching]. He could take a mediocre team and make them champions . . . . He knew how to treat his boys to get the best out of them, and he knew how to have them play football to have fun, which is what a student ought to do. 'We'll win and we'll have fun doing it.' After it was over, it was over. If you won, fine. If you didn't, you found out why and came back and won the next year."

Except for the absence of his mother, Dad's boyhood was pleasant and unremarkable. "The south side of Minneapolis was a beautiful area," recalls one of Dad's oldest friends, Jack Boos. "We had nice neighborhood schools. We knew everybody all the way to school. You'd know people all along the way and you'd pick up your friends and walk with them. Where Bud lived was right near the end of the tree line, where the farming began."

Between school and sports, Dad's young life was full. And six years later, when C.P. married his second wife, Ethel Grace, a woman Dad later described as being "just as perfect as it's possible for a person to be," he once more had a mother. Ethel was a petite, lovely brunette, reserved and proper. But she could be roused. One of the family's favorite stories revolves around a day Ethel came to see Dad play football at the University of Minnesota. When the man in front of her in the stands happened to make a disparaging remark about Dad and his team, Ethel quietly rolled up her program, bopped the offender over the head, and told him in no uncertain terms he was to cease and desist from that behavior—at once.

à

Unfortunately, Dad had little time to enjoy being in a two-parent home again. One of the cousins who lived next door had enrolled at the Shattuck School, a military school in Faribault, Minnesota. Though Dad and Bill were enamored with his uniforms, neither brother had any desire to leave home and attend Shattuck. C.P. decided, however, the discipline they would receive at Shattuck would be beneficial to their development—and in the twinkling of an eye, the Wilkinson boys were enrolled.

Shattuck was a beautiful school, with lots of trees and Gothic architecture, but the first thing Dad mentioned about the school was that it was cold. In the frigid Minnesota winters, the heat in the dormitories was turned down every night to save money, and when Dad rose in the morning, his room was so cold he'd find the ink frozen in his pen.

"Let me put it this way," remembers Jack Boos, who also enrolled at Shattuck. "We weren't permitted to have pets. But I had some goldfish and they would freeze in the bowl every night. When I'd get back to my room at noon, they'd be thawed out and swimming around."

Dad's second memory was of regimentation. "It was a real regimented life compared to public school," recalls Ed Eaton, a Shattuck classmate. "You didn't like it much. You got used to it. You'd get up in the morning, and boy, you'd have to dash to formation. You had to be on time and dressed for that. Then you went to the dining room in lock step formation. You'd line up in a column of twos. Each guy was close behind the other guy, and you took off. You'd better stay in step or there were going to be some guys falling over. We had formation before lunch, too, and we'd march to the dining hall."

Demerits were common. "If you were late for formation or something, the Commandant would give you demerits and you'd get so many hours of 'squad.' You'd report to squad after lunch and you'd fall in and have to carry a rifle on your shoulder and walk in a little triangle. You'd just walk around this thing for an hour [or more]. It behooved you to obey the rules," says Eaton.

Since Dad was already well acquainted with the discipline and perfectionism of his father, the regimentation was not too burdensome for him. What was difficult was the separation from his family. Because of the warmth and closeness of the entire clan, being away from them was difficult and, until he was a senior, he spent many hours in solitary tears at the beginning of each school year and following every break. C.P. advised him to tough it out.

Sports helped. "Everybody had to go out in the afternoon for sports of some kind," says Eaton. Every boy at Shattuck was a member of one of two intramural teams, and if he was not on a varsity squad, he competed for his intramural team in one of fourteen seasonal sports.

In his freshman year at Shattuck, Dad played only two sports—baseball and football. By his sophomore year, however, he was 5'10" and playing on the football, baseball and hockey varsity teams. At 15, he'd grown another inch, put on 10 pounds, and was signal-calling tackle on the football team, the position he played for three years, captaining the team his senior year. Also in his senior year, at 6'1" and 186 pounds, he added another sport, basketball, playing center. At his graduation, he'd earned four letters in baseball, three each in football and hockey, one in basketball, and was the only four-sport letterman in his graduating class.

Studying also kept him from being too homesick. Motivated by the rigors of the curriculum and the demands of the teachers, he maintained high grades, graduating cum laude and receiving the Harvard Cup for highest excellence in combined athletics and scholarship and the Williams Cup for being Shattuck's best all-round athlete. He was particularly affected by the teaching style of Duke Wagner, who taught English. "Regardless of the quality of the paper," he later recalled, "if the T's weren't crossed and the I's not dotted, he failed it. I didn't agree with that or understand it then. I do now." Though he was strict, "The Duke" instilled in Dad a love of words that later would form the basis for his exceptional skill as a teacher and communicator.

For two years, Dad was also a member of the Crack Squad, a nationally-known precision drill unit, and he took part in various other school activities. "He was a real leader," Eaton says, "one of the biggest men in the class. I don't know how Bud got everything done that he did."

It wasn't all work, study, and activities. Even though Boos remembers the sister school, St. Mary's, as being "absolutely forbidden territory; you couldn't even walk by," the 1933 yearbook, *The Shad*, says Dad was "a triple threat man, not only on the athletic field, but in the halls of St. Mary's as well." Obviously, the Wilkinson positive attitude worked off the field, too.

≈

After graduation from Shattuck in 1933, Dad headed for the University of Minnesota, where he came under the tutelage of coach Bernie Bierman. Modern theories of leadership and management all point to the importance of mentors, and Bierman was Dad's. Many of the coaching innovations Dad brought to Oklahoma were pioneered by Bierman, and Dad was an apt and willing pupil.

"Bernie was very quiet, very close to himself," says Dad's teammate Dan Elmer. "I almost think if he saw part of his team coming, he'd walk across the street. You'd meet him and all he would say was hello. He was very, very strict. He treated everyone the same. You were just another football player out there, and everybody had to learn . . . . Yet when you were through as a player, you could go in and talk to Bernie for an hour. He was just great. He kept the respect of his boys all the time."

"Bierman recognized Bud as a good man," says Jack Boos, who also attended Minnesota and was a Psi Upsilon fraternity brother of Dad's. "He recognized Bud's qualities, and he sent him over to the track coach, who taught him how to run. Bud was too slow, and the track coach got his speed up. Bierman wouldn't have sent him if he hadn't seen something in Bud, because he had lots of people to pick from. Getting his speed up was one of the keys to getting Bud on that football team."

Dad played freshman ball with at least 150 other young men who were hoping for places on the Golden Gopher squad. The recruiting of those young men, if there was any, was certainly casual by today's standards. Babe Le Voir, who played both halfback and quarterback at Minnesota, says, "Biggie Munn was on the staff of the University of Minnesota coaching the freshmen. I got a call one day, when I was a junior at Marshall High, and he said, 'Babe, how would you like a couple of tickets for the Ohio State game? . . . . You come on over in an hour and I'll give you two tickets.' That was the only recruiting that was done."

Running back Pug Lund had a similar experience. "My cousin and uncle arranged for Biggie to meet me and give me a ride around the campus. In about ten minutes the ride was over. He dropped me off and said, 'I hope you come here.' I never heard from anybody."

When Dad made the team in 1934, he began to learn the lessons he would carry with him throughout his coaching career. The cornerstone was fundamentals. Though most coaches just warmed up their teams and began to scrimmage, Bierman organized the practice schedules so the team worked first on fundamentals and drills. Football, like other team sports, is in large measure, reaction to movement; Bierman understood that repetitive drills helped his players react more rapidly and contributed to their success.

Next came dedication. During spring and fall practice, players hit and hit again, so Bierman could find those who were willing to work hard to play for Minnesota. Dad absorbed this lesson well, and later, those who played for him learned it, too. You either went all out all the time or made way for someone who was willing to do so. There were always people ready to take your place if your dedication faltered.

The third Bierman trademark was conditioning. The teams ran and ran—wind sprints, jogging, then more wind sprints. Dad discovered from Bierman that the way to become a proficient runner was to run. A generation later Oklahoma players were doing the same, sometimes losing their lunch in the bushes, but ending up the best conditioned athletes in the country.

Rest was critical to the Bierman plan. Once team members had proved their mettle in practice, he husbanded their energy. Ten days before the first game, scrimmages stopped. While other teams were scrimmaging every day, becoming sore and worn out, Bierman's teams were drilling and running. Consequently on game days, they were fresh and rested, while their opponents were bruised and beaten up before the game even began.

Bierman's unusual strategies resulted in three consecutive national championships—in 1934, 1935, and 1936. Dad was part of all three teams, first as a guard, and in his senior year, as a quarterback. "Bud's interest in football at that time was almost like a coach," says Lund. "He enjoyed the involvement and the strategy."

According to Dr. John Kirklin, who was team manager at the time, Dad's transfer to quarterback occasioned some controversy. "As manager, I was good friends with the sportswriters, who were always seeking some kind of favor. I used to chat with them and they'd say, 'It's not going to work out at all. It's a lousy idea, probably the worst idea Bierman ever had,' but, of course, Bud was a star as a quarterback as well.

"Probably his single greatest moment as a quarterback was the day Bud received the punt—of course the quarterback receiving the punt is unheard of today—but after he received and the opposing team converged on him, he threw a lateral to Andy Uram for the 70-yard touchdown that won the Nebraska game, 6-0."

The Nebraska game was exciting, certainly, but did not compare to the drama that occurred at the team's hotel prior to their game with the University of Washington.

Dan Elmer says, "We took a long train trip going out to Seattle. We got into Miles City, Montana, and Bernie was going to have us practice there. It was so windy the center had to keep the ball, go and put it down and hang onto it.

"Then we went into Missoula, Montana and went to the big hotel . . . . Ray King played the piano. Everybody was around singing, and we had a real good evening. We hit the sack.

"We were up on the third floor, and we heard a noise. We went to the window and looked out, and there was a fire truck. We heard [the firefighters] remark that they had the wrong [hose] fitting . . . . All of a sudden, everyone's pounding on our door to get out of there. It was the middle of the night. There was a lot of smoke in the hallways. Bud and I got out; we threw towels over ourselves. Everyone was there, some in a bathrobe, some bare-footed . . . . We had to go down to the train, which was across the river. We laid there in the train and watched the fire gradually go, go, go. It went right up the elevator shaft. Sure enough the next morning they took us for a bus ride, and the hotel was down to the ground. We were very fortunate."

Minnesota's consecutive national championships would be remarkable in and of themselves. What makes the achievement all the more outstanding is that athletes who comprised the teams were full-time students who took their studies seriously.

Dad's teammate, Glenn Seidel, was an engineering student. "Bob Tanner and I were excused from practice one or two days a week because we had classes. They don't do that anymore.

"Friday nights the team used to go down to Stillwater. We'd go have dinner and the chalk talk, and then go to bed. The next morning, they'd take us back in a bus, but I always had to get back early because I had a lab class on Saturdays. So they'd send me back in a cab. I'd go to the lab and then walk over to the stadium."

Because it was the height of the Depression, many players also were working at demanding jobs. Le Voir says, "I worked down at the Northwestern National Bank [along with several other team members] . . . . We got $50 a month; we'd work five days a week. We'd hit the adding machines from noon until about 3:30, and then we'd take the street car to practice. We'd practice until about 7:30 p.m., and then I'd walk the mile and a half to get home. We had very little social life."

Though the Wilkinsons were better off than many during the Depression, Dad worked at a Ford assembly plant, a clothing store and a gas station during his college years.

What social life there was usually revolved around the fraternities, but Dad's Psi U brothers don't remember him as being a party animal. He attended parties and hung out with the guys, but he was much more reserved and quiet than his brother, Bill. "He was a pretty private person," says Dad's All-American teammate Ed Widseth.

Obviously versatile and coachable, Dad ended up a two-time All-American, and as he had done at Shattuck, took away Minnesota's highest honor for combined scholastics and sports—the Big Ten Medal.

Following graduation, he played in the college All-Star game, quarterbacking the collegiates to a 7-0 victory over the Green Bay Packers, the first time in history the All-Stars had triumphed over the professionals. He was also part of the Galloping Gophers, a basketball team that traveled around Minnesota, North Dakota and Montana, playing independent teams, including the Harlem Globetrotters, whom they defeated. They earned five to ten dollars a game, and things were occasionally a little disorganized.

Dad's good friend, Otis Dypwick, was the ticket manager. At one of the games, says Helen Dypwick, "Otie was counting the money when they came and asked him to referee. He put on the referee's uniform. Then one of the players didn't show up, so he quickly put on a uniform to play. He kept switching back and forth. Then the player arrived, and he was the referee again." Dad recalled a considerable amount of booing when the fans saw that the referee was associated with the Gophers in so many other capacities.

≿▲

Dad's scrapbooks show clearly that although he excelled in several sports, football was his first sports love. "Football," he said, "combines the combat of wrestling and boxing, the speed of track, the ball handling of baseball and basketball, the ball judgment of tennis and the incredibly difficult skill of kicking." Yet, during his college career, he also continued to play golf, making the golf squad during spring football practice and serving as captain his senior year; and he played goalie on the hockey team, as well.

It was his hockey playing that eventually led to his marriage to my mother, Mary Shifflett. Mom was a student at Carlton College when Dad came with the Minnesota hockey team to play against Carlton. "I was dating a Carlton hockey player," Mom says, "and I was waiting for him and was all dressed up. My buzzer rang, and I went downstairs expecting my date. Instead it was the whole Minnesota hockey team. I didn't know any of them. It was obvious I was on exhibition, but I had no idea why. I was so embarrassed."

Mom's intuition about being on display was accurate. Somehow the rumor had swept through the Minnesota team that Carlton was the home of a beautiful Indian princess—Mom—and that the team should go over to the dorm and get a look at her. Though the Indian princess rumor was a falsehood, the beautiful part was correct. Mom was, and remains today, an exceptional beauty. "Bud told me he didn't know himself why they came over, except someone said there was an Indian princess they must look up."

"The next fall, my junior year, I transferred to Minnesota. Bud was a senior. He didn't call me until after football season. By that time, I knew what his name was because he was such a big guy on the campus. When he called, I said, 'I don't really know you. Is this a joke?' He said, 'No, I do know you . . . .' He told me the dress I had on that night at Carlton. He came over that evening, and that was the beginning."

The romance progressed slowly, however. "I went with him that spring," Mom says, "and then he went to Europe the summer after he graduated as director of deck sports for one of the Holland America Line ships. After that he went to Syracuse to coach. I really didn't start going with him again until the next winter after being away from him."

The European trip clearly distracted Dad from his pursuit of Mom. Otis Dypwick recalls the aftermath. "[I went to see Bud at Syracuse, when he was in his first year as assistant coach]. He had been on a student trip to Europe and had met a lot of young ladies, one of whom was Kitty Ann. Before they parted company, he invited her to come to Syracuse for the weekend of the football game with Colgate. Bud had to be away the night Kitty Ann said she'd be arriving. He asked me to meet her, and gave me a very detailed description of her. He also gave me a ten dollar bill to buy her a bottle of Bushmill's Irish whiskey, her favorite beverage."

After accosting several young ladies who alighted from the train, Dypwick approached the last woman on the platform. She was indeed Kitty Ann, but since she'd had a nose job, Dad's description was way off base.

Later in the season, Dad invited Dypwick to the Army-Navy game. "We checked into the hotel, and he found several telegrams from girls he had met on the summer cruise, each one saying she was going to arrive for the game. Obviously, there was no way we could accommodate them unless we made some quick changes in our plans." Apparently Dad continued to have the appeal that had been evident as far back as his Shattuck days.

As Mom mentions, Dad's first after-college job was a part-time coaching assignment at Syracuse University. C. P. was not thrilled, as he felt coaching was not a proper occupation for someone with Dad's skills—that he was simply frittering away his time. Thus began a tug-of-war between the two men that lasted several years.

C.P. enlisted the aid of friends to try to talk Dad out of his career choice; Dad gracefully declined their advice. Over the years, he did try intermittently to get interested in the family business, taking only part-time coaching contracts, but as he said, "I couldn't. I wanted to coach. Paperwork was boring, and I disliked the monotony." C.P. didn't fully embrace Dad's profession until 1950, when Oklahoma won its first national championship, but once he was convinced of the seriousness of Dad's career path, C.P. told him, "I know you'll be the greatest coach of all time."

Dad wasn't sure he believed him, but he took great pride in C.P.'s confidence in him. As Dad's star ascended, he and C.P. often greeted each other with a rousing rendition of "Oklahoma," and C.P. loved being involved with the Oklahoma program, if only peripherally.

After his first year at Syracuse, Dad returned to Minneapolis to work for C.P. There he renewed his courtship of Mom; they were married in 1938 and returned to Syracuse, to stay until 1941.

ಶಿ

At Syracuse, Dad was an assistant coach to Ossie Solem, whom he admired and respected. Dad coached the golf and hockey teams as well, and he received his master's degree in English, which had also been his undergraduate major.

In a departure from coaching, but as a precursor to his later career in broadcast communications, Dad also had a weekly 15-minute radio show on WFBL. The program grew out of a classroom assignment.

"Bud had a communications class with one of those personality professors who was fun and bright and attractive," recalls Mom, "and their assignment was to create a radio show. The professor liked it so well he thought Bud should talk to the radio station. They liked it and hired Bud to replace the regular sports show on Sunday nights. It was very popular."

And what was the first purchase Mom and Dad made with the money from the radio program? Not surprising to Mom, it was a piano.

Dad's primary duties at Syracuse centered around football, and at a very young age, he was already beginning to affect not only the on-field activities of his players, but their off-the-gridiron lives as well.

Sportscaster Marty Glickman played on Dad's first Syracuse team. "He had an enormous effect not only on me, but also on all the guys. We knew all about him—a two-time All-American under Bernie Bierman. We were impressed with his background. When this handsome blue-eyed blond with the rosiest cheeks you ever saw turned up . . . we were all rather surprised, until he began to move around the field on occasion. We were really impressed with him as a man and as a human being. He was a very quiet coach. I never heard him raise his voice.

"I like to say I made Bud as a coach. I was the starting tailback, and he was the backfield coach. Naturally, I was one of the first, if not the first guy he coached. I brag about the fact that I made him," Glickman chuckles. It's possible, however, some other teammates, like Duffy Daugherty, who later coached at Michigan State and became Dad's partner in the Coach of the Year Clinics, also added to the team's luster.

The biggest game in Dad's Syracuse career was against Cornell in 1938. Cornell had won its first three games, Syracuse its first two. Though it was highly unusual for an Ivy League team to defeat a Big Ten opponent, that year Cornell bested Ohio State. They were national contenders and highly favored to defeat Syracuse.

"We played at Ithaca, and we upset them 14-6," says Glickman. "I had the best day of my life. I scored both touchdowns, intercepted a couple of passes, made some touchdown-saving tackles. . . . The reason I did so well in that game is because Bud took me aside before the game . . . and he said, 'Marty, go out and have a good time. Have fun. Enjoy it.' I'd never heard that before. It was foreign to the coaches' way of talking to kids. Usually they tell you to go out and kill them, fight like hell, give 110 percent and all that stuff.

"All through that game," Glickman remembers, "I kept saying to myself, 'I'm having a hell of a time.' What's happened since then is that when I coach broadcasters, I've always told these young men that their enjoyment of the game is going to be projected to the listener and to the viewer . . . . The thing I want to hear most is, 'Marty, you sounded as if you were having a great time during the ball game.' You've got to have the attitude that this is fun, this is having a great time . . . that you'd rather be there playing that game or doing that broadcast than anything else in the world on that particular day. That's what Bud taught me."

ᘏᕹ

It was a nice life in Syracuse. The coaching was going well, and Mom and Dad welcomed their first son, my brother, Pat, to the family. In 1941, however, Dad returned to Minneapolis for a brief period to become an assistant coach at his alma mater. In 1942, Mom, who was pregnant with me, decided she would rather deliver in her home town, and so she spent several months in Grinnell, Iowa. I was born there in April.

Outside the United States, the war was heating up. Though Dad's Shattuck experience had predisposed him to the Army, he instead enlisted in the Navy in 1942. He was assigned to the Navy's pre-flight program.

The pre-flight—or V-5—program was designed to improve the physical skills of young men who wanted to be pilots.

A drastic improvement in fitness was required before most of them could handle the demanding responsibilities of the cockpit, and the pre-flight sports program brought prospective pilots to peak physical shape before they were trained in highly expensive aircraft. The curriculum included boxing, wrestling, football, and soccer.

The program fostered the competitiveness necessary for warfare and was also a tool for weeding out those who weren't willing to fight, or in one of Dad's favorite phrases, to "pay the price." It was a cost-effective way to find the strongest pilot candidates.

Dad was assigned to Iowa Pre-flight School at Iowa City in 1943, where he worked with Don Faurot, who had been coach at Missouri and who would return there after the war. Joining Dad and Faurot was Jim Tatum, who later became head coach at Oklahoma, taking Dad along as his assistant.

"Players would be at pre-flight only about three to four months," Faurot says. "They'd start to play and then they'd get transferred out."

Short duration or not, the Sea Hawks learned some inventive football from Faurot. Faurot had won two championships at Missouri using his newly created split-T offense. Dad learned it, too, and after the war, transplanted it to Oklahoma, where he and Tatum were in the vanguard of coaches using the new formation.

The pre-flight schools were folded up in 1944, and Dad was assigned to the aircraft carrier *U.S.S. Enterprise.* He joined the ship in San Francisco; Mom went to see him off, filled with all the emotions every service wife knew well.

The "Big E" was dubbed "the fightingest carrier in the fleet," accounting for 911 Japanese aircraft shot down, 71 enemy ships sunk and another 192 damaged by her pilots, while steaming more than 275,000 miles. According to a history of the ship published in August, 1945, "nothing was tougher than the last 19 action-packed months, taking her through the bloody victory of Okinawa." Dad was hangar deck officer during part of this time. His friend, Bob Fischer, was also aboard.

"During the Iwo Jima campaign," Fischer says, "we were in general quarters on the *Enterprise* for more than a week." From February 23 to March 2, in fact, the *Enterprise* had planes in the air for more than 174 consecutive hours. "I can tell you, when our ground troops finally established themselves, there were more than 3,000 totally exhausted people [on the *Enterprise*]."

By now, Dad, like everyone else, was feeling enervated by the stress of war and the torrid climate of the South Pacific. He wrote to Mom, "This is the first time in my life I've ever missed winter . . . . You lose your pep and vitality out here if you don't keep constantly reminding yourself that you have to keep moving. When there will be a job to do, it will be better, but now our life tempts us to sack out all the time."

Not only was Dad missing the change of seasons, but he was also missing all of us, especially Mom. He wrote, "I've been thinking a lot lately about how my heart is always with you at home, and yesterday for some unknown reason, I tried to write a poem about it . . . . Here goes:

I'm living these days with a 'lady of war,'
A grim, grey ship of the fleet.
A lustful mistress who lives to destroy,
Whose food is the cannon's heat.

She's demanding of strength from my body and soul,
A hard task master is she.
And I serve her with honor and pride as she fights
To make this a world for the free.

Yet whenever I pause in this life based on strife
My thoughts take wing and are prone
To take me in dreams, straight to my heart
Which I left with my dear ones at home.

And I dream of my Mary, my beautiful wife,
So lovely and gorgeous and true.
A woman of courage and strength and of faith,
And my heart is with her anew.

As my fantasy grows, I see my two boys,
Unburdened by cares as they play.
And I join them and rough-house just as I did
Before the war came our way.

But the notes of the bugle are calling me back
Away from my home and its joys.
Away from my heart; the things that I love;
Away from my wife and my boys.

Though I'll serve her as well as I humanly can,
This 'lady of war' while we roam.
She never will capture the love of my heart
For that's with my loved ones at home."

Soon, there was a "job to do." The *Enterprise* had been the target of Kamikaze pilots over several weeks. She was hit on March 18, March 20 and April 11, 1945. After repairs, the ship headed for Kyushu and on May 12 joined in an intense two-day bombardment of the Kamikaze bases there. On May 14, the Japanese counterattacked. As the crew watched, one Kamikaze streaked toward the *Enterprise*. When it was clear to the pilot he would go past the ship, he flipped the plane and crashed onto the flight deck, his bomb detonating under the forward elevator. Dad was in general quarters on the hangar deck.

Bob Fischer paints the picture. "It hit the elevator. The elevator was up, which means it was part of the flight deck . . . . My gun group was on the starboard side of the stack, so I just heard it . . . . It actually landed abreast of where we were, and all of my sailors were undisciplined enough that they ran to the edge of the ship, because they couldn't believe they were looking at this great big piece of deck. Of course it sank fairly quickly and was gone."

The forward elevator flew 400 feet into the air. Fourteen men were killed and thirty-four injured. Dad was standing behind a beam at the time and was unhurt. Had he been positioned only three or four feet away, he would have been killed. "Five or six men were killed on the hangar deck," says Fischer, "and quite a few injured just from the explosion."

A well-trained crew braved their way through the flames and smoke and brought the fires under control within seventeen minutes. Inside a half hour, all the fires were out, but the day was just beginning. Twenty-one more raids had to be driven off in the course of that terrible day, nine by the ship's own guns.

By the end of the day, the ship was at eighty percent efficiency, and the decision was made to bring her to Puget Sound Naval Yard for repairs. "We came back to Bremerton," Fischer remembers, "around the tenth of June." Dad and Fischer were then on thirty-day leave.

After the leave, "the train ride back to Bremerton was incredible," Fischer says. "Bud's father had some influence with the Northern Pacific Railroad, so we all gathered in Chicago, and we had our own car on the North Coast Limited, which was the Chicago to Seattle train. We had three great days of partying across the country. There must have been 18-20 guys."

Those like Dad and Fischer, who had taken the first leave, were in Bremerton for a little over a month waiting for orders.

"Most of the sailors thought they'd be going to Japan," Mom says. But on August 14, after the attacks on Hiroshima and Nagasaki, the war was over.

Fischer was on a ferry coming into Seattle when the sirens signaled the end of the war. "There's a building in Seattle—it's almost the shape of the Washington Memorial, only shorter. The only way you could describe it that afternoon is that building looked like it had exploded because of all the confetti and torn paper people were throwing."

Mom was walking through the Navy Yard on her way to the Officers' Club. "There were hundreds of employees in the yard. When the whistles went off, I was right in the middle of it. You can imagine . . . . It was just like the pictures you've seen of Broadway on that day. Everyone was beside themselves with joy."

From Bremerton, Dad was ordered to Pensacola and after about six weeks, he was honorably discharged. Now, with a wife and two young sons, it was time for him to look for a post-war job.

# 2

## Oklahoma: Beginning the Tradition

*"To be prepared is half the victory. . . ."*
—*Cervantes*

In 1946, when Dad moved our family to Norman, home of the University of Oklahoma, the town was just a dot on the map and looked like any other heartland settlement. Two-story brick and wooden structures comprised the business district that lined the main street; that street led to the square, where the Cleveland County offices were located. Ranches and farms surrounded the town, pressing in on every side; the proximity of the prairie lent a real frontier feeling. The university, with only 6,500 students, was Norman's largest institution.

At the time we arrived, the people of Oklahoma were suffering from a collective inferiority complex. John Steinbeck's novel, *The Grapes of Wrath*, had portrayed "Okies"—those folks who migrated west after the Dust Bowl storms—as stupid, incompetent rubes, and citizens of the state were having a hard time shaking the image. There was a sense of embarrassment about being a resident and a mild paranoia about what the rest of the country was whispering about Oklahoma.

As Billy Vessels, Oklahoma's first Heisman Trophy winner says, "That name, 'Okie,' was one of disdain; it wasn't a joke. Steinbeck's book really put us in a bad light. We were a new, young state. We weren't all Princeton graduates out there, but we had people that were very proud and ... with good fiber. Those who left the state, fine, good luck to them, but we stayed. It was like coming back and beating Texas in the last minute of the game. We won. We beat down Mother Nature. We survived. We stayed and fought the elements."

Two things began to change Oklahomans' view of themselves. The first was Rodgers and Hammerstein's ground-breaking musical, *Oklahoma!*, with its message that the state was "doing fine." The second was the fact that the University of Oklahoma's football team started to win, and with the victories came a rebirth of the people's pride, enthusiasm and self-esteem. Those early victories were the beginning of the first Oklahoma football dynasty—a dynasty that eventually captured three national championships, twelve conference championships, seventy-four straight conference games without a defeat (1947-59), six post-season Bowl victories, a won-lost tally of 145-29-4, and two winning streaks of thirty-one and forty-seven consecutive games, the longest streaks ever seen in collegiate football.

Today, if an entire state were collectively depressed, whole teams of psychiatrists would be dispatched to the area and massive psychological studies conducted. In those simpler days, a member of the Oklahoma Board of Regents suggested a winning football team might turn the tide and make Oklahomans feel less apologetic about where they lived.

The idea grabbed hold. Dad recalls, "Everyone was so charged up . . . . It was a belief that 'by golly, we want to do this.'"

Because the war was ending, hundreds of college-bound men with four years' eligibility would be returning home, as would the coaches of armed services football teams. The regents decided to go after one of the service coaches—one who'd have access to a pool of top-notch athletic talent that could be recruited to Oklahoma.

The university's athletic director, "Jap" Haskell, had served with the United States Navy, and suggested the board talk to Jim Tatum, a coach he'd observed in Jacksonville, about coming to Oklahoma.

Tatum demanded an unusual condition for his interview with the regents. He insisted on bringing a prospective assistant coach along with him to the interview, a coach he'd worked with in the Navy's football program—Bud Wilkinson.

This request set in motion a chain of events that almost cost Tatum the job. On January 9, 1946, the two men were interviewed jointly and then left to attend a coaching conference in St. Louis.

According to *Presidents Can't Punt*, Dr. George Lynn Cross' book about his days as president of the University of Oklahoma, following the coaches' departure from the regents' meeting, board discussion centered on Dad rather than Tatum; consensus began to build that Dad should be offered the head coaching job. Dr. Cross had serious ethical reservations about such a move, however, and after more discussion, the regents' unanimous decision was to make an offer to Tatum with the stipulation that he bring Dad along as an assistant coach. Without Dad, there was no deal.

Tatum was furious, and said that after the St. Louis meeting, Dad had told him he was returning to Minneapolis to go into business with his father. That was true. According to Dad, "I'd been in the war, at Okinawa, Iwo Jima, and other places, and I wrote my dad that if the war were good enough to me that I would come back, I would not be a coach. I was certainly going to follow his lead and that the Wilkinson Home Finance Company would be fine for me." Besides, Tatum argued, he needed the freedom to choose his own staff. Cross replied he had no choice but to offer the job as the regents dictated.

Within a few days Tatum accepted the position, after making an agreement with Dad the regents knew nothing about. He asked Dad to come with him for one year only. After that time he'd be free to resign, return to Minneapolis and go into business with his father. In order to help his friend get the job, Dad went along with the plan. "The first contract I was under at Oklahoma was a part-time thing," said Dad.

But a year later Tatum moved on to the University of Maryland, and coaching was once again in Dad's blood—so much so that he had agreed to take the head coaching job at Drake University. There was a contingency, however. Dad stipulated he would go to Drake only if the Oklahoma job Tatum was vacating was not offered to him. When Oklahoma made their proposal, his acceptance of the Drake position was moot. In 1947, at the age of only 31, Dad became head coach and athletic director of the University of Oklahoma.

❧

"I was delighted, of course, for the opportunity," he said. "I had reservations only from the standpoint that I was young, and I knew that the people you need to have support you, if we didn't do very well, might feel I was just too young."

In his new position, Dad was coaching both war veterans and college boys. Many members of his teams were only a few years younger than he. All-American Wade Walker, a tackle on the 1947 team, says, "[I was recruited by Tatum because] I'd played for him at the Naval Air Station in Jacksonville. I happened to be in Dallas and came up for the weekend to see the campus and to see Tatum and so on . . . . Jap Haskell was the Athletic Director, and he had a den or basement or something where Tatum was staying. When I went in, Coach Wilkinson was there . . . and Tatum says, 'Meet Bud Wilkinson.' I said, 'Hi, I'm Wade Walker. What position do you play?' He looked at me and said, 'Well, I'm the coach.' The irony of it is, heck, he looked a lot younger than I did."

All-American halfback George Brewer represented the other end of the age spectrum, but his introduction to Dad was similar. "I was pre-enrolled at SMU . . . but Eddie Chiles had been courting me since between my sophomore and junior year in high school . . . . He came by . . . and he wanted me to go up to Oklahoma. He had been so darned nice to me and my family that I agreed to go up and spend the weekend. I knew I wasn't going to go there.

"I flew into Oklahoma City, and I was met at the plane by the biggest, best-looking guy I'd ever seen, and he had on a t-shirt that said 'Property of University of Oklahoma Athletic Department.' He had a Dodge, which was really rare at the end of the war; very few cars had been built. It turned out it was Jim Tatum's car.

"So," Brewer continues, "we're halfway to Norman and I asked, 'What position do you play?' He said, 'I'm the backfield coach.' He had introduced himself as Bud Wilkinson, and I knew zero about OU when I went up there that weekend. I was so embarrassed, I thought, 'Oh, my God, here I am, a crewcut seventeen-year-old, trying to play with a bunch of men.' I was really embarrassed. He got a kick out of it." After a grueling tryout, Brewer decided to go to Oklahoma, after all.

Once on the field, the age groups got along well, according to Harry Moore, a veteran who graduated at the age of twenty-nine and was the oldest member of the team. "The younger kids that had never been to the service ... all looked up to the veterans, and anytime they had a problem, they would come around and counsel with us." Myrle Greathouse, a fullback from Dad's first team, agrees. "The pattern we showed came through to the new guys. They respected us and kind of idolized us."

The fact that Dad was so young created a coaching challenge, but according to Walker, "Coach had enough knowledge or enough sense to realize . . . he wasn't dealing only with eighteen-year-olds. I was a twenty-one-year-old freshman, and I wasn't the only one. I think thirty-six of us were married. He knew he was talking to mature guys who'd been in fox holes, been shot at . . . . He was smart enough to make rules and regulations for adults . . . . It was not regimentation. He had enough foresight ... to communicate with experienced, worldly people in a way that molded the greatest camaraderie that's ever been. I have no closer friends. I had no more love for anybody other than my immediate family. And Coach, he was the leader of it."

Dad was quick, however, to give credit to his teams. As he told a reunion of his 1949 team, "The greatest compliment [you] paid me was to have confidence ... in my coaching. If the team doesn't believe, the coach has not got a chance to ever, ever make anything happen. The fact that the team believed what the assistant coaches and I said and were willing to go for broke for us, football-wise and every other way—that was a marvelous, marvelous compliment, which, of course resulted in our being an undefeated team."

But in 1947, Oklahoma's undefeated seasons were in the future, and Dad had to do more than make the team believe. He had to make the regents, the administration, the faculty, the parents, the students, the sportswriters, and the fans believe, and to do that, he had to win. Until his teams started to win with regularity, Dad had no real job security.

He knew he couldn't get the job done all by himself, so he began to assemble his coaching staff. Over the years, he was blessed with superb assistant coaches, such as Pop Ivy, who went on to become head coach of both the Edmonton Eskimos in the Canadian Football League and the Chicago Cardinals. But as other assistant coaches came and went, Gomer Jones remained.

Jones, who'd been an All-American center at Ohio State, was Dad's line coach, mainstay, friend and confidant throughout his entire Oklahoma career. The two men's coaching styles were complementary, and they were an unbeatable team.

Harry Moore knew Jones from St. Mary's Pre-flight football. "There are very few coaches you can go through life and never hear anybody say a bad word about . . . . Gomer was one of those people. He was a professional guy, and he had the respect of everybody. He handled people completely different than Bud did . . . . Bud made everybody better or try to improve . . . . He had a great feeling for getting the most out of a guy. Gomer was a little different . . . more jovial. The two of them were a great, great combination."

Dad appreciated both Jones' relationship with the players and his coaching skills. He was quoted on more than one occasion as saying that if Jones ever quit, Dad would have to quit with him.

&

The 1947 season began strongly, with Oklahoma defeating Detroit and Texas A&M. The third game of the season was Texas. The Oklahoma-Texas rivalry is one of the greatest in football; it's unique because it is not played at either school, but at the Cotton Bowl in Dallas. The games of that era were blood baths, the margin of victory usually being only a touchdown or an extra point. For Sooner fans, the only game that really matters is Texas. Oklahomans will forgive their coach a losing season if that season includes a win over Texas. Conversely, a winning season without a Texas victory is dust and ashes. The fans had swallowed the bitter pill of defeat for seven years prior to the 1947 game. They wanted a win, and they wanted Dad to deliver it. It was not to be. And with this defeat, a new word—"Siscoed," meaning betrayed—entered the Oklahoma vocabulary.

Prior to the game, the coaches agreed the scoreboard clock would be the official time. In the first half, with the game tied 7-7 and twenty seconds on the clock, Texas was on the Oklahoma three-yard line. On the next play they gained one yard. Lining up quickly, they made one more scoring attempt, but Texas back

Randall Clay was stopped for no gain as the seconds ticked off the clock. Sooner fans erupted in jubilation.

At this point, one of the officials, Jack Sisco, signaled first a touchdown, then a time out. He maintained the Longhorns had called for the time out from the pile-up, with three seconds left, and there had been no way to notify the clock-keeper.

The Texas "bonus" play resulted in a touchdown, in which Sisco also had a part. Texas' Jim Kennedy was carrying the ball; he fumbled, and one of the Texans lateraled the ball to Clay, who scored. Oklahoma fans—and Dad—protested that at least one of Clay's knees had been down when he received the lateral and that Sisco should have blown the ball dead at that point. Sisco, however, defended his position, and Texas entered the locker room 14-7 at the half.

In the second half, Texas scored again. Oklahoma returned the favor, and the score was 21-14. Texas came back, but deep in Oklahoma territory, All-American Darrell Royal intercepted a Longhorn pass. Sisco declared a holding penalty against Oklahoma, which returned the ball to Texas on the Sooner 23-yard line. Texas went in for the touchdown. The final score was 34-14.

In retrospect, Dad said he made an error in not taking his team off the field and into the locker room when the scoreboard clock indicated time had run out in the first half. The agreement had been made, and he insisted that had he been a more experienced coach, he would have demanded the agreement be honored. Clock or no clock, however, it was an ugly game for Oklahoma, with the Sooners turning over three fumbles and racking up sixty-eight yards in penalties.

It was nasty off the field, too, as Oklahoma fans threw bottles onto the gridiron and supporters from both schools punched each other out in the stands. Sisco was escorted from the field under guard, but not until he knocked out an Oklahoma fan who had dashed from the stands to attack him.

The rookie head coach was beginning to feel some pressure. He had not won The Game, and that loss was followed by a tie with Kansas and a loss to Texas Christian. The next two games, Iowa State and Kansas State, were Oklahoma victories. The season was becoming a roller coaster, and that was bad news for Dad.

"Generally," he said, "if you don't win quickly, and with consistency, you're not going to be around long. Missouri was the key game." Indeed, by this point in the season, the heat was on. All-American Jack Mitchell, who was quarterbacking the team, was approached just prior to the game by the university president. "He asked me, 'Jack, how do you feel about the game?' I said, 'Dr. Cross, I think we're ready to go.' He said, 'Well, I don't know if you know it or not, but this game is probably one of the most important points in Coach Wilkinson's life.' I thought to myself, 'It's pretty damned important to me, too.' I didn't appreciate what he said."

"Missouri was expected to beat us," Dad said, "but during the game, [our halfback and punter] Darrell Royal punted out of bounds three times in the second half—at the five-yard line, the three-yard line, and the two-yard line. The third time, Missouri fumbled the ball and our great offense made two yards. We scored the touchdown. Once we crossed that bridge, everything was on a relatively even keel." The season was closed out with two more victories, over Nebraska and Oklahoma A&M.

Darrell Royal, who later became head coach at the University of Texas, remembers the Missouri game clearly, too. "It probably meant more to Coach because he was . . . establishing himself. We hadn't done too well, and we needed to win that ball game. He . . . wasn't totally accepted yet. We had that shaky start, and then finished with five straight victories."

Though the Oklahoma football machine was yet to take shape, the 1947 season of 7-2-1 was the second best in Oklahoma's history and gave fans a taste of what might be in store. Even without a Texas victory, they were willing to string along with Dad a little longer.

❧

Although he hadn't had a lot of experience, Dad came to Oklahoma with his coaching philosophy pretty well jelled. The focal point of that philosophy, from which he never deviated, was the "will to prepare."

"The will to prepare is the key ingredient to success," he said. "When the game starts, all the people in the stands and the players hope they will have the will to win. If you lose, all too many times media people and fans say, 'The team wasn't ready today. They didn't have the will to win.'

"At game time, everybody has the will to win, believe me. Everybody does. The band is playing, the parents are in the stands, the girls are there, families are there.

"The will to prepare is getting out of bed at 5:30 . . . for the morning practice, and you're stiff and sore and you don't want to practice. If you do not practice totally productively, you've wasted that time. That's what I characterize as the will to prepare. It's not the flags flying at game time; it's the off-time situations when you have got to know that this is important enough to you, that you say, 'I can't waste this time and ultimately be able to be the best.' So the will to prepare is tantamount, really, to the ability to win."

Dad felt no one better exemplified the will to prepare than Ben Hogan. Dad, an avid golfer, was privileged to sit next to Hogan at a banquet before a golf tournament. Throughout the dinner, he noticed Hogan gripping and handling his knife as if it were a golf club. When Dad asked why, Hogan replied, "There are so many good players on the professional tour that I have to be better prepared than any of them. Tomorrow morning when the tournament starts, the players will tee off and hit their first shot." He gripped his knife again and said, "I will have played the course thirty times in my head before I go to bed tonight." Many of Dad's teams heard that story as an illustration of both physical and mental preparation.

In *Modern Defensive Football*, a book Dad co-authored with Jones, they defined the will to prepare as: *mental toughness—the willingness to pay a price in practice for victory. Mental attitude creates within the player the will to win, the desire, through proper conditioning, to develop his physical ability to the fullest possible extent.*

Dad observed his team throughout spring practice. Obviously, he was looking for players with athletic talent, but more important, he was deciding which players had the itch to succeed. "If an individual doesn't have the desire to excel in his own psyche," he said, "there's not much a coach can do about it. The coach can improve upon what's already there, but he can't manufacture something that isn't inherent in the individual."

Many of those who coupled the overwhelming desire to achieve with a willingness to hit hard were sophomores, and Dad frequently had fairly young teams. "The public thought that if a first year player were inexperienced, he could be forgiven for mistakes," he said. "That person would learn and get better as he had more experience. But I thought the opposite. If a player wasn't good enough as a sophomore, he wasn't ever going to be good enough."

With the toughest players in place, the second part of Dad's coaching philosophy kicked in—simplicity, built around a core offense. "We didn't have many plays," says Wade Walker. "Four to the left, four to the right, a fullback counter and a halfback counter. It modified as we went on and got better and did more, but basically, that's all." Dad's teams practiced those plays until they were virtually hardwired into their brains.

Darrell Royal explains the results. "No one was ever confused. A football player that's confused you can't tell from a so-called coward—a guy that doesn't like contact. They look exactly the same. They don't know where to go or what to do; they stand around a lot on the edges and they're never in the eye of the storm .... One thing about Coach Wilkinson's teams—they were never confused. They knew exactly where they were supposed to go and why they were supposed to go there."

The simplicity of his approach meant Dad didn't have to work his teams to death. Instead, his practices were very efficient, a trait he brought with him from his college mentor, Bernie Bierman.

Jack Mitchell says, "Bud had a schedule. There was never a period of time when anybody stood around. Practice never went more than two hours, and he got more done in those two hours ... than anybody could ever believe. And on that schedule, he never wore you out completely."

Instead of exhausting the whole team by scrimmaging for hours every day, Dad ran specific drills, such as quarterback/halfback handoffs, for specific combinations of players. Mitchell says, "One thing I learned from Bud was repetition. We'd run that handoff over and over and over again until we got it right."

Drills also were essential for eliminating mistakes. "If you have the ball thirteen or fourteen times in a game, fumble three times and have three penalties, you only have seven opportunities to score," Dad said. "Penalties, fumbles, and missed assignments are things you can control, and you must control them so you don't waste your scoring chances."

Drills require a degree of patience and persistence that is foreign to most players—and to their coaches. "There's no telling how many coaches came to Oklahoma to study Bud's offensive thinking," says Royal, "but when they would go back home, they wouldn't have the patience to do what he did or stick with that philosophy. The way I heard it from Coach, football was a series of first downs; it was a game of ten yards. You make ten and move the chains. If your offense is well executed and you . . . take care of the ball, ultimately you'll get a touchdown. The more you drill that way, the more efficient you become."

Oklahoma players were expected to give everything they had to every drill in every practice, every time. Dad believed once they got used to playing all out, no matter what the drill was, they would develop the habit of playing against themselves, rather than the opponent. He always said it didn't matter whether the other team was wearing red, green or white jerseys. The key was to pay attention to yourself, to make sure you were playing your best, and not to worry about who was across the line.

He emphasized that if you looked at the film of two teams and cut out the big plays, you couldn't tell which was the better team. Football is a game of big plays, he said, and the only way to make big plays—or prevent them—is for all eleven men to give their utmost to each and every play. With that kind of discipline in place, victory takes care of itself.

The efficient use of drills and practice time saved energy. Because that stored energy was available for game days, Oklahoma became known for the speed and quickness of its offense.

"His emphasis," says Mitchell, "was on speed, rather than size, for the entire team, not just the backs, but the linemen, too. The sprints after practice, God almighty. We'd go four 50s and then two or three 100s."

"Take two teams that are evenly matched," Dad said, "and theoretically each team will have the ball thirty minutes of the game. However, if we run fifteen more plays during our thirty minutes, the yardage we make on those plays is the yardage that will result in our victory. We really believed that and taught it and went to great pains to make the players believe it."

Moving fast also demoralizes the opponent, says Walker. "He had the simplest philosophy of how we were going to win. We're going to pour the pine to them so hard and so severe, and the pace is going to be fiery for three quarters . . . . If we poured the pine to them, if we kept the pressure on them for three quarters, then the fourth quarter was ours. He kept saying time and time again . . . never worry about what's happening in the fourth quarter. If we've done what we think we should, the fourth quarter is ours. We'll win because they won't be willing to pay the price."

Any Oklahoma player not willing to "pour the pine" consistently would find himself disciplined. Dad disciplined the team by moving players up and down the depth chart throughout the entire season, based on the constancy of their effort. Assistant coach Pop Ivy says, "Usually, he moved a player who was on the first string and played poorly and gave a bad effort. Nothing was said to them by any of the coaches, but on Monday morning, they were down on about the fourth team."

Most coaches don't bother with this type of up and down movement. They set their teams and forget about it for the season. But, as Ivy says, "It was a very effective way of getting effort out of players. The biggest thing Bud was looking for was what kind of effort a player was making. If a guy didn't play, he just didn't play, that's all. But if he *did* play and *wouldn't* play and wouldn't give his best every play—well, he could find himself down on the third or fourth team.

"As a matter of fact," Ivy says, "the first thing Bud would ask every one of the coaches on Sunday when we got through looking at the pictures of the game was, 'Is there any player that should be moved up or down?' He was very concerned about getting the best players playing football and not sitting them on the bench."

Dad was always concerned with what was right for the total team. In a book he later prepared for *Sports Illustrated*, he said:

*"Linemen prefer to play defense because they get more personal recognition by making tackles than by blocking on offense. Backs prefer to play offense because they get more recognition by being ball carriers than by being defensive players. Nonetheless, each player must be willing to subordinate his personal goals for the good of the team if that team is to achieve its maximum potential."*

Simplicity, preparation, practice, speed, appropriate discipline, heart and teamwork, then, were the watchwords as Dad began to build the Oklahoma football tradition. Many coaches stress those same qualities, however, and don't have the same kind of success. As Royal says, though, "Bud was different from all the rest."

The difference between Dad and other coaches was his ability to innovate, communicate, and motivate. The Oklahoma 5-2 defense is a premier example of his innovative style.

"If I contributed anything to football of an original nature," Dad said, "it was the Oklahoma 5-2. We evolved it from the seven-man line, which in that day and time was one of the standard defenses. In order to add a little fluid ability, cover passes, and make adjustments, the 5-2 dropped the ends off the line of scrimmage, so they became linebackers. Now we had five linemen, not seven—two inside linebackers and now, two outside linebackers. We were able to funnel everything to the middle guard. It was awfully hard to go wide against us.

"The defense has stood the test of time. It's something that every team plays today."

Offensively, Dad was in the vanguard of coaches using the split-T, which he'd picked up from coach Don Faurot at Iowa Preflight school. "It proved to be the offense of the future," he says. "The splits in the line divided the players enough that if you could stand off with them, you didn't have to create the hole; the hole was already there. My experience in football was playing single wing football where you had to double-team people and knock them aside to open the holes .... The split-T was the wave of the future, where the holes were created before you snapped the ball. Today's option football is totally an extension."

Ivy mentions, "Bud wanted to do things differently. He wasn't content to settle with the same concepts .... We were always talking about something this team might be able to accomplish that the team before wasn't able to. He was constantly looking for the things they could do best."

All this innovation could have been confusing to the players. To work successfully, innovation has to be combined with good instruction. As Royal notes, "I don't care how smart a coach is, it's how you teach. Some people can just teach the game. That was the genius of Coach Wilkinson. He expressed himself extremely well. Coach once thought he'd be an English professor. He would have been a good teacher whatever his subject was."

Walker concurs. "Coach had a great, great command of the English language. Why is that important? If you don't give players the where and the why, you're not going to sell them. Coach Wilkinson had the ability to define what we're going to do, how we're going to do it, and then why we do it. He was just the best at that."

For Dad, communication and motivation worked together. During the summers, he wrote weekly letters to the players, urging them to keep up with their conditioning and reminding them about offensive and defensive fundamentals. Instead of keeping the letters and recycling them for the next team, he purposely destroyed each set and rewrote them from scratch every summer. He believed this discipline was important for him—that he should concentrate on his present thoughts and feelings rather than rely on his past notes.

During the football season, Dad also wrote weekly letters to the members of the Oklahoma Alumni Association. These letters, which Dad put together with Harold Keith, the university's sports information director, gave him an opportunity to pat specific players on the back, which was an extra motivational boost for them. It also kept him in touch with the alumni, for Dad was enough of a realist to know that a coach needed their support if the going ever got tough. His letters made alumni feel they were right on the sideline with him at every game.

Dad's motivational techniques were especially meaningful because they were always based on respect for the other person.

As Royal says, "He never really jumped on a player. I agree with Coach that the most important thing a player has is his pride. A coach can destroy pride. The player is in an indefensible position. If he's cursed or yelled at in front of his teammates, he either has to take it or rebel. If he rebels, then he's probably kicked off the squad. Coach always allowed us to keep our pride."

Walker adds, "The worst I ever heard him say to a player was, 'It just looks like you don't want to play.' Is that strong medicine or is that strong medicine? You can't shun them worse than that. You couldn't have called him a low-down gutless son of a bitch more explicitly . . . . Coach never raised his voice; he never got overexcited other than for joy and praise of you. He never downgraded you."

For Mitchell, the memory is similar. "He wouldn't get out there and just cuss and give you hell and kick your ass around. If you weren't cutting the mustard or were dogging it or something, he'd say, 'Jack, you'd better take a rest.' Of course, he had the players to replace you with. Dave Wallace and I were the two quarterbacks. I didn't want to hear him call for Dave Wallace."

Perhaps Dad's most effective motivator was the fact that he truly believed on any given Saturday his team could be beaten. Where most coaches fire up their teams with dreams of glory, Dad was more pessimistic. And he had a remarkable capacity to generate respect for an opponent.

For a man who put such stock in the power of positive visualization, Dad's own imaginings were unusual. Each Sunday night, he would visualize one of the next opposing team's very good players running up and down the field for touchdowns.

Then he would visualize the scoreboard, with the opponent far ahead. He said if he could convince himself defeat was possible, he could convince the team, and they would run a little scared. This tactic was especially useful when Oklahoma was regularly pulverizing the opposition.

He was also a master of motivational storytelling. Most of his players remember—and they remember in astonishing detail—one particular motivational story Dad used to tell. The players call it "the bird story."

As Dad related it:

There was a group of people back East who enjoyed one another's company and frequently got together just to talk. There was one especially brilliant man, and they often met at his house to hear what he had to say. To this group came a new young man. He attended one of the meetings and said to the others after the session broke up, "This old man is a phony, and I'll prove it to you."

The others asked him how he would do it. He replied, "Tomorrow, I'm going to go to him and I'll be holding a bird in my hand. I'll say, 'What do I have in my hand?' I'll let the bird's head peek through, and the old man will say, 'You have a bird in your hand, sir.' Then I'll ask if the bird is alive or dead. If the old man says, 'It is dead,' I'll open my hand and let the bird fly free. If he says the bird is alive, I'll squeeze it to death. I'll show you this man is not as brilliant as you all suppose."

The next day all went as planned. When asked, the old man said, "You have a bird there, sir." The young man said, "Well, is it alive or dead?"

The old man looked at him intently and said, "As you wish, my son."

Different people took different lessons from that story, but most players agree it was one of his best and a potent source of inspiration before a game. They went out of the locker room with a real sense that their fate—in life, as well as on the field—was in their own hands.

&

The 1947 record made it easier for Dad to recruit outstanding athletes. Tatum was a demon recruiter, and Dad inherited a great group of men. To build a winning tradition, however, he had to keep them coming.

A good recruiter is part diplomat, part father confessor, and part salesman. Dad turned out to be an ace. Pop Ivy, Bill Jennings and other assistants generally made the first contact with recruits. "Bud was pretty smooth," Ivy says, "when it came to talking to players themselves and talking to parents. We did a lot of the leg work, but he could wrap them up pretty quick."

"In those days we'd center a compass at Dallas and swing it 150 miles," Dad said. "Anyone within the circle we had a pretty good chance of getting."

Dad's recruiting philosophy was typical of the great college coaches of that era. "You have to recruit young men with athletic ability, but because football is a game of heart and morale, you first have to have a boy of good character who is able to handle college work. He should be able to graduate. If he doesn't have the academic ability to graduate, he shouldn't be in college." One of Dad's early prize recruits was Jim Weatherall, an All-American tackle who won the Outland Trophy in 1951. In the late '40s, Jim already appeared to have great talent. In those days, he was considered huge at 6'4" and 230 pounds, and he had superb lateral movement.

Recruiting is always a crap shoot, however. A kid who looks good in high school just may not cut it in college ball. It's a risk coaches take in recruiting and a situation parents don't always understand. Parents are always sure their boy will play first team.

Jim Weatherall's father was an exception. When Dad visited the Weatheralls, Jim's father said, "Coach, he's a good boy. I don't know if he'll ever be good enough to make it with you, but please treat him well." Dad always cited Jim's father as the ideal football parent and wished there were more like him.

One of the major emphases of Dad's recruiting was each player's education. Proud as he was of his teams, he was prouder still of the fact that he graduated more than ninety percent of his scholarship athletes. He also stressed excellence and the relative insignificance of material things. In the early '50s, he went after a young man named Jack Ging.

"My father was killed early in World War II ... my mother was a waitress in Alva ... and we never had a car," Ging says. "It's a pain in the ass when you're a senior in high school and you wanted to date and you always had to double date because you didn't have a car. I'd had a very successful high school career, and one of the colleges that recruited me guaranteed me a car. That meant a lot to a boy like me.

"Bud came to the Texas-Oklahoma high school all-star game in Wichita Falls, Texas .... He asked me if I'd like to ride home to Oklahoma with him in the university plane. On the airplane he said, 'Jack, I know about you and your mom and everything. I even know that you've had offers from a couple of other schools .... I'm going to tell you something. You're very young now and a car seems like an important thing. As you get older, you can always buy a car. It's the easiest thing to do—buying a car. I'll tell you something that will never happen to you again. The next four years will never come again, and the only thing we're going to give you to come to Oklahoma is the chance to be a champion. You can never buy that. If you come to Oklahoma, we're going to give you your books, tuition, and $15 a month, but it's going to be great.'

"We came into Norman," Ging continues, "and I came to his home and met Mary, who I absolutely loved .... I called my mother and said, 'Mom, we're not going to get that car.' She said, 'What happened?' and I said, 'I'm going to Oklahoma.'

"Bud made you start looking at the value of everything you do."

 ❧

What resulted from all the preparation, motivation, and recruiting was better and better football. The 1948 season, however, opened with an unfortunate loss to Santa Clara. Sportscaster Curt Gowdy, who was covering Oklahoma, found Dad outside the dressing room, dejected, head in hands. Gowdy put his arm around him and said, "Tough loss, Coach." Dad lifted his head slowly and wearily, but as Gowdy recalls, he suddenly snapped out of his funk and said, "Oh, hell, we probably won't lose again for three years."

The next week, on October 2, 1948, Oklahoma defeated Texas A&M, and Dad's prediction started to become reality. From that date until January 1, 1951, Oklahoma would win an unprecedented thirty-one straight games. It was the longest win streak by any collegiate team in history and would stand until broken—by Oklahoma—in 1953-57.

But first they had to get by Texas. Once again, the Oklahoma-Texas game was the third of the season. Oklahoma had now dropped eight straight to the Longhorns. With one victory and one loss going into the game, Sooner fans didn't know what to expect, but they were nervous. Texas had blown out its previous two opponents and looked loaded for bear. On October 9, 70,000 people thronged into the Cotton Bowl—the largest crowd ever.

Jack Sisco was nowhere in sight, and the game was exactly what it had always been—hard-hitting and hard-fought, but this time, Oklahoma was on the winning end of the 20-14 score. They would lose to Texas only once more in the next eight years.

The 1948 Missouri game was as exciting as the previous year's tilt, but for a different reason. It was the first time an Oklahoma game was nationally televised, and it was rated the day's No. 1 game. Though his mentor, Don Faurot, was head coach at Missouri, once again Dad's team showed no sentimentality regarding the two coaches' previous affiliation. The Sooners stomped Missouri 41-7, and went on to defeat Nebraska, Kansas, and Oklahoma A&M. They finished the season with a 10-1 record, won the conference championship, finished fifth in national polling, and defeated North Carolina 14-6 on January 1, 1949 at the Sugar Bowl.

During the 1949 season, the Sooners were undefeated and unstoppable, scoring 399 points to their opponents' 88. Dad was named the American Football Coaches Association's Coach of the Year. Winners of the Big Six title and second in the national polls, Oklahoma made their second consecutive appearance in the Sugar Bowl on New Year's Day, 1950, drubbing Louisiana State 35-0.

This game was notable for the "spy incident" that preceded it. Ned Hockman, who was in charge of filming the Oklahoma games, was fully involved as the scenario unfolded.

"Bud and Mary were in the dining room. Loretta and I were at an adjacent table when a man came in and said something to Bud. Bud got up and left. When he came back, he came right over to me, and he had tears in his eyes. I said, 'What's the deal, Bud?' He said, 'I just got a call from a man who lives in a house that's adjacent to our practice field, and he says that in between two garages there's a ladder with a board on it, and there's a man there taking notes and pictures. He has a telescope and he's taking pictures."

The next day, Hockman; Dr. C.B. McDonald, a dentist from Oklahoma City; John Askin Jr., a policeman from Biloxi, where the practices were being held; John Scafidi, a professional player; and Bill Dennis, a photographer, slipped up to the garage.

"McDonald pulled the door open," says Hockman, "and the guy saw us and jumped down. I took a motion picture of him running out and the still photographer took a still photograph. This big guy, who they said was Piggy Barnes, had a handkerchief over his face. So McDonald reaches up and gets this handkerchief and pulls back, and the picture you see looks like McDonald is getting ready to hit him.

"Actually what's happening is he's just pulling the handkerchief off, and he's in a hitting position, and I put my camera down and the other guy put his camera down and we all charged this guy and tackled him. He hit me across the chest, and I went rolling about twenty feet. He swung McDonald out of the way and he ran into this house . . . . He never did come out. So we all got in the car and the photographer processed the still shots and brought them to Bud."

When the picture was shown the next day, Darrell Royal identified Piggy Barnes, a former LSU player Royal knew, as the spy. Accusations and counter-accusations flew. As was his style, Dad kept relatively quiet about the whole incident, although he did publicly challenge Barnes and Elbert Manuel, supposedly an accomplice, to present themselves to a panel of three neutral witnesses for identification. They didn't show up.

As far as the Sooners were concerned, the final score was the final vindication, and many Oklahomans consider the 1949 team the best in Sooner history.

In 1950, Oklahoma again went 10-0 in regular season play and received their first national championship. Dad was tapped as Coach of the Year by the Associated Press, and three players made All-American. A highlight of the year was quarterback Claude Arnold's passing. He threw 114 times with only one interception.

Arnold was at the helm during the 1951 Sugar Bowl. Kentucky, coached by Paul "Bear" Bryant, had, says Arnold, "a very good scheme for us. We had a young line that year and he took advantage of the fact that they didn't pick up on the cross stunts and things he devised. We had like eight fumbles in the game from . . . people coming through the line completely untouched, from our linemen picking up the wrong guy . . . . We outgained them on the field, but we had eight fumbles. You've got to give them credit for that." Kentucky triumphed 13-7.

ঽ▲

And so the first streak came to an end. For Dad, however, a new life was about to begin. In 1951, Dad had emergency surgery for a bowel obstruction. During the course of the surgery, doctors discovered a testicular lump. The biopsy revealed cancer. "When Bud found out," my mother says, "he wanted to go to the Mayo Clinic because that's where his best friends were. He had such confidence in them . . . . We went on the train, and he was flat. I mean he was really, really sick . . . . He was really glad he had the bowel obstruction, because he didn't know [about the cancer]; if he'd waited a long time later, it might have been too late."

At the Mayo Clinic, the cancerous testicle was removed and Dad returned to Norman. Though there was nothing ever written about his illness, everybody in town knew about it, because, according to Mom, people who shouldn't have talked about it did. "I found it very disappointing that professional people wouldn't keep a confidence," she says.

"It was such a shock at the beginning," Mom continues. "I'm sure it always is when they tell you. He didn't want any publicity. I think he didn't want people thinking he was going to die right away . . . . He wanted to find out how it was going to turn out."

Dad thought it was best just to tell people about the bowel obstruction and to say there were complications from that, and that's what Mom did. "I never told anybody he had cancer," she says.

Dad, as was his habit regarding private matters, kept his own counsel, and involved only those who needed to be involved. Just before he left for the Mayo Clinic, he confided in Gomer Jones, and Jones promised to look after my brother and me, no matter what.

Once the surgery was completed, his friends and coaches had very little discussion about it. All-American Eddie Crowder, who had just become the starting quarterback, says, "I just remember him coming to spring practice looking less healthy. He was always such a vibrant, healthy-looking person . . . . In later years, he told me he had felt so fortunate . . . and so blessed to have been going to Mayo's. He said he was fortunate to have the kind and quality of doctors and good friends that they had at Mayo's. I know he felt he had kind of been given a second life."

What he would do with that second life was amazing.

# 3

## Oklahoma: The Invincible Years

ॐ

*"Nothing can seem foul to those that win . . ."*
—Shakespeare

In 1951, the Sooners, though their ranks were badly depleted by the Korean War and by the graduation of several players who'd been instrumental in bringing Oklahoma its first national championship, were able to craft an 8-2-0 season and win the Big Seven championship. They were ranked tenth in the national polls.

Also in 1951, Dad made another crucial addition to his staff—Port Robertson. Robertson already was established as the wrestling coach, and his teams ultimately won three national championships; for the football team, he served as freshman coach and head of the study program. Dad believed deeply in the student half of the student-athlete equation, and he was vehemently opposed to freshman eligibility.

"I was disappointed in '51," he said, "when the rules changed and made freshmen eligible, and I'm even more disappointed by what I see today. I understand the situation now—they're on scholarship, and if they're capable of playing, we should play them and so forth—but there is a change when a young man doesn't have to prove his academic integrity prior to being eligible. I was very much in favor of the rules change after the '51 season [that once again made freshmen ineligible]."

Bill Carmack, a professor who came to Oklahoma in the late '50s, says, "Bud established a kind of idealized image of what a football team could be like. It was fun to have the athletes in class. They were scholarly. Bud is often quoted as saying, 'If you're too dumb to do well in college, you're too dumb to play the kind of football we play.' "

It was Robertson's job to see that the players proved they were capable students. "It's hard work for students," he says. "People don't realize that going to college is so much harder than trying to get out on a job. It takes discipline to study . . . . I know I wasn't very popular, but you get a bunch of guys who were kind of big shots in their high school and then they come up here and find there are some other big shots . . . they're not quite ready for it.

"I interviewed every athlete and his parents. I told them that I expected those youngsters to go to class and to make an honest effort, and I explained the rules . . . . I told their mamas that if they didn't go to class, they were going to join the Navy. Then I explained what the Navy was like, and Junior would kind of squirm around a little bit. I'd say, 'This is the way it is, and there's not going to be anything changing. If it's not what you're looking for, why, we need to discuss it further or you need to look somewhere else.' "

The punishment for infractions of Robertson's rules was running the seventy-two rows of the stadium steps. The number of trips up and down varied with the seriousness of the sin, and many players made those round trips for many reasons. Carmack recalls one student athlete in particular.

"The players had been told they were never, ever to approach the faculty using football as the basis for a special favor. The second year I was here a football player came to me and said something about how they had an away game, and I'd scheduled a quiz, and he was leaving . . . . All he wanted to do was take it early. I said sure. I'd been on the debate team in college and I was often gone on debate tournaments—sometimes for ten days to two weeks. If the faculty hadn't been completely understanding, I'd never have graduated. I thought it was wholly appropriate. So, by God, the next thing I knew, someone told me the kid was running the stadium steps because the word had gotten out that he had taken a quiz early. That's how strict Bud was about the student athlete."

Many of the players who ran the steps today credit Robertson for their graduation and subsequent careers, and they smile when they recall him. Jimmy Harris, who quarterbacked the team in the mid '50s says, "He was the kind of guy that made you appreciate it and made you do it .... He'd break your neck if you didn't. I have tremendous respect for Port, and I think I wouldn't have gotten the degrees I've gotten if he hadn't been there right on top of me." And Brewster Hobby, a former halfback, laughs when he says, "I was thinking about Port the other day, and my chest started hurting from where he used to poke me with that finger of his."

ᘒ▲

If football players were students first, Dad viewed the coach as a teacher whose job was to develop young men to their fullest potential—to be the best they could be—and not just to win games. An article in *Collier's* quotes him as saying, "Too much emphasis is placed on a coach's winning. The professor who flunks half his students in an academic class is judged not only tough, but good. But if a coach flunks half his players by losing half his games, he's apt to be fired. A coach is always trying to make an A player out of a C player. The professor just flunks the C if he doesn't come through."

So, Dad set out to teach the game of football and to create the challenges that would raise each player's level of performance until the whole unit could say they were getting an A in desire, heart and execution. He did it, as all great coaches do, by expecting the best and somehow getting players to believe the best was within them. All they had to do was reach down and find it.

Halfback Jack Ging has a vivid memory of Dad saying, "You have a great opportunity here to do something most people go through life and never get a chance to do, and that's to test yourself .... If you go out in a football game and make a long run for a touchdown, you're going to be in the headlines, but any of you could have blocked for that run and then gotten up and blocked again and again, and nobody knows it but you—the headline in your own heart and soul. You know you did something really special . . . . You have to give it all—all the time. The mark of a man is what that person will do when nobody's watching . . . . Go out and find out what kind of man you are. Are you really the kind who would sacrifice your body for your teammates for the whole sixty minutes? . . . You can fool the coaches most of the time. You'll fool me most of the time, and you can fool the fans all the time. Never fool yourself. Why waste a moment of time? Find out what kind of person you are."

He inspired his teams to believe in themselves off the field as well, and to conduct themselves as gentlemen, with honesty, humility and kindness. He was smart enough to know, however, that "do as I say" teaching wouldn't work. He had to model the traits he expected, not just give them lip service. He continued, therefore, with only a few exceptions over the years, to praise and support his players, rather than to berate and intimidate them.

Eddie Crowder mentions one player he thought was going to have a hard time. "He was just a little too moody and temperamental. He became unbelievable. He just responded so noticeably to this positive, loving support. . . . Bud would never put him down. As a matter of fact, when he was in his more moody periods, I would see Bud with his arm around him . . . . The noticeable growth in this guy from the time he arrived as a freshman until his senior year, when he was a spirited, positive, consistent performer, was just awesome."

Too much praise without counterbalancing correction, however, can result in swelled heads. If Dad saw his players getting too impressed with themselves, he had just the remedy. The message would be delivered quietly, but it would sting nonetheless. Ging remembers an incident in 1951 that had an effect on the whole team and particularly on him.

"[Like all the sophomores, I was playing my first season; freshmen hadn't been eligible the year before, and we were on our way to the Oklahoma-Texas game]. We were the defending national champions, and we were really cocky little shits. We got on this big Braniff airplane and the stewardesses were really nice to us . . . . I had never been to Dallas, and here is the band playing for us, and we get off the plane, and there were a bunch of little kids getting autographs . . . . We work out and we go to the hotel in Ft. Worth, something I'd never seen in my life.

"We got off the bus, and it had already hit the front page of the paper—the picture of us landing in Ft. Worth. In Alva, we got a paper once a week. Here we hadn't even been there two hours and our picture's on the front page. We walk in through the lobby and people . . . are patting us on the back. I had just ridden in a four-engine plane, had good-looking clothes on my back, had arrived in a big city, signed autographs. God damn, I felt like I was really something, and so did we all, and that's the way we walked."

Things went downhill from there. "[Before games] Bud did everything the same way. At the hotel we would have our defensive meeting, and then we'd get our seventy-five cents for the movie. Then we went to the movie and came back in. The next morning we'd have our offensive meeting.

"So," Ging says, "we went down to our defensive meeting, and we were all in there kind of visiting and joking and talking about everything—really feeling great. Bud came in and he walked up to the chalkboard. He stood there in front of the board and turned around and said, 'We're not going to have a defensive meeting tonight.' He put the eraser and chalk down and said, 'If you'd like to know why, I'll tell you.'

The room became very still. 'You people aren't ready to play. You think you're something really big. You remind me of a great American story called shirt sleeves to shirt sleeves in three generations.

'Many years ago,' Dad related, 'there were a lot of destitute people in a lot of countries. All they wanted was a chance to work—to make a living so they could claim a decent life and have a family and raise their children. They came to America . . . they worked hard, and they taught their children the same discipline. But the children became a little more successful . . . . They were able to go to school. They even had a good change of clothes.

'So these children,' Dad continued, 'grew up and the family business became much more prosperous. Some of the children went to college . . . . They were pretty well educated. That was the second generation.

'Now came the third generation. They were driven to school, they had hot lunches, and then they decided they were going to go to college— like it was owed to them. The parents were proud and happy, and they sent their kids off to college. That generation came home and took over the business because that was owed to them, too . . . . That's the way they ran the business. With that attitude, they lost everything they had. At that time, they were no different from their grandparents who came over here in the first place. That's shirt sleeves to shirt sleeves in three generations.' "

At this point Ging remembers how Dad personalized the story. " 'The reason we're not having a defensive meeting is because you're going to lose tomorrow, not because you're not good, but because you think you're so much better than you are. You think you're so special.'

"Players began to sweat and shift in their seats. 'I watched you talk and laugh on the plane as though you deserve that. You think I didn't watch you land in Ft. Worth and see boys *who have never hit or been hit in an Oklahoma uniform* sign autographs? The boys who were getting the autographs didn't know who you were, but they knew you represented the University of Oklahoma . . . . You thought they wanted *your* autograph. I watched you come into the hotel and I watched you getting your money to go to the movie. You don't deserve the money you got for your tickets, you have not earned those clothes on your back, and you have not earned the right to sign an autograph for anyone. Good night.' "

Ging continues, "Now, I'm sitting there thinking he was only talking to me, but . . . everybody sat there with their heads down . . . . Nobody knew what to say . . . . Everybody pushed their movie money back. I went to my room so infuriated and so embarrassed. I said to myself, 'I know one goddamn thing. I'm the first generation. If anybody gets my autograph again, I'll have earned it.' We didn't have TV then, so we sat and thought about what the old man said."

Pete Elliott, who joined the coaching staff that year, remembers the meeting well, too. The 1950 team had won a national championship, but Elliott says, "these [younger] players had not earned it. The point was, which generation were they? Were they willing to make the same sacrifices as the players who gained Oklahoma's reputation? . . . . It's a great story, really, when you apply it." According to Elliott, though the shirt sleeves story was one of the most memorable, "Bud had a way of expressing himself that was always understandable and believable. It wasn't put on . . . . In locker room talks, it was always a 100 percent honest thing. Why are you playing? Is it worth it to you? He could explain it better than anyone else .... He just told you as it was, and you could say, 'Yes, that's correct, I'm ready to go.' He was a genius at that."

"He was so classy in his presentation of his thoughts," adds Crowder. "He was a wizard of expression .... While he had an awesome vocabulary, he didn't have to overpower you with multiple syllable words. He had the unique ability to arrive at one or two or three themes that had remarkable relevance and a wonderful ability to come up with illustrative stories or examples that made it so meaningful."

It would be nice to report that following the shirt sleeves talk, the team went out and destroyed the Texas opposition, but as Dad had predicted, the game ended in a 9-7 defeat. Nonetheless, the talk seems to have had the desired effect. In his letter to the alumni, he said, "I'm as proud of the way our team fought against Texas in defeat as I've ever been when we won during the past three years." Though beaten, he still believed his team to be real "first generation" men. After that loss, they pulled themselves together and remained undefeated the rest of the season.

Dad might not have liked freshman eligibility, but in the 1951 Texas game, he had reason to be grateful for it. After halfback Billy Vessels tore the ligaments in his knee in the fourth quarter, freshman Buddy Leake stepped up to replace him and went eleven yards the first time he touched the ball. That play led to OU's only touchdown and was the start of a great career for Leake.

&

If Dad was a wizard with the words, he also taught by example. Dick Ellis, a lineman, tells of a day when "we were doing calisthenics and I was on my back doing leg lifts. I thought we were never going to stop, and I had my eyes closed because I was straining, and I let out an expletive. Bud was standing right over me, and I didn't know it.

"The next day I went into practice and my locker was empty as it could be. I went to the manager and said, 'My uniform isn't in there.' He said, 'You have to see Coach Wilkinson before you can get it back.' I thought, 'Oh, my God.' I went in and he read me the riot act.

"I just said, 'Oh, shit.' He didn't like that," Ellis continues. "He said, 'You're a senior. You're supposed to be some kind of a leader and here you are doing that. Now you go back there, and if you ever do that again . . .', well, I don't remember what he told me, but I do remember my uniform being gone."

Though discipline was never-ending, Dad continued his efficient use of players' talents into the decade of the '50s.

"To the extent," Crowder says, "we wouldn't put on any hard gear at all. It was unheard of at that time. The normal leader might think if doing these tough things is good, then more of them has got to be better . . . whereas high intelligence and wisdom says, 'OK, enough is enough.' Where other people would be loading their guns for firing some more practice time . . . he was doing just the opposite."

Conditioning was essential for success in this kind of compressed practice situation, and if Dad ever had a player who exemplified the "will to condition," it was Tom Carroll, who returned to Oklahoma in 1952, after his service in Korea. His conditioning effort was so extraordinary that Dad held Carroll up to future teams as the model to emulate. As with all role models, a mystique, some of it now known to be apocryphal, grew up around him. Generations of players heard the story of how Carroll's feet were frostbitten in Korea and there was concern he would never play again, but how, through Herculean effort, he rebuilt his body and became a standout. I grew up with that story.

Carroll today finds the tale surprising. "I don't think I ever got frostbite at all," he says. "I did get cold feet." Nonetheless, he continues, "When I came back from the service I was in terrible shape. When I was a freshman, I probably weighed 175 or 180, and when I came back from the service I was probably on the order of 210. You can imagine how much more bulk I was trying to carry around . . . . In 1952, I struggled, but I didn't even make the traveling squad."

Carroll dug in. "I was terribly disappointed that I couldn't perform like I knew I used to. It was hard on me, so I decided that I either had to get in shape or forget the whole thing."

Through the next winter and spring, he ran the indoor track, practicing sprints and hurdling. In the summer, he worked for an oil company, and went to the track before and after work.

"I went over to the stadium steps," he says, "and I started trying to run them. That was quite an ordeal; there were seventy-two rows. By the end of the summer, I got to where I could run ten times up and down the steps without any resting .... During the fall, I could feel myself improving .... I was getting back to where I was before.

"One Monday, we went out and scrimmaged the freshmen .... I had a good scrimmage; I was real proud of myself—I didn't let anybody know that—but I was very proud of what I had done. The very next day Bud called me out with the first group. I was very delighted and elated to say the least."

Whether his feet were frostbitten or not, Carroll's effort *was* Herculean, and it was the kind of effort Dad rewarded with playing time.

ॐ

The innovations Dad was making and the success of the program he was building made him attractive to other football programs, and he fielded many inquiries about his availability. Rumors ran so rampant, sports information director Harold Keith prepared and sent the following tongue in cheek news release to papers around the state:

*Norman, Okla.*—Bud Wilkinson, Oklahoma football coach and athletic director, today denied that:

He is breaking his contract at Oklahoma to accept a job at ... (Please fill in the name of whatever school is mentioned in the next rumor).

"I am very happy at Oklahoma. My contract at Oklahoma still has three years to run. When it expires, I hope the Oklahoma people will want me to stay longer," Wilkinson says.

In fact, Dad was approached to replace his mentor, Bernie Bierman, at the University of Minnesota, but he turned down the job. The U.S. Naval Academy was also in touch, but once again, Dad stayed put in Norman. He did, however, according to Dr. Cross, briefly resign in 1951, in order, he said, to accept a position in public relations with a company owned by Eddie Chiles, who had been instrumental in recruiting many fine players. Cross relates in his book that in a private conversation, he began to sense Dad really didn't want to leave, and Cross poured on all his powers of persuasion. Within two hours, Dad had rescinded his resignation and broken the news to Mom, who, Cross says, "had just spent the evening explaining to Mrs. Cross why her husband had decided to leave OU."

ॐ

As head coach, Dad spent a great deal of time with the quarterbacks. Eddie Crowder says he was often amazed by what he termed Dad's "second sight." He seemed to know what was going to be thrown at the Sooners in any given game, even if the offenses or defenses were unusual or quirky.

"I remember one time we were playing Colorado in Norman and it was supposed to be close," Crowder says. "Bud told me in a final meeting on Saturday morning, 'I just have a feeling they're going to try to load the defense .... I want you to be particularly alert in observing the secondary, and be prepared to use play action passes.'

"I walked out there and on the very first play, I looked up and their three deep guys were all within five yards of the line of scrimmage. I couldn't believe it . . . because Bud had said not three hours earlier that's what they were going to do. We hit four [play action passes] in the first seventeen minutes of that game."

Crowder was present for a similar, more dramatic episode later in his career. "I think we were getting ready to play Oklahoma State," he says, "and Bud had been going over all the preparation, and he said, 'I had a premonition that we might see something called a 10-1 defense. Probably you've never seen this because it isn't very sound, but let me show you this thing.' He drew just a basic formation on the board, and showed us how it worked," Crowder says. "Somewhere years before, he'd seen the formation in a clinic, and he said, 'It's the kind of thing . . . if somebody just used it as a surprise deal . . . it could make things difficult for us.' "

The defense Dad described was exactly the defense that lined up against the Sooners, but because he had "known" it was coming, the team was prepared for it—and the trick defense was a bust. According to Crowder, the opposing coach believed he'd been spied on, because the 10-1 defense was almost unheard of. "I talked to Bud about it, and he said to me, 'Honest to goodness, I had knowledge that they would want to do it.' He said he woke up in the night with this in his mind. He said he felt terrible someone would think we would spy, because we didn't need to do that."

In 1952, the season opened with a tie at Colorado, a series of wins, and then a closely-fought 27-21 defeat by Notre Dame. The Sooners came back to win the last three games, and the 1952 team boasted some of OU's most impressive records. The team won the Big Seven—its fifth consecutive conference championship—and led the nation in scoring, with 407 points; Billy Vessels was named Heisman Trophy winner; four players made All-American; and the team was fourth in the national standings.

The unquestioned highlight of the season was the 49-20 victory over Texas. Smarting from the previous year's defeat, the team played as if they were possessed, scoring twenty-eight points in the first quarter. I was only a youngster at the time and was not at the game. I went to the movies, but found I couldn't concentrate on the screen. Every couple of minutes, I'd run to the concession stand to check the score. I was sure the concessionaire was pulling my leg when she'd tell me we'd scored again every time I asked her. In fact, though, OU was scoring that rapidly— at 2:15, 7:44, 9:44, and 10:50 of the first quarter.

"Listen up," Dad said at halftime. "You have an opportunity to do something unique. You can go back out and double the score." They nearly did.

For Vessels, of course, the Heisman hoopla was very exciting, but nerve racking, too. "I'll never forget sitting on the plane to New York City," says Vessels, "saying I'd never made a speech before and I didn't know what to do. Bud said, 'Don't worry about your delivery. As long as you believe what you're saying, the audience will accept you. They will know that you're not just saying words, but that you really believe what you are saying.' "

Vessels goes on, "He said, 'You're going to have these writers talk to you and make this production about you at the dinner . . . . Don't pay any attention; what really counts is what you are twenty-five years later.' Believe me, I never forgot that remark."

ё▲

The 1953 season began inauspiciously, with a second consecutive loss to Notre Dame and a tie with Pittsburgh. The Texas game turned the tide. A new chapter in Oklahoma football was about to be written.

In the first quarter, Oklahoma led 6-0. They added a second touchdown in the second quarter, entering halftime with a 12-0 lead. The third quarter brought another touchdown and conversion for a 19-0 score. Things looked great.

After Texas roared back, scoring with 6:14 left in the game, the Sooners were backed up to their own goal line. Dad made the decision to kill some time and gain decent field position by taking a safety and kicking off again.

Tom Carroll carried the play in to Gene Calame. "I was the messenger. 'Get behind the goal line and drop down to your knee. We'll take the safety and I'll punt it out.' "

Calame, however, didn't do it. He ran out of the end zone and was downed at the Oklahoma three-yard line. The story goes that one of the linemen told Calame, "If you see any daylight, go for it," and that, seeing a hole, he tried to dive through it. That story is not true. Dad made it up.

As Calame relates it in Harold Keith's book, *Forty-Seven Straight*, "I was running around the end zone trying to kill time and forgot where I was. I was close to the goal when a Texas player hit me, knocking me back on the field. Texas tackled me there. It was their ball."

"Bud made up the lineman story," says Calame today, "just to keep me from being embarrassed about the entire situation, and it gave me an excuse . . . . He made it up on a moment's notice to keep the press off me.

"He told me not to be the least concerned about it," Calame says. "He firmly believed that you never did anything very well if you didn't practice it numerous times to where it became almost rote memory. He said that it was the coaches' fault, because we had never practiced taking the ball and running around the end zone, although I really don't know if you need to practice that play very often.

"[One thing I remember]," Calame continues, "is that I was on the ground and I looked up, and those white cards—the 10x12 white cardboard cards Gomer carried that had all the defenses and all the offensive plays we were going to use—all I could see was Gomer throwing those cards. They were landing everywhere."

Texas scored and converted quickly. They tried an onside kick, but were offsides. Their next attempt at an onside kick was too short. Oklahoma took over, and went on to win 19-14.

That hard-scrabble victory was the beginning of Oklahoma's 47-game winning streak. From that day—October 10, 1953—until November 16, 1957, they would not be beaten or tied. Small, tough Gene Calame would win every game he started at quarterback, as would Jimmy Harris. Players who graduated in 1956 never saw anything but W's in their entire collegiate won-lost column.

Except for a scare at Colorado and a defensive squeaker at Missouri, the scores for the remainder of 1953 were lopsided, and the team was selected to play Maryland, coached by Dad's old boss, Jim Tatum, in the 1954 Orange Bowl.

J. D. Roberts calls that Orange Bowl the biggest game of his career. "We'd had our chance to be No. 1, and we got beat by Notre Dame, so that did it. The tie with Pittsburgh knocked us completely out, and in those days the No. 1 team was picked before the bowl games. So as the season ended, it was Maryland, Notre Dame, UCLA, and then we were fourth. It's No. 1 and No. 4 playing. This was the opportunity for us to get back ... and of course we did it with a 7-0 victory."

Calame remembers the game for different reasons. "When Bud coached with Tatum, they would always send somebody to the opposing team's hotel to see if any of their players just happened to leave some material around ... like their playbooks or their defense. So Bud made up a fake offensive report and a fake defensive report. We laid them all over the lobby.

"After the game, somebody told me Tatum said, 'Bud, you son of a bitch, that wasn't your offense or defense.' "

The 1953 team finished the year as conference champions and led the nation in scoring; Roberts won the Outland Trophy.

It was a great triumph for Roberts, and a real piece of luck, too, because in 1952, he'd been booted out of school for disciplinary reasons. It was only when Dad went to the president of the university and took personal responsibility for Roberts' behavior that he was permitted to return to school. By the time he was a senior, Roberts had become such a solid citizen Dr. Cross had the suspension expunged from his transcript.

ঽ▲

Roberts says, "I think that '53 team was probably as good a coaching job as has ever been done." One reason for Dad's great success that year and throughout the years of the streak was a rules change that dictated a return to one-platoon football, in which one group of men played both offense and defense, rather than having two specialized squads, one for offense and the other for defensive play.

Dad was elated. The rules change played right into his hands. Since he always stressed conditioning—which is critical for success in one-platoon ball—his teams were well-positioned to win. In addition, one-platoon ball was more conducive to Dad's major strengths—organization, teaching the game, and motivating the team.

Quarterback Jay O'Neal says, "It was completely different [from today]. You didn't have a coach for the right guard and the left cornerback and all when you were trying to organize a practice. It's one thing to go out there and spend four or five days getting ready to run an offensive attack … and that's all you have to worry about. But when you have to get the team ready to play offense and defense, and then also to do all the kicking aspects of the game … with a coaching staff of maybe six people, it takes an amazing organizational talent."

"I thought I knew a lot about football until I met Bud," says Jimmy Harris, another great quarterback of the '50s. "He spent so much time on so much detail, it was like going to school with the greatest professor in the world."

Roberts echoes, "Bud's big thing was that we weren't only told what to do, but how to do it, and the most important thing—why."

Harris continues, "I think if you've got any intelligence you want to know … why …. Bud could make you feel like you were doing it for a reason."

The players had to learn everything in short, intense bursts of practice. "We weren't on the field as much as the band was,"

Gene Calame says. "I can remember them marching over to the practice field before we started, and we'd be through and eating, and here would come the band marching back, going through their drills. Bud thought coaches made a serious mistake in overworking their players and wasting a hell of a lot of time."

Calame continues, "It was Bud's approach to coaching to get it down into short drills—five minutes on this, three minutes on that, where other coaches were scrimmaging their whole team for an hour or an hour and a half. He never understood how you could beat up your players all week scrimmaging and have them enjoy the game . . . . He'd say, 'See how tired those people are, and how quick we look. We're so much quicker than everybody else . . . . I really believe those other people are overworked.' "

That isn't to say practices were easy. Roberts recalls, "Once the season got started, it was mostly drills and going over how to do it . . . . It was hard work and an awful lot of running. The other thing that Bud did was that we would run plays—I mean six, seven, eight, nine, ten in a row—until we got that thing down, until we knew everybody was together . . . . We got the timing just right. It was timing. Everything was timing. It was repetition, repetition, repetition."

"The return to one-platoon football was a difficult transition," Dad said, "but a necessary one. I delighted in it, because the game is a totally different game. If you have to play both offense and defense, you have to learn to do things you are not naturally adapted to do and may not want to do. Very few quarterbacks want to play defensive halfback, but they have to play someplace on the defensive team . . . . I just think it's a far better game because of the fact that it's a discipline . . . . Getting a true feeling of excellence in something you don't want to do is one of the factors that *should* be the highlight of the experience."

Preparing players for one-platoon football also made another of Dad's tenets very clear—that the game of football is first and foremost a defensive exercise. "There's an old cliché," he said, "that if they don't score, you can't lose; you don't get fired for ties. If you're good enough defensively, you're in the game and you maybe can win. Offense is important, but not nearly as important as the defense." To build his teams, he chose his strongest defensive players and taught them offense, rather than the other way around.

All-American Jerry Tubbs was at first disbelieving about his new assignment. "All through high school I was a center and linebacker. In my sophomore year, Coach Wilkinson called me into his office. I was second string center playing about one-third of the game. He said, 'I think we're going to move you to fullback.' My heart just fell. I thought, 'Is he trying to get rid of me? Is this the way they do things?' I didn't know what was happening. [I found out], of course, that they put me . . . at fullback strictly for defense—so Kurt Burris and I could both play."

"Defense is harder to play and harder to teach," said Dad. "The offensive team has the signal set, the starting count set, and the offense has the ability to fake and do other maneuvers that, hopefully, will help them make yards. The defense is handicapped at the start of every play. They don't have the starting count; they have to adjust . . . to be good enough to stop the opponent for no gain . . . . That requires a totally different skill from the offensive lineman's or offensive back's."

Players who needed to be taught the skills necessary for one-platoon play often learned them from Dad himself. "He was teaching me how to block as a fullback," says Tubbs. "They put a dummy up and he would go out there himself and roll at that dummy to show me precisely how to get it done.

"That really impressed me. He didn't have on any pads or anything, but he'd go out there and show us exactly how to do it. He was a great teacher, and so was Gomer. They were just excellent teachers."

Because he believed so strongly in the importance of defense, Dad tried to vary his defense with every game. He thought the worst thing he could do was allow the opposing team to line up against a defense they'd studied all week. He'd change and modify the alignment, even if it weren't particularly strong, just to give the other team something new to chew on and try to figure out. Oklahoma would stay in the new defense until the other team had adjusted to it, and then they'd revert to their own game plan. The opposing offense would then have to adjust to that, too. It was very confusing.

Dad wasn't just a defensive coach, though. He was a wily competitor when it came to designing innovative offenses. The Swinging Gate, a formation that involved diverting virtually the entire line fifteen yards from the center, was very effective and a real crowd-pleaser, too. Since Oklahoma usually gained a lot of rushing yardage, many people didn't realize that about seventy-five percent of the team's plays were options. It made for terrific flexibility and was good for mystifying and demoralizing the opposition.

♣

By 1954, the Oklahoma juggernaut was invincible. That year brought Dad's second unbeaten season, with the Sooners outscoring their opponents 304-62; another conference championship and a third place ranking in the national polls.

It was an exciting time for Oklahoma athletics. As J.D. Roberts says, "It was something even as kids you got caught up in . . . . Oklahoma all of a sudden was in the spotlight. Bud put it there, and then along comes Mickey Mantle from Commerce, Oklahoma . . . and [pitcher] Allie Reynolds . . . . It just seemed like everything fell in place."

There was a fly in the ointment, however. The Sooners' amazing performance had caught the eye of Walter Byers, the NCAA executive secretary. A variety of speculations had arisen, particularly in the press, about the activities of the university and the Touchdown Club regarding player recruitment and retention. According to these published reports, great sums of money were being spent on athletes beyond their scholarship aid. It was charged that players were receiving "walking around" money, clothes, and cars. Some of the discussion surrounded Buddy Leake, and he was asked to testify before the NCAA.

"The four points were," says Leake, "[My dad had written to family friend, Dr. Phil White], who he'd played football with, and who lived in Oklahoma, and said I was being recruited at Tennessee; how about Oklahoma? So Dr. White told me if I made a C average, he'd buy me a suit at the end of the school year. Then he told me that anytime I had tickets I couldn't get rid of . . . he'd buy them for ten dollars apiece . . . . That was pretty good money in those days. It wasn't like today; we'd get three comps or something, and he said he'd buy them from me if I couldn't get rid of them.

"Then, in the summer of 1953," Leake says, "he let me use his '41 Cadillac to go down and visit my sister in Dallas, and then we drove it home one time to my father's funeral. It was a twelve-year-old car, a nice car, but it wasn't any new convertible."

The NCAA Committee on Infractions found Oklahoma guilty of "offer[ing] students cost-free education beyond the athlete's normal period of eligibility" and "paying medical expenses for wives and children of student athletes." They found that "patrons have provided student athletes . . . with fringe benefits in the form of clothes, miscellaneous gifts of cash . . . and in the case of two athletes, paid the charges of the periodic use of a rent-a-car."

Oklahoma was placed on probation for two years, but as Dr. Cross reports in his book, "No serious charges against the university's athletic policies had been sustained . . . and the action taken by the NCAA had not included barring the institution from . . . bowl games."

Though Dad clearly was angry about the probation and felt the university had upheld all Big Seven policies, publicly he said nothing, as he went about getting the team ready for 1955.

And in 1955, even with the cloud of probation hanging over their heads, the team just got better. They won another national championship, another conference championship, and on January 1, 1956, returned to the Orange Bowl to face Maryland, and to defeat them once again, 20-6.

Dad prepared quarterbacks Jimmy Harris and Jay O'Neal to run Oklahoma's rapid offensive style. "You suck air so hard," says Harris. "We would run it just boom, boom, boom. We did it in practice especially before the Orange Bowl game our junior year."

The constant running had the desired effect. "We were in tremendous shape when we got down there that year," says Harris. "I don't think anyone was in better condition than we were. I know Maryland certainly wasn't . . . . [I remember a Maryland player groaning], 'Oh, my God, here they come again.' He hadn't even gotten the defensive call out and here we were back at the line of scrimmage, ready to go again."

Dad said, "A lot of people still feel that in the 1956 Orange Bowl, Oklahoma didn't huddle, and that simply wasn't true. They huddled every time; they made up for it in the speed factor.

After the whistle blew . . . they ran back to the huddle. That was time they saved. Most teams adjust their paths and walk back."

Though Dad had always emphasized speed, it was All-American Tommy McDonald who made it the Oklahoma trademark. "McDonald," Dad said, "was a marvelous football player—not a very big boy. When he was in high school, since he was slight, he adopted the attitude that no matter how hard he got hit, he'd get up and run to the huddle. So while the people who had hit him were lying around stunned, he was back in the huddle and ready to go. He was the catalyst that made the other people believe in it."

Dad liked McDonald's attitude. Ned Hockman tells the story of McDonald's first practice with the team. "The first scrimmage, they kicked the ball to McDonald and they tackled him. [After practice, Bud saw McDonald was upset and went to find out what was wrong.] He came back to me and said 'Great, great, Ned. You know what? He was crying because he thought he had let me down, because when he first touched the ball, he didn't run it all the way for the touchdown.' "

Pete Elliott says McDonald was a powerful example. "I think the speed just evolved, and once it got going, it was a phenomenal thing to look at . . . . Other teams just couldn't stay up with it. McDonald was the guy who epitomized everything. The rest of the players did it too, and it was a great source of pride. Man, oh, man, when they got to be known for it, they couldn't wait to get back into the huddle and up to the line of scrimmage."

As well as preaching the speedy offense, Dad spent hours with the quarterbacks, teaching and reteaching, until they were able to know intuitively what was called for in every situation.

"In one of the Texas games," Harris says, "Bud wanted us to call a time out . . . . At that time, there were limited substitutions, so I had already called the play I thought we should run. He brings in a play, and it's exactly the same play. You knew exactly what his thinking was, because you were just a copy."

Jay O'Neal adds, "We were pretty well programmed. Bud had pictures and slides taken of where the quarterback would stand and look at the defense, and then we would call a play, and he would flash a defense up there . . . just like flash cards. We would either let the play go or check it . . . . Actually, it was so sophisticated that some of the pictures would only show you what was right in front of the guards or center, whether it was defense or non-defense . . . It was well thought out."

ঌ

1956 brought, incredibly, another undefeated, untied season and probably the most satisfying win of Dad's career. Notre Dame had been his nemesis, and now, after blanking opponents, including Texas, in their initial three games, and thumping Kansas 34-12, Oklahoma was to meet Notre Dame once again. Preparation was fierce.

"He always gave a hell of a talk when we were at Notre Dame," says Jimmy Harris. "Talking all about the pride of Notre Dame and having to beat them in South Bend and about how there is no way we could win unless we were just really lucky.

"Later he had the quarterbacks meet and he said, 'You know, that speech may have been a little tough. You know we're going to beat the hell out of them. There is no way they can beat us.' That was one of the few times I can remember him being real confident. Hell, he knew it."

The game was a rout. Oklahoma 40, Notre Dame 0. "I think he took more personal satisfaction out of that 40-0 than any game he coached," concludes Harris. The team awarded Dad the game ball.

Standing atop the national polls, the Sooners next met Colorado. This game was marked by Dad's actually showing a flash of anger to his team. Obviously, pressure had been building, as the win streak wound from team to team and year to year. Dad was always a realist; he knew eventually someone would cut the string, but when it happened, he wanted to be defeated by someone playing tougher and with more desire. He wouldn't tolerate Oklahoma's backing into a loss.

At halftime Colorado led, 19-6. Though Dad's style was to use halftime only to review mistakes and make technical corrections, on this day, Jay O'Neal says, "Everyone was sitting on the floor, leaning up against the walls. We were all kind of quiet and morbid. Bud came in and I remember him saying, 'Gentlemen, you ought to take those red and white jerseys off. You don't deserve to wear them.' And then he turned around and walked back out."

As the halftime ended, however, Dad relented, and after giving out the second half assignments, built the team back up again. "Look," he said, "there are 60,000 people out there who know you're beaten. There's only one person in the entire stadium who knows you're going to win. That's me."

Dad's anger—and his rebuilding of the team's confidence—were effective, as Oklahoma came back to win 27-19. "He wasn't hostile," recalls O'Neal. "He tried to make everyone feel like it was just a dishonor, the way we were playing . . . . If you're an Okie, you need to get out and really play . . . . We knew we could beat them. It was just a matter of going out and doing it. We did."

As All-American halfback Clendon Thomas puts it, "He made sure we understood that some other guys had paid the price to get as far as we had gotten . . . . There was some obligation there. I think what hurt me the most when we finally lost in 1957 was that I had to be part of it. It's one of those deals where you say, 'Don't let me be part of that one.' "

After the Colorado scare, the team rolled on, outscoring their remaining foes 218 to 20. They retained their national championship ranking for a second consecutive year and led the nation in rushing, with a 391-yard per game average. Thomas was the major college scoring leader with 108 points. With 102 points, McDonald was the nation's second highest scorer. McDonald and Jerry Tubbs won multiple honors and joined teammates Bill Krisher and Ed Gray as All-Americans.

ᶻᵃ

Faculty reaction to the win streak was interesting. Roger Nebergall, Ph.D., said, "There was enthusiasm for the team and for Bud," but he also remembered a fascinating conversation that took place during a Faculty Club presentation Dad made. "I went to the meeting, and when Bud said what he had to say, he opened the meeting for questions, and there were questions, of course.

"One fellow said, 'Bud, I would not change a thing you're doing, but it occurs to me that young men who go through four years of college football and never lose a game have lost something.'

"Bud," Nebergall continued, "said, 'Yes, I think that's right. There's a great deal to be learned from doing your best and losing. On the other hand, losing when you're not doing your best teaches you nothing at all.' I've reflected on that often and I cannot imagine another circumstance in which that exchange would have occurred."

ᣡ

The years since 1953 had been rewarding, but not without stress. A streak of the kind Dad was building puts the coach and his team in the crosshairs every week. Fans expect only victory; opponents wait for their moment to pull off an upset. The media clamor for interviews; the administration wants the program to make money.

Added to these kinds of pressures was the drive for perfection that characterized every aspect of Dad's life. "Perfection was one of his consistent themes," says Clendon Thomas. "He would give an example of how many players we had and what would happen if we each made only one mistake . . . . The goal was to have a perfect ball game . . . . The only pressure I ever felt was that I would fail ... that I would not do my job or perform like I should perform."

"My goal," Thomas relates, "was to do everything I did, every play, as hard as I could do it, with no reserve. He was so good at explaining that if you got tired, better that somebody replaced you. Don't ever take a loafing step. He would recognize that it was an impossibility ... but I don't think there was a player I played with who didn't know what his job was when he went to the field."

Dad applied that all-out standard to his own behavior as well. It was a tall order, and though his demeanor was always polished and his attitude always positive, he was often tense. After an eighteen-hour day, sleep frequently eluded him. He would tempt it by playing the family's chord organ or by reading. When that didn't work, he'd head off to the training room, to take some steam and stretch out on the automatic massage table. He'd often wake there in the morning.

Beyond physical stress management techniques, Dad also relied on the power of prayer. In an article for the *Episcopal Churchnews*, Tom Siler writes that "self-denial ... pinpoint[s] the foundation stone on which Wilkinson builds winner after winner."

Self-denial was indeed a theme of Dad's, but not simply self-denial for its own sake. In a speech for the Campus Crusade for Christ, Dad shared the reasons for his belief in the importance of self-denial. "Jesus said we must deny ourselves. An athlete who practices Christian self-denial will not be swayed by popularity or material appeal and has the proper perspective desired in a good athlete.

"Prayer places sports in its proper perspective," he continued. "It helps the player find the right place for himself on the team, and gives the team a unified spirit it can never attain in any other way."

It's not surprising Dad was sympathetic to the Fellowship of Christian Athletes, later becoming part of its governing board. All-American Bill Krisher was an FCA member at Oklahoma. "Clendon and I would go out and speak to churches all over Oklahoma. We were sharing our witness here, there and everywhere. The coaches were great . . . . Bud was very supportive of FCA, which was our Christian commitment . . . . We had monthly meetings at the dorm and we had the Bible study and everything going on, and I think that was part of the strength of our team."

≈

In 1957, it looked as if the undefeated tradition would be continued for another year, but some chinks were beginning to appear in the armor. That year's win over Colorado was by only a one-point margin, and the Sooners looked—and were—vulnerable.

Three weeks later, Notre Dame visited Norman. They'd been humiliated the year before, and humiliated Irish are dangerous Irish. They were coming to play—and to win.

According to Ned Hockman, "We were all waiting for Notre Dame to come to practice. Their bus came in, and it was weird, because as the bus stopped, we [heard them] chanting 'Beat Oklahoma, Beat Oklahoma.' Those guys said that all the time they went to the dressing room, while they were dressing, and when they came out exercising, they continued to say 'Beat

Oklahoma.' . . . . They were doing all these maneuvers chanting, and then they got on the bus and left, still chanting."

At the game, Hockman, looking through the lens of his camera, had a different view from the one the fans saw. "Nick Petrosante would go over guard or tackle . . . and whoever our guy was—he had a big body but little legs, I remember—he was bloody. They kept running right over him, and he was fighting the best he could, but they just moved down the field . . . because he was a little bit smaller . . . . He fought his heart out, but he was just too small on the base."

Petrosante had a brilliant day, recovering an OU fumble and rushing well, especially on critical third downs. But it was Irish halfback Dick Lynch who blazed past right end into the end zone, with under four minutes to play. Monte Stickles kicked the PAT. Oklahoma battled back, but an intercepted end zone pass brought collegiate history's longest winning streak to an end as the Sooners lost 7-0, ironically to the team that had last defeated them before the streak began.

Oklahoma fans sat stunned and silent. My friend, Gary Rawlinson, son of OU trainer, Ken Rawlinson, says, "Did you ever experience such disbelief? Surely they'd extend the game so OU could come back and win. How could it happen? There was no consolation. It was over. No one would ever do it again. Never. OU would never be the same again, nor would any of the people whose lives were intertwined with the program."

Suddenly, however, the crowd rose in a sustained, thunderous standing ovation of appreciation for all that the Sooners had accomplished before this day.

In the locker room, Dad was telling the team, "I'm very proud of you. You guys have been part of something that nobody will ever do again. You've won forty-seven straight major college football games. In life, if you're going to play, you're going to lose. If you don't want to lose, don't participate. Just remember that the only ones who never lose are the ones who never play." Halfback Jakie Sandefer says, "He was very classy [about it]."

Clendon Thomas recalls, "We played well. We played as hard as we could. It just didn't go our way that day . . . . We were a little flat for some reason. There are times when you get so ready that you do a little bit too much and you're not really fresh enough to go out and bang away. Bud was a class act, but I know he didn't like to lose .... He's a nice guy, but ... he didn't take any loss casually."

Indeed not. Tim Cohane, in a 1982 article in *Modern Maturity*, wrote that Dad's "grace was matched by the inner furnace of a white-hot competitor."

"After the press conference [following the Notre Dame contest]," Cohane quotes Dad, "I had a dinner date at the home of Dean Earl Sneed, our Faculty Representative of Athletics. When I got out of the car, I kicked a brick wall in front of Earl's house and had an extremely sore foot for about a month. Temper, temper, temper!"

Temper or not, accolades flowed in. When Dad went to the Monday meeting of the Oklahoma City Quarterback Club, all three hundred attendees stood and counted in unison to forty-seven. Notre Dame's Father Joyce, who had represented Father Hesburgh at the game, commented on Dad's graciousness in defeat, saying, "I've never heard a losing coach ... say that his team played as well as it could."

That's what made the defeat bearable for Dad. His team had played with heart and soul and blood and grit, and they had been defeated by a superior team. It was over and it was time to get on with the rest of the season.

Of course, not every Oklahoman took things in stride as well as Dad did. Cohane overheard two men leaving the stadium, saying, "Wilkinson hasn't got it anymore. He's been around too long." A nasty letter to the editor in the Oklahoma City paper credited the team's four years of success to a walkover schedule and called for a "young hero able to cope with modern football." The old hero was, at the time, forty-two years of age. A few other armchair quarterbacks publicly questioned Dad's coaching ability—just after he had finished piloting his teams through the longest win streak ever, one that has stood for nearly four decades.

Guided by his own internal gyroscope, Dad took what little second-guessing there was with poise and courtesy, as he prepared his team for the games that followed. They regrouped, gathered up their pride, and won them all, defeating Nebraska 32-7, Oklahoma State 53-6, and Duke in the 1958 Orange Bowl, 48-21.

The team took the conference championship and was ranked fourth in the nation. The string had been broken, but the team's heart was still intact.

And they were working on a three-game winning streak.

# 4

## Oklahoma: Glory and Change

*"A circle that took them in ..."*
—*Markham*

Although, of course, in 1957, football fans in Oklahoma and across the nation were mesmerized by the Sooner winning streak, Dad was involved in an activity that ultimately would mean much more to him and to the university than his won-lost record. He was breaking the color line in Oklahoma football, and he was doing it in the person of Prentice Gautt.

"At the University of Minnesota, I'd never experienced any segregation problems," Dad remembered, "because I'd always had black teammates in 1934, 1935, and 1936, when I was playing. At the time [Gautt came], the Big Eight never admitted they were a segregated conference. They somehow just hid behind the status quo, and nobody was playing blacks.

"Prentice," he continues, "was the best high school player in the state of Oklahoma. A group of black doctors in Oklahoma City knew Prentice was this good, and they said they would contribute to the scholarship fund to pay for Prentice's scholarship the first semester, and then, if he could make the team, OU would pick up the scholarship. I knew he could make the team all right . . . . He matriculated and was the best player on the freshman team and was on scholarship after the first semester."

Gautt remembers the excitement of being recruited by Oklahoma after the state's high school all-star game, the first all-star game in which a black athlete was permitted to play. "It was like a kid's dream," he says. "I wasn't even supposed to be there—had only been told [I was allowed to play] two days before the game. I got the Most Valuable Player and made two or three touchdowns . . . had a great game, and after the game, Kurt Burris, an All-American, was talking to *me*, and asking me to come to Oklahoma . . . that Bud was interested. I very much was walking on Cloud 9."

But life on the campus, as on the field, was tough. Gautt's addition to the team was taking place, after all, only three years after *Brown v. Board of Education*, and integration was proceeding very slowly. Though there had been a handful of black graduate students at Oklahoma, Dr. Cross had to improvise separate entrances and even self-contained classroom booths to comply with the state's segregation laws. Gautt was the first African-American undergraduate athlete at the university.

Early in his freshman year, Gautt became discouraged, to say the least. Freshmen who had scholarships were kept separate from walk-ons, and because Gautt's scholarship was non-conforming, he was considered a walk-on. "What kept me going," Gautt says, "was looking over at the first team and telling myself that someday I would be on that team."

Meanwhile, Port Robertson was on hand, taking the freshmen "under his wing," as he put it, and dispensing his unique brand of discipline. "I was sure he and [freshman coach and former OU captain] Norm McNabb were trying to run me off. They ran us so much. I was determined to stay, though. He would have had to kill me before I'd leave. I think I gained a lot of respect from those guys for just hanging in there."

If Gautt thought the team wanted to be rid of him, the freshman game with the University of Tulsa quickly reassured him. Stopping for a restaurant meal on the way to the game, his teammates were outraged when the wait staff refused to serve Gautt. "It's so vivid in my mind," he says. Team members informed the restaurant that if Gautt couldn't eat there, they weren't going to eat there either, and they walked out. "Several guys—Brewster Hobby, Jim Davis, Jere Durham—" Gautt says, "led the support for me there." Gautt also remembers Morris Tennenbaum, for years the gatekeeper at the OU stadium, meeting him at the bus outside the restaurant. As a Jew, Tennenbaum was well acquainted with prejudice. "He walked up to me when I got on the bus. He was one of the first ones to come up to me, and he said, 'You and I have experienced a lot of similar kinds of things. You're going to be much better for it.' He was cheering me on."

Though Gautt began to make inroads with the team, he ran headlong into Dad's high expectations. After the first year of spring practice, "Bud called me in," Gautt says, "and he told me, 'You're not living up to your abilities; you aren't even going to make the travel squad.'

"I thought I was working hard. Of course, being out there with all those guys as a freshman, I'm thinking, 'My goodness, I shouldn't be out here. These guys are all tremendous players.' You've read about them all your life, and here they were, and you were out there on the same field. It was a real adjustment."

By telling Gautt he wasn't living up to his abilities, Dad lit a fire under him. "Because at the same time he was telling me that, he was saying to me, 'I believe you can do it. I want to see you do it, but now you're not going to.' You don't say that to a guy unless you're behind him and believe he can. His bringing me in and preparing me to really put out—that's all it took."

Gautt knuckled down and made the varsity squad in 1957, his sophomore year. The majority of his teammates applauded his achievements. A vocal minority did not.

"He didn't receive acceptance from some of the Texas players at all," recalls halfback Brewster Hobby. "They had had no affiliation with a black player, and we in Oklahoma only scrimmaged against them. The black schools didn't play the white schools. I got acquainted with Prentice during the all-state camp ... and then down in Norman, and he was just such a heck of a gentleman .... I saw him go through the mental and physical abuse he was having to go through in practice, with people hitting and so forth."

Hobby goes on, "Then some very, very strong verbal statements were made to him. I just admired the guy because he had such character. It would have been easy for him to quit .... He was just a true gentleman who gave 110 percent all the time, kept his mouth shut and went about his business."

The minority's problems with Gautt stemmed not only from lack of knowledge and prejudice, but also from jealousy.

"It was a tough time for Prentice," says guard and team captain Leon Cross. "I was right next to him in the dorm. I'd been in an integrated high school in New Mexico . . . so I'd been around black athletes . . . . That helped me—actually being close to a lot of black kids. But some people from strictly segregated situations made things tough, especially when Prentice beat them out of their positions . . . . That didn't set too well with them . . . . Prentice certainly won their respect eventually."

Hobby adds, "Some players were very vocal about their feelings that Prentice was given his spot because he was black, which was just not true."

Halfback Jakie Sandefer was an exception to the Texas resistance to Gautt, and in fact was Gautt's roommate when the team traveled. "We were on our way to play Pittsburgh . . . and they passed out the depth chart. [You roomed with whoever was behind you on the chart]. Prentice was playing behind me and Bobby Boyd behind him. But they had me rooming with Boyd. When I got to the hotel, I saw Bud walking across the lobby, and I said, 'Coach, if Prentice is second team, I don't mind rooming with him.'

"Well," Sandefer says, "Bud said, 'I'll tell you the truth. When we were working out, Prentice dropped some punts and . . . we have moved Bobby back to second team.' When I volunteered to room with Prentice, I thought they'd not roomed us together because he was black, not because they'd moved him down."

The next week, Dad asked Sandefer if he'd room with Gautt full-time. "I said, 'Sure, I'd be happy to,'" says Sandefer. "I roomed with Prentice the rest of that year on trips. The next year, they moved him to fullback. We still roomed together every game. Prentice and I had a great relationship. He's a class guy. He and I became very close friends, and he was a delightful person."

Notwithstanding Sandefer and some others, the undercurrent of discontent and prejudice continued. "Things had surfaced to the point where it was hurting the team overall," says Hobby. "I think we were beginning to choose up in groups. The group that supported Prentice had taken the time to get to know the guy; the other guys just ignored him and stayed away from him.

"It kind of spread through the ball club. We had a couple of weeks where we hadn't had great success, and morale was very, very low. Bud called the captains in and told them they needed to do something because the attitude was starting to harm the team."

After a midweek practice, which Dad said was the worst he remembered in his entire coaching career, he called the team together and confronted them about their denigration of Gautt. He insisted that if they were men they would have the guts to say to Gautt's face what they were saying behind his back—and to get on with it. He left Gautt and the rest of the team in the locker room.

Cross picks up the story. "Prentice got up in front of the team and said, 'In no way do I want to be a detriment to this football team. I want it to be successful, and if it will help team unity for me to leave, I'll do that.' Of course, he walked out. The team then met and there was no one except two or three guys that really . . . wanted Prentice to leave. The rest of us—well, it really solidified the team."

"I popped up in that meeting," says Hobby. "[I liked and admired Prentice], so I said, 'This is the way I feel, guys.' From then on other people got up and admitted they were wrong— even some of the Texas guys—and said they were glad to be teammates and a part of the Sooners with Prentice. We then went into having a real solid football team."

Gautt was fighting for respect off the field as well. When the team journeyed to Texas for the big game, "Dallas law was that a Negro could not stay in the same hotel overnight with whites," Dad said. "Prentice would go to the team meeting and then to the show; then we would put him in a cab and drive him over to the black hotel, where he would spend the night."

"Ken Farris went with me the very first time," says Gautt. "Bud told him to give me money and to make sure I was able to get back . . . . A different cab driver would pick me up in the morning and bring me back to the hotel where I could eat with the team. That worked out just fine."

Things were not much different in Oklahoma. "We spent the night before home games in Oklahoma City at the Skirvin Hotel," Dad said. "At the time of Gautt's first appearance with the team, we had had practice and gone to dinner. We went to the Skirvin and registered. Rightfully, the black press were there, and they snapped a myriad of pictures of Prentice registering.

"Dan James, who was my friend and the manager of the hotel at the time, was so overwhelmed the next morning. His switchboard just lit up with people saying, 'Now that the hotel is integrated, can we have this party or that function there?' The situation evolved until the next week when Dan said, 'I'm sorry, we can't accommodate you because it's just too tough.' "

The team found another Oklahoma City hotel and did not return to the Skirvin again until after Gautt had graduated.

While Gautt was fighting his uphill battle, so was Dad. "I had so much hate mail," he said, and there was vociferous alumni criticism, all of which he kept from Gautt as much as possible. "I know Bud protected me quite a bit," Gautt says, "and it was as if the two of us were in it together. When you're going through it, you just go through it; subsequent to that, you look back and someone says you were pioneering, and I guess they're right. I certainly didn't look at it that way at the time."

Pioneering it was, however, and Gautt paved the way for other black athletes at Oklahoma. "Prentice is in a class all by himself," says Hobby, "and no matter what, he would have weathered the storm."

Port Robertson agrees. "It was a tough thing, but the attitude that Prentice had . . . well, I'm sure they only made one of him. I don't have the words to describe what he's made of, characterwise."

"I truly love Prentice," says halfback Mike McClellan. "He helped me so much when I got to start; he was always there. Besides being a great football player, he was a great human being, one of the finest there is. A lesser person couldn't have done what he did."

Dad's assessment of the Gautt situation was that "it was the most significant thing I did when I was coaching; there's no question in my mind. But all the credit belongs to Prentice, believe me. It was so damned tough for him that anything I could do was after the fact.

"The rapid change in the segregation situation is one of the marvelous things that has happened in America in my lifetime."

≀▲

Beyond the addition of Prentice Gautt to the team, in 1958, Dad was facing turmoil on another front. The NCAA once again was sniffing around the Oklahoma football program. Though the situation was not resolved until 1960, when the NCAA slapped Oklahoma with a probation that included post-season games and television appearances, it drew Dad's attention during the entire period.

In 1958, NCAA Executive Secretary Walter Byers wrote to President Cross and asked him for information concerning a "slush fund" Oklahoma boosters had used to recruit athletes in 1953 and 1954. The fund had been administered by Arthur Wood, an Oklahoma City accountant.

Wood replied that he had managed a fund used to transport athletes back and forth to Norman for recruiting purposes. Wood further said when he could not support the activity from his own funds, he enlisted the help of friends, and he disbursed the money.

Byers then demanded the records of the fund, including names of contributors and amounts. Wood refused to give them up, saying the release of his confidential client records would be a violation of federal law.

After nearly two years of back and forth negotiations, the NCAA announced an indefinite suspension, and stated the matter could be reconsidered when and if Wood opened his books, which he adamantly refused to do.

≀▲

In spite of all the distractions in 1958, the Sooners continued to win, with the notable exception of the Texas game, which was decided by a two-point conversion. The Longhorns, in their second year under Dad's friend and former player, Darrell Royal, won the game 15-14. According to Dr. Cross, who spoke to Royal after the game, Royal was thrilled to win, but devastated it had to be against Dad.

Dad was a big proponent of the rules change that brought the two-point conversion to college football. "I was on the rules committee, and I felt when the suggestion came up . . . that it would be something that would make the game more interesting and would make it easier to come from behind in the culminative parts of the games. I was a very sound exponent of the two-point conversion rule. The evening of the Texas game, however, I obviously wasn't very satisfied with my vote," he said, with a rueful smile.

The rest of the year went well, however, with the Sooners picking up the conference championship, while holding four conference opponents scoreless. They were ranked fifth and defeated Syracuse in the 1959 Orange Bowl, their fourth consecutive Orange Bowl victory.

Though it ended with a win, the Orange Bowl was notable for the absence of David Baker, who'd been quarterback, defensive back, punter, placekicker—a gifted and popular member of the team. He hadn't been going to class, however, and the university bounced him. Baker's eligibility lasted through the end of the season, and legally, Dad could have played him, but his concern for the educational message he'd be sending led him to forbid Baker's participation in the Orange Bowl. Fans howled over the decision, but Baker understood and accepted it. He graduated from another university and became an outstanding player with the San Francisco '49ers.

ða

Later in 1959, things began to sour. The regular season opened with a defeat that was one of the most controversial in Oklahoma history. Playing their first Big Ten opponent, Northwestern, in a nationally televised game, the team traveled confidently to Evanston.

After a Wednesday arrival, there was a Thursday workout and then a special treat—dinner and the early show at the Chez Paree.

"When we first went in," says Brewster Hobby, "there was a beautiful blonde and a couple of old guys in the restaurant. As we went in, they were positioned such that these gentlemen introduced the woman to each of the players. She was very quick to ask, 'What position do you play?'

"Of course everyone was trying to be polite. We told her what position we played and what team we were on."

What happened next is etched forever in the brains—and stomachs—of those who were there.

"They started serving the fruit salad," Hobby says, "and instead of going down the row like they normally did, it was sporadic throughout the area. Evidently the drug was in those salads. They got twenty-two of the top thirty-three players."

Just moments after eating the salad, team members began peeling off for the men's room. "It affected us within three to five minutes," says Hobby. "I remember going into the rest room and there were so many people in there vomiting, it must have been heel deep . . . . We were just piled on top of each other."

Seven players were hospitalized; nine had to have their stomachs pumped. One suffered shock and a circulatory collapse.

The entire incident might have been chalked up to simple food poisoning, except for the fact that the betting line on the Sooners changed dramatically a few hours before the incident occurred. "Somebody made a lot of money on that game," says Hobby.

Further compounding the mystery was the fact that the stomach contents of all the players who had their stomachs pumped mysteriously disappeared, even after demands from trainer Ken Rawlinson and the team physicians that the samples be kept for investigation.

"About the only thing they came up with [as a possibility] was a drug that used to be used to sober people up when they'd been on a four- or five-day drunk. If you hadn't been drinking, it induced . . . uncontrolled vomiting," says Hobby.

Prentice Gautt, worried that he might not be served, stayed away from the dinner, and obviously was not affected by the poisoning. Neither was All-American guard Jerry Thompson. "I was the only one they didn't poison. They only poisoned the good players. Or maybe I just have a strong stomach," he laughs. "We had about twenty-five guys who couldn't come to practice on Friday."

According to Thompson, game day "was the worst we ever had. You'd see players on the field trying to key normally, and then a guard would pull *here*, and you're supposed to go *there*, and instead they'd go the opposite direction. It affected them in such a way that they just did strange things."

The game was played in a driving downpour, and even if the Sooners had been at the top of their form, they would have had a hard time handling Northwestern. The Wildcats, under coach Ara Parseghian, had an outstanding day; the final score was 45-13, with Oklahoma fumbling 12 times, and losing the ball on nearly half the fumbles.

The next week, their health restored, Oklahoma beat Colorado. The Texas game was another defeat, however, and the record was not shaping up as Dad wanted. Though the next two weeks brought victory, the Kansas game was a 7-6 squeaker, and the following week, after seventy-five consecutive conference wins, Oklahoma was defeated by Nebraska.

Dad's letter to the alumni that week stated, "I must not be doing a good job of coaching or the team wouldn't continue to make the same type of basic mechanical errors so repeatedly in every game. I have always believed they were controllable if a team had the morale and discipline which results from proper leadership." As always, he took full responsibility for the team, injuries and food poisoning notwithstanding. His 1959 record now stood at 3-3.

The Sooners went on to win their remaining games, including a thriller against Army at Norman. Though the team once again won the conference, the record of 7-3-0 was the poorest since 1947, and the NCAA was about to lower the boom, which would have repercussions until the end of Dad's Oklahoma career.

᠄ᴥ

By the 1960 season, I had left Norman to study and play at Duke. I agonized, not only over the Duke games, but also what was happening to Dad. For the first time in my memory, and in the memories of many Oklahomans, he was contending with a losing season.

Recruiting had not gone particularly well. "It would have been different if I'd been a little more farsighted," Dad said. "I never realized that Oklahoma had earned enough publicity and

enough accolades that we could recruit beyond our own geo-
graphic area. We felt our recruiting was the state of Oklahoma
and the Texas panhandle. In '60 and '61, I didn't have the normal
athletic talent graduate from high school. If I'd been more farsighted . . . we could have expanded that recruiting area quite a
bit, but at that time, I didn't do it. And the natural flow of talent
just wasn't that good, and we didn't have it."

Some players also feel Dad's heart wasn't in recruiting to
the degree it had been previously. For one thing, he was heavily
involved in his Coach of the Year Clinics. Dad and Michigan
State's Duffy Daugherty founded the clinics, which were annual
weekend coaching workshops for high school and college coaches
and were held in twelve different cities across the country.
Clinics were held in three cities at once—with the clinic staff,
always including Dad, Daugherty and whoever was the American Football Coaches Association's Coach of the Year—rotating
in and out of the three cities over the weekend. One day of the
weekend Dad might be in Boston, the next day in Denver and the
last in Pittsburgh. Obviously, the clinics involved a tremendous
amount of travel and speaking, and they were exhausting. Sometimes, when potential recruits were on the Norman campus, Dad
wasn't there. Boys who had come to meet him were often
disappointed, and that undoubtedly hampered the recruiting
effort.

As Leon Cross remembers, "We just didn't have the talent
in 1960, but I also remember that we had people who didn't make
their grades and an unusual number of injuries. I think sometimes you go through these cycles."

Of course, the '60s were an era of tremendous societal
change, and many athletes' attitudes changed along with the
times. Some players were less likely to take coaching and to
deliver the kind of discipline and dedication to the team and to
their education that Dad required. There was no open rebellion,
and only a few players questioned the system, but the seeds were
planted.

"Maybe it's the old story of the third generation," says
Cross. "We won so long and [then] we got people who really
didn't want to pay the price. The leadership wasn't there. Everybody was worried about 'me' and not the team. Bud was very
frustrated with the 1960 team. He would try different things. He

called us all a bunch of quitters once. A few choice things like that, trying to motivate this team. The talent was there, but the leadership wasn't. We were probably a 7-3 or 8-2 team that went 3-6-1."

Jerry Thompson adds, "It was a period of time when it was obvious we didn't have the quality of player ... we had had. We were just shy a couple of players."

The Sooners lost to Northwestern again, this time without outside interference; they lost to Texas; to Colorado; to Iowa State; to Missouri; to Nebraska. They tied Kansas and defeated Kansas State, Pittsburgh and Oklahoma State. The team placed fifth in the conference.

ᐧᐁ

Putting the grim performance of the previous year behind him, Dad went out and recruited again, this time with slightly better results. And early in 1961, after Art Wood·shared some of his nonconfidential records with them, the NCAA lifted its sanctions against Oklahoma. If the Sooners could improve their record, they could once again play in post-season competition.

Though he was delighted about the end of the suspension, Dad's horizons were widening beyond football. President Kennedy had tapped him to be the director of the President's Council on Youth Fitness. During the summers, he was in Washington, rather than in Norman, and there were meetings to attend and programs to supervise during the year. His exposure to the Washington scene was opening his eyes to the political process, and it both repelled and intrigued him.

Nonetheless, his first loyalty was to Oklahoma, and the team prepared carefully for the 1961 season. It began abysmally, with five straight losses. Strangely enough, however, as Leon Cross recalls, Dad wasn't soured on the team the way he had been on the 1960 squad. "It was a unique time to see his reaction. With the '61 team he didn't have quite the talent he had before, but he knew he had some motivated people. He was a different person than he was in '60, because he realized that we had given the effort. Even though we lost, he was always encouraging. He made us feel good because he was never down on us."

After the fifth loss, sportswriter Dick Snider remembers walking home from the stadium with Dad, listening as Dad told him he was doing his worst job ever as a coach. "We're going to get some players in here next year, or I won't be here," he said.

It was only to his good friend, however, that Dad showed his discouragement, and, in fact, following the fifth defeat, he did something unprecedented. Well-known and sometimes taken to task for his professional pessimism, Dad went on his post-game television show and stated that the Sooners were through losing for the year. They would win the next five games.

Howard Neumann, who co-hosted the show, was shocked. He and Dad worked tirelessly preparing every show, but Neumann always had a couple of extra questions that lent more spontaneity to the telecast. "I asked him," says Neumann, " 'How do you look at the season? This is the first time we've been faced with five losses in a row.' He said, 'I think we're going to win the next five.'

"It floored me," Neumann continues, "because it wasn't at all like him. He'd worry more about Kansas State than he would about Nebraska."

Surprised as people around the state might have been, the Sooners weren't. "He'd already told us the same thing," says Mike McClellan. "He told us, 'This is it. We're not going to lose any more.' "

Nobody believed it could be done. No coach had taken a team from 0-5 to 5-5, and the next five opponents were tough— Missouri, who was ranked in the top ten, Army; Nebraska; Oklahoma State; and Kansas State. The skeptics, however, hadn't reckoned with Dad's "second sight," nor with the *esprit d'corps* and determination his prediction brought to the team.

My childhood friend, Geary Taylor, who later became a Sooner halfback says, "What he said surely came to be. I don't know if he was lucky, or just good at it, or just paid attention. I believe the old saying that he'd forgotten more than most people knew."

The Sooners defeated Kansas State 17-6, and moved on to the Missouri game. "Bud had perception and the ability to foresee," Taylor says. "Before the Missouri game, he sat us all down, and he said, 'This game's going to be won, boys—by inches. Every play, every time you carry the ball, or every time you make a tackle, you're going to have to follow through and steal that one extra inch.' I believe during that game they measured the first down nine or ten times. It was unbelievable. We won 7-0."

Next came the Army game, played at Yankee Stadium. Dad always had one or two trick plays up his sleeve, and one of them proved the margin of victory in the Army game.

When on defense, Army tended to huddle far from the line of scrimmage and to come up to the line slowly. Dad designed a two-part play to take advantage of the weakness. First, the quarterback would hand off to the halfback, who would gain two or three yards and go down. The Sooners would then hand the ball to the referee and act as if they were returning to their huddle. There would be no huddle, however—simply a quick return to the line of scrimmage, a fast count, and a lateral to McClellan, who would go the distance.

"It worked like a charm," says McClellan. "The play was set up so Page gave it to Carpenter and Carpenter was just going to run to a spot and get tackled. Everybody knew where he [would be] .... We practiced lining up on that spot.

"When they called the play, Carpenter got up, and Page and everybody was still; the line was already there. Carpenter just reached down and picked up the ball and pitched it to me, and here we went."

Using the trick play, McClellan scored the Sooners' first touchdown. Later in the game, a delayed count twice drew the Cadets offsides at their own one-yard line, resulting in Oklahoma's second score. The game ended 14-8.

Dick Snider was with Dad following the Army victory. "After the game Bud and Gomer were in a suite at the old Manhattan Hotel in New York, and after the last of the well-wishers left, the two of them shook hands and embraced like they had just won a national championship. It was more emotion than I had ever seen from either of them."

In the next two weeks, Nebraska and Oklahoma State fell to the Sooners. The impossible had been accomplished. Coaches and sportswriters around the country hailed the comeback as the top sports story of the year.

Most people concur that 1961 was Dad's finest coaching performance. According to him, "When a coach loses the majority of games during the first half of the season, the biggest dilemma is the perplexity and frustration of the coach himself. Leadership then becomes even more critical, because if the leadership turns sour, if the coach gets frustrated . . . it's like a contagion . . . . The team is very susceptible; they are ready to have an excuse."

Dad's response to continual defeat was to turn his leadership skills up a notch, telling the team, "Don't worry about defeat. Do not become impatient with yourself or the public. This is when we're being tested to be at our best."

1961 wasn't a winning season, but it wasn't a second consecutive losing season, either. Oklahoma was on the move again.

ఇ

The 1962 season was the culmination of the years of rebuilding. Except for losses to Notre Dame and Texas, the Sooners were on top again, recapturing the Big Eight championship. The feat was particularly amazing because of the youth of the team; only two starters from the previous year returned. The majority of the team were sophomores.

On January 1, 1963, Oklahoma journeyed to the Orange Bowl once again to meet Alabama, under the leadership of Bear Bryant.

"Bud wanted to win so bad," says halfback Charley Mayhue, "he like to have killed us. The hardest practices I had at OU were down in the Orange Bowl . . . . He wanted to beat Bear so bad, we changed our offense, we changed our defense, we changed coverage. I went in there weighing 178, and I played the game at about 169 pounds. I had to put my hands in my pockets to hold my pants up.

"When I went out to warm up [on the day of the game], I came in as tired as if I played a ball game . . . . Other people have told me the same thing . . . . Everybody was just drained."

The immediate pre-game period was highlighted by a locker room visit from the President of the United States, John F. Kennedy. Rumors had been flying that Kennedy was coming to the game, and according to sportswriter Bill Connors, Bear Bryant was concerned about it, for an unexpected reason.

"I knew Bud and Bryant probably talked together every day ... but one day Bryant said to me, 'I've heard the president's coming to the game. I'd like to know what Bud's going to wear because he always looks like he just came out of the barber shop .... I always look rumpled and everything. I don't want to look bad in front of the president. Do you think you could find out what Bud's going to wear?'

"I'm stunned," says Connors. "I thought he could find out easier than I could. That day ... I was riding back to the hotel with Bud. I said, 'I have a request to ask you.' He looked at me kind of funny. I said, 'Bryant wants to know what you're going to wear, because he doesn't want you to show him up in front of the president.'

"Bud started laughing. 'You tell him I'm not going to tell him. Just let him guess for himself.'

"The next time I saw Bryant, he said, 'Did you find out?' I said, 'He said he wasn't going to say.' Bryant said, 'I just know he'll look like he just stepped out of the tailor shop.' "

Connors continues the story. "If you recall, Bryant had been wearing what he called his lucky blue sleeveless sweater all through his long win streak, and, of course, he always wore a sport coat, too. He said, 'I'll just send Mama down to one of those Palm Beach stores and try to guess what kind of Florida clothes Bud would wear. I'm going to try to get dressed up.'

"It was a day game, and it was hot, and when Bud comes out he has on a white short-sleeved shirt with a tie, and, as Bear said, he looked fresh and cool and everything. Alabama comes out and Bryant has on a long-sleeved shirt—you can see the cuffs. He still has on his light blue sweater and he's got him a new Palm Beach sport coat. He just looked like he was burning up."

The clothes, however, didn't make the man. And the president's visit, exciting though it was, might have been a distraction. Alabama, behind Joe Namath's superb passing, defeated the Sooners 17-0.

ॐ

In the early '70s, Dad made a speech called *The Coach's Relationship to His Players*. During the talk, he posed a coaching dilemma. "You have a player, a great athlete, and you know it.

You also know that he is not doing the proper thing; his attitude toward the team and toward his teammates, and the effort he is making, are not what they ought to be. Do you put up with this player or do you wash him out after ample opportunity to correct his ways? . . . . I feel more strongly about this than anything else in coaching. Anybody who lacks discipline, who doesn't want to be part of the team, who doesn't want to meet the requirements, has to go."

During the 1963 season, Dad was forced to put this belief to the test as he dealt with halfback Joe Don Looney.

Looney was a junior college transfer, the only one Dad ever had taken at Oklahoma. And he was talented. In the opening game of the 1962 season, against Syracuse, he ran sixty yards for a touchdown; by the end of the season, he had made All-American.

But Looney didn't like the discipline required at Oklahoma. He was vocal about it, too. "I didn't have the courage and still wouldn't today, because I wasn't raised [to challenge authority]." says Geary Taylor. "You just went out and did it . . . . But if it didn't suit Joe Don, he would challenge you or he wouldn't do it."

Dick Snider says Dad told him about one particular practice with Looney. "He came to Bud one day and said, 'Coach, I know all the plays, don't I?' Bud agreed. And Looney said, 'And I'm in good shape, aren't I?' Again Bud agreed. 'So,' Looney said, 'why do I have to practice?' "

"Some days," says Jerry Thompson, "Joe Don would practice hard, but if he didn't think it was necessary for him to practice hard that day, he really wouldn't do it."

That kind of inconsistent preparation was anathema to Dad, but he was stuck between the rock of discipline and the hard place of Looney's athleticism and the desire of the team to keep him.

Charley Mayhue remembers the exchanges between Dad and Looney well. "Joe Don had so much to contribute, but he was only interested in himself. He was a 'for me' type person, not a team player.

"Bud kept working with him, believing in him, thinking if Joe Don just had a chance to be good he would be good. The problem is, when Joe Don had a chance to be good, he took

Dad (far right) with his father, Charles Patton (C.P.), and older brother Bill. C.P. taught Dad the self-discipline and positive outlook that helped make him such a successful coach.

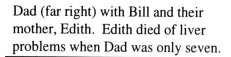

Dad (far right) with Bill and their mother, Edith. Edith died of liver problems when Dad was only seven.

Dad's stepmother, Ethel, who Dad described as being "just as perfect as it's possible for a person to be."

At Shattuck School, a military academy in Minnesota, Dad was awarded the Williams Cup as the school's best all-around athlete.

Dad was a standout football player for the University of Minnesota. A two-time All-American, he also won the Big Ten Medal, Minnesota's highest honor for combined excellence in scholastics and sports.

*photo by Minneapolis Star*

After enlisting in the Navy in 1942, Dad was assigned to the aircraft carrier U.S.S. Enterprise. He witnessed some of the bloodiest fighting in the war at Okinawa.

Dad at home, prior to his leaving for the Pacific, with his two sons, Pat (L) and me.

*photo by Ned Hockman*

Dad's first coaching victory over Texas in 1948 brings joy to the Sooner locker room. The Oklahoma-Texas rivalry is one of the most celebrated in all of college football.

Dad, Pat, Mom, and I relax at home with our dog, Spot. Spending time with his family was very important to Dad.

*photo by Bob East/Oklahoma Publishing Co.*

Every football season, Dad mailed weekly letters to OU alumni. The letters made them feel they were right on the sideline with him at every game.

*photo by Ned Hockman*

The Sooner players never sat on the bench. They knelt on the sidelines, close to the action, their teammates and their coach.

*photo by Ned Hockman*

Dad poses with the team after arriving for the 1949 Oklahoma-Texas game. Darrell Royal is to his right and Wade Walker to his left.

Dad will always be remembered for the trademark hat and tie he wore on the sidelines.

*photo by Ned Hockman*

*photo by Ned Hockman*

Dad and his father, C.P., watch the Sooners practice.

*photo by A.Y. Owen, Life Magazine © Time Warner*

Dad instructs the players during practice. For Dad, the will to prepare for the game was the most important aspect of his coaching philosophy.

Dad and the rest of the team celebrate after a surprise score. Assistant coach Gomer Jones hides his face in disbelief.

*photo by Ned Hockman*

*photo by A.Y. Owen, Life Magazine© Time Warner*

Speed, speed, speed. It was always a hallmark of Oklahoma football, even when they were only making substitutions.

*photo by F.M. Bauman/Look Magazine*

The Sooner Football staff: (left to right front row) Ken Rawlinson, Pete Elliott, Dad (back row) Ted Youngling, Sam Lyle, and Gomer Jones.

Prentice Gautt was the first black player at the University of Oklahoma. Dad said that breaking the color line at Oklahoma was the most significant thing he did while coaching.

photo by Ned Hockman

Dad watches as the team practices in 108° heat before the game against USC in 1963. The USC players practiced in full gear—and lost to Oklahoma. The victory gave the Sooners the nation's number 1 ranking, but they lost it the next week after losing to Texas.

At one of his last games as Oklahoma coach, Dad cheers on his team.

photo by A.Y. Owen, Life Magazine©Time Warner

Dad helps Pat and me sharpen our skills. This was a rare occurrence, because he wanted us to listen to our own coaches.

*photo by F.M. Bauman/Look Magazine*

Dad, Pat and I went on this fishing trip to Canada.

Dad congratulates me at the *Look Magazine* All-American awards. I won the award in 1963 as a senior at Duke. I was also voted ACC player of the year and was eighth in the Heisman Trophy balloting.

advantage . . . of Bud, the university, everybody. He was a taker, not a giver. It was real sad because Bud bent over backwards to help him . . . . When he had finally had enough and couldn't go any further with him, he did just lower the boom. I know it was hard on him, and it was hard on the team to an extent, but it really helped the team in the long run."

Dad finally dropped the hammer on Looney after the 1963 Texas game. The season began with victories over Clemson and Southern Cal. U.S.C. was No. 1 at the time, and Oklahoma's victory vaulted the Sooners to first place in the national rankings. Looney had a good game against Southern Cal, but according to All-Big Eight end Rick McCurdy, "He had a bad week of practice before the Texas game."

Just prior to the kickoff of the Texas game, the one game everybody in Oklahoma cared about, and the game at which Oklahoma was ranked No. 1 and Texas No. 2, Looney sidled up to Dad, saying, "Sorry, Coach, I can't go in. I have a pulled muscle."

That was it. After Oklahoma was defeated, Dad called a meeting of the team captains, and though the seniors actually voted Looney off the team, it was simply the ratification of a decision Dad had made already. As McCurdy says, "We were trying to promote leadership, but the guy we're maybe depending upon the most, Joe Don, isn't there . . . . Bud perceived the buck stopped with him . . . . Ultimately his decision was that to compete and win the Big Eight, we could no longer have that type of situation. That's not to take anything away from Joe Don. He was really a good friend of mine, and I respected him, but at the same time, you've got to look out for the overall team morale."

After the Looney decision was made, Oklahoma won its next six games, and prepared to play Nebraska on November 23, 1963. The Presidential assassination intervened.

Most games were canceled, but Dad, after speaking with Kennedy family members who encouraged him to maintain the playing schedule, decided the game should go on. Nebraska won.

"It was the most cold day; it was an awful day to be there," remembers McCurdy. "I think we should not have played the game. I think we were all ready to go back home . . . . Had we been in Oklahoma with our own family and our own friends, we would have been the victors . . . . If they had been the visiting team, I think they would have lost just because of the situation."

During the ride home from Lincoln, Dad called several of his players, including McCurdy, to the front of the plane. "He said, 'We aren't going to the Orange Bowl now; the Blue Bonnet Bowl is interested.' He wanted to know what I thought. I said, 'Coach, I'm so tired right now . . . . As far as I'm concerned, let's beat OSU, and if we can't go to the Orange Bowl, I don't want to go anyplace.' He made the decision the next week that we wouldn't be going to the Blue Bonnet."

By the next week, it was also clear the Oklahoma State University game would be Dad's last as head coach at OU. Though Dad had given his utmost to the team for seventeen years, he was a student and scholar who'd always had a wider world view than just the gridiron. In some important way, the assassination had shaken him loose from the game.

After the Oklahoma State game, Dad spoke with Bill Connors in the kitchen of our home in Norman. "I come from a political family," Connors says, "and I really had been interested in President Kennedy. Bud and I were talking and I said, 'Bud, I was thinking that just over a week ago how terribly important the Nebraska game seemed, and then how all at once it didn't seem as important as we built it up.' He looked at me and said, 'Bill, it never was.' "

Oklahoma ended its season second in the conference and rated eighth in the nation. Two Sooners, Jim Grisham and Ralph Neely, made All-American, and the seventeen-year saga came to an end.

ॐ

Throughout his years at Oklahoma, Dad was more than a coach. He was a builder, building relationships with his players and coaches, with the administration and faculty, and with the media and the fans.

Perhaps because he had a master's degree in English and was a fine communicator himself, Dad had an appreciation for the work the sports media performed, and he was relaxed with them, able to discuss words and literature.

"Bud was great with the press," says sportswriter Volney Meece. "At his house after the games, before all the boosters would get there . . . he'd be in the kitchen mixing drinks and telling us what really happened in the game, so we could write a story and look like the experts we weren't . . . . You could paraphrase anything he said and make it look like you knew what the hell happened.

"I remember one night," Meece says, "when Mary was in the hospital and Bud was going to see her after all the fans and everybody left. He insisted Dick Snider and I stay until he got back from the hospital . . . . He scrambled some eggs for the dog and went into the study and talked about different books he was reading. He insisted that Dick . . . take a book with him and read it."

He had the same attitude toward fans. Bill Krisher recalls, "Coach would stand outside the bus and visit with anyone and everyone before he ever got on the bus. He never shunned a fan; he never shunned a person at all. He was very, very polite to them . . . and with the sports media . . . he'd stay as long as needed to get the interviews out of the way. He was very gracious to them after every game."

He was equally gracious to his assistant coaches. Though Dad and Jones made the final coaching decisions, they listened to the assistant coaches and often incorporated their ideas into offensive and defensive schemes. Pete Elliott says, "We weren't just coaches together. We were friends . . . . He made his coaches enjoy being part of the staff.

"One of the things he did that was a little different was to meet very early in the morning. The great thing about it was I was one of those who had young kids, so while we got up real early in the morning, when practice was over, we basically would go home, except during double sessions. We had a chance to be with our families, and I appreciated that. There are times when, until your work is done, you have to stay with it . . . but there are times when you can make the schedule to be with your family."

Jay O'Neal, who coached with Dad later in his career, recalls his first coaches' meeting. "Each coach got his turn to go to the board and put up what he thought we should do offensively and defensively. Bud sat there with a pad. He would take notes and ask questions when he saw something he wanted to know more about.

"He came to me and said, 'Jay, what do you have?' I said, 'I don't have anything, Coach.' He said, 'I'm really surprised.' I never went back again without something.

"He really did watch what was happening. Now, you might not get anything in, but two weeks later, something like the idea you had would appear, or it would be adjusted even that week .... He really did very seriously believe in listening to what was happening and what people had to say."

જ

If there is a watchword that describes Dad's entire coaching career, that word is consistency. "The coach has one aim," he said, "and that is to get the best out of each player and to help the player develop in every way.

"This is what a coach is trying to do with the people who play for him. He first tries to have them understand their potential, and next he presents a challenge to them to be as good as they can be. He hopes this will carry over into other activities in life in which they may become involved.

"The players' attitude toward you hinges on one thing, and that is respect. If they do not respect you, you have lost them. If you have their respect, you have it made.

"The coach has to conduct himself on and off the field in a way to gain respect. That involves a consistency of performance on the coach's part. Closely related to respect is discipline; you can't have respect without discipline. You *must* be respected and you *must* have discipline."

Dad was able to create that respect and discipline with amazing consistency. Players who were on his early teams often speak of the life lessons they took from him in virtually the same words as players he coached in the '60s.

Listen to Jack Mitchell. "If it weren't for Bud—my life, I don't know what it would have been. I would just have gone into business some place, no telling, just been another guy. He's totally responsible for any success I've had, no question. Not only on the football field ... the discipline and the organization. He just had it all. The Lord gave it all to him."

And Billy Vessels. "Coaches can't afford to get too close to players, because then they're going to depend on you for the rest of your life. You have to make them believe in you, but there is that point where they're going to have to do things on their own. [It was as if he was trying] to help teach you about life to come. He was the most loving individual in the world, but you have to distance that from being the football coach."

And Jimmy Harris. "The values—the moral values—the leadership .... Bud instilled a confidence in you that carries with you for the rest of your life. I've patterned a lot of my life after him .... He was a tremendous father figure to me."

And Bill Krisher. "He showed wisdom and advice to young men on which way to go with their lives and what they should do. Bud would be the epitome of a great father and a great coach and a great individual."

And, finally, Charley Mayhue. "Other than my father and the good Lord Jesus, Bud had as much influence on me as anybody. When I was around him, I felt a feeling of security and greatness. I felt inspired to do things more than ... I really had the capability of doing. He could get the best out of players when the first person you have to defeat is yourself.

"To be able to defeat yourself ... when you're fatigued and keep it ongoing; when you're discouraged and keep it ongoing, when everybody else is complaining and you don't complain. You get the best out of your abilities that you can."

えひ

In the Oklahoma locker room was a sign the players used to jump up and touch, as a sort of talisman, on their way to the field. It read, "Play like a champion today." For seventeen years, they did.

# 5

## Letters From My Father

ða

*"You'll be a man, my son . . . "*
—*Kipling*

My older brother Pat and I grew up in the '40s and '50s, and our experiences were the stuff the American Dream was made of. We lived with our parents—a working Dad and a homemaker Mom—and a dog in a single-family home right in the center of middle America. My friend, Gary Rawlinson, remembers it as "the time when mothers were always there; weekend touch football games; the smell of burning leaves in the air; innocent pranks, with no guns or violence—a time when the body stuffed into the trunk of the car was really Eurton with ketchup smeared on him."

In many respects, Pat and I lived the same idyllic life the other kids had and one very like the childhood our father had enjoyed. We swam and had barbecues in the summer. We took fishing trips. We invited our friends to play pool in our converted garage. Dad, an avid golfer, cut a putting green into our back yard; we all practiced there. We were campers at Camp Lincoln in Brainard, Minnesota, where Dad had once been a counselor. We visited our grandparents. When we were teenagers, we spent our summers working in landscaping or construction.

Our lives, then, were pretty much like other young people's, with our parents, school and church being the major influences. But with all the normalcy of our upbringing, there was one big difference between Pat and me and our friends. Our dad was well-known, not just in Norman, but all over the country. His picture graced the cover of *Sports Illustrated*. He starred on the first televised college coach's program in the United States. Other sports legends, such as Bear Bryant and Woody Hayes, visited our home, and we were privileged to meet superstars like Mickey Mantle.

Great stuff, no doubt, but it had its downside. Pat and I never could be anonymous. No matter where we were—in school, on the street, in a restaurant, or messing around with pals—people knew us. We were "Bud's boys," and as his sons, we were expected to excel in whatever we attempted.

Even though Pat and I loved and admired our mom and dad, sometimes the spotlight was too bright. There were times when we just wanted to fit in with our friends and not be singled out. I remember the first night game ever played at Owen Field in Norman. It was a professional game, and the Detroit Lions quarterback was Bobby Layne, who played at Texas during my Dad's first season at Oklahoma. Doak Walker, who was a star for Southern Methodist during that same period, was also with Detroit, so Dad decided he wanted to sit on the sideline for the game. As he and I walked across the field, there was sudden spontaneous applause. People stood in unison and began chanting his name. I was mortified and told Dad I'd run ahead and find our seats. I just couldn't bear the attention and applause, even though it wasn't for me.

Mom had a mink stole she wore from time to time. I always hoped she wouldn't wear it where our friends would see it, because we didn't want them to think we were rich. And when the Muskogee Boosters Club gave Dad a Cadillac, Pat and I worried even more about the "rich kid" tag. Pat used to de-tassel corn in the summer, and the one time Dad drove him to work in the Cadillac, Pat made him stop 100 yards from the field, so his co-workers wouldn't see the car.

While there was considerable pressure from the outside world for Pat and me always to measure up to Dad, inside our home the pressure was off. There we found laughter, love, warmth, learning, and discipline. And at the center of it all was Dad.

This in no way detracts from my mother. Like all coaches, Dad was away a great deal of the time. In the football season, he was preoccupied with practices and games; during the off-season, he was engaged in recruiting and clinics, and he was in heavy demand as a banquet and motivational speaker. Mom was always home, reading to us, making sure we ate properly, keeping our house immaculate, encouraging us in our homework, making our friends welcome. Mom was lovely, kind and soft-spoken. Whatever credit—or blame—our parents deserve for Pat and me, much of it belongs to our mother.

When Dad was there, however, another dimension was added to our lives. A warm, demonstrative person, he was emotionally available to us at a time when the man in the gray flannel suit—the self-contained, buttoned-down, emotionally dead man—seemed to be the national norm. The only thing Dad had in common with that man was the flannel suit he wore on game days.

ja

When I remember my earliest childhood, all sorts of vignettes come to mind, but one of the most vivid is Dad telling Pat and me bedtime stories about Bossy Beaver and Happy Beaver—stories Dad had learned when he was at Camp Lincoln. Happy Beaver was a team player who could get along with others; Bossy Beaver was a disruptive character with an impertinent attitude. Sometimes the stories were mysteries, with Bossy Beaver using his big tail to cover up the clues that would show he'd done something wrong. Sometimes the stories were just pleasant accounts of the two beavers swimming in the lake and caring for one another. But whatever the details, each tale incorporated Dad's philosophies about how people should treat each other, and every story had a positive theme. It became obvious to Pat and me at an early age that Happy Beaver was clearly the hero and the one we should emulate. After the stories, Dad would wrestle with us as we giggled and laughed and finally hollered "uncle."

One constant in our family life was church. Dad was reared as an Episcopalian; in Norman, we belonged to St. John's, and we rarely missed services, even during the football season, when Dad and the team were traveling. In a 1953 article in *Forth* magazine, our rector and friend, Joseph Young, related a particularly telling example of Dad's faithful attendance:

> Everybody, it seemed, had gone to South Bend for the [1952] Oklahoma-Notre Dame Game. I told myself I'd be fortunate if one communicant showed up for services. But the next morning when I walked in to begin, I knew I had one. Bud Wilkinson was the first person I spotted. He and his whole family were there. I've never known a more sincere churchman who is ever working for the growth of the church.

It certainly would have been understandable if Dad had skipped church that morning. He hated to lose, and Oklahoma had lost the game to Notre Dame, in an upset Notre Dame coach Frank Leahy later called "my biggest coaching thrill." Father Joe was right about attendance at the game; more than 9,000 Oklahomans, many from Norman, had traveled to Indiana.

Besides being a visible churchman, Dad also practiced his faith privately. Often I'd go into Mom and Dad's room to say good night and find Dad kneeling next to his bed in prayer, his face in his hands. Feeling embarrassed and as if I'd intruded, I'd tiptoe out and return a few minutes later.

As little kids, Pat and I were given Oklahoma jerseys with the numbers 26 and 44, which were the numbers of Jack Mitchell, the great Oklahoma quarterback, and Myrle Greathouse, the outstanding linebacker. That was about as close as we got to them. Neither Pat nor I had special privileges regarding the team. We weren't permitted to sit on the bench or act as water boys, because Dad felt the father-son relationship should be separate from practice and game conditions. We were allowed to come onto the field to meet our heroes only on picture days or when practices were open to the public. Once, though, during the off-season, as a very special privilege, I got to go with Jack and Myrle on a fishing trip to Lake Texoma. I caught a four-pound bass and couldn't have been more proud. And we were allowed to fly back to Norman on the team plane after the Oklahoma-Texas games, because Dad always allowed the players to remain overnight in Dallas to blow off a little steam. Pat and I never understood why the players would want to party in Dallas when they had the opportunity to take an airplane trip. We figured it out when we were older.

As we grew up, my brother and I were included in more activities involving the team and coaching staff. One of our favorites was "Old Fashioned Night." Once a week during the season, Dad would invite all his staff to put their coaching disagreements behind them and to relax and come together over a couple of Old Fashioneds. It was a time to solidify the staff and get them emotionally ready for the game. Our dog, Ginger, a red-haired setter-Labrador Retriever mix, would amble in and out between the living room and the kitchen, wagging her tail and occasionally knocking drinks off the coffee table. Spirited discussions about personnel, practice and the upcoming game resounded through the house. Because from the time I was six until I left home at eighteen Oklahoma never had a losing season, laughter was the hallmark of these evenings, and Old Fashioned Night was a time Pat and I anticipated eagerly each week.

And there were the games themselves. Gary Rawlinson and I would listen to the games on the radio, and sometimes we'd get so nervous we'd turn off the game and go outside to throw a football around until we could bear to check the score again.

Football, of course, drew a major portion of our attention, but our lives, like all kids', revolved around school. Though Dad had once received the Big Ten Medal and believed in lifelong learning, he never stressed grades. We didn't have to make straight A's or be at the top of the class. The only thing Dad demanded was that we be the very best we could be. We were expected to work hard and to do our best, all the time, in all our activities. If our best wasn't as good as someone else's best, that was all right, but our best was expected.

If we didn't do our best, discipline was swift and sure, but never really punitive. Neither Pat nor I remember Dad ever hitting us, swearing or even raising his voice. If we stayed up too late or failed to complete an assigned chore, his usual quiet admonition was, "If you don't want to pay the price to live by the standards of the University of Oklahoma football players, that is your choice." We knew Dad had established a special code of behavior for the team; we wanted so much to be like them that our failure to uphold the team's principles was much worse than physical punishment. Sometimes, when we shirked our responsibilities, Dad would simply do the task we were supposed to complete, without comment. The sight of him quietly cutting the lawn we were supposed to mow or clipping the hedges we were supposed to trim was a much more powerful admonition than his yelling at us would have been. We'd rush outside, apologize and try to take back our jobs. Sometimes it was tough, though. Dad had a thing about hedges. We called him the Mad Clipper, because once he got the trimmers in his hands, he was likely to cut down every twig in sight.

Pat, doing his best at all times, was co-valedictorian of his high school class. During this period, Woody Hayes came to Norman for a brief visit. Woody, who, like Dad, had a reverence for learning and education, was impressed with Pat's performance, and when he returned to Columbus asked his son, Steve, "Why can't you make straight A's like Coach Wilkinson's son?" It's reported Steve replied, "Dad, I'll make straight A's when you win forty-seven straight games."

ই

Even though Dad could have drilled it into us that we were to follow in his footsteps, much as a musician or a businessman might encourage his sons to carry on the family tradition, he made it clear to us that sports were an option, not a duty.

Nonetheless, we both chose to play football. Pat's high school football career, strangely enough, was one of the factors that led to his becoming a doctor. Pat suffered five football injuries, all of which required surgery. One knee was operated on twice, and he needed surgery on the other knee and both shoulders, as well. Each time, he was operated on by the renowned orthopedic surgeon, Dr. Don O' Donoghue, the Oklahoma team orthopedist, who was affectionately called "The Knife." Because of his more than nodding acquaintance with surgery, Pat became interested in medicine and today is a nationally-known retinal surgeon in Baltimore, where he heads the department of ophthalmology at Greater Baltimore Medical Center.

It was typical of his concern for us that during Pat's first surgery, Dad insisted on being in the operating room. Donning his mask and striding in confidently, he became nauseated at the sight of the first incision and had to depart quickly. But he tried, and Pat knew it.

I, too, played football and basketball and was fortunate enough not to be knocked out by injuries. I did have one fleeting health problem, however. In the summer of 1959, I developed a mysterious allergy. For about a month, whenever I mowed the lawn or engaged in any physical activity, I developed a rash and severe itching. I was alarmed, but when Dad insisted I go to the Mayo Clinic to be evaluated, I angrily refused. Perhaps because he had seen Pat bear so much pain and discomfort, Dad actually wept when he told me he only wanted to be sure I was healthy and well. I finally agreed to go to Mayo's within a few weeks; fortunately, during that period, the allergy cleared up as suddenly as it had appeared.

With Dad being one of the nation's most successful coaches, my high school sports career could have been a nightmare. He might have chosen to lurk around every corner, telling the coaches what to do and generally making a nuisance of himself. He didn't. After Norman High School won the state basketball championship in my junior year, my coach, Chet Bryan, told me my parents were the only ones who didn't call him during the season, either complaining or offering advice.

On only one occasion did Dad break his rule about supporting our coaches. When Pat was a junior, a new football coach, trying to instill a sense of raw-boned Oklahoma *machismo* in Pat's team, decided no one on the team should have soap to shower with after practice. Somehow, not using soap became equated with being tough. Dad, however, felt it was just plain unsanitary and interceded behind the scenes to make sure there was soap in the locker room. He took care of it so quietly that when soap reappeared in the showers, none of the players knew Dad had intervened on their behalf. In general, though, Dad and Mom knew they needed to remain in the background, if Pat and I were to become anything but "Bud and Mary's kids." We both appreciated their forbearance.

Dad did more than offer quiet moral support at our state championship basketball game during my junior year, however. About two minutes into the game against El Reno, Dad and Mom walked in with Charlie and Liz Coe. Charlie was one of the greatest amateur golfers of all time, having won the U.S. Amateur in both 1949 and 1958. I was amazed when the four of them sat down right behind the Norman bench, because Dad never drew attention to himself at one of our games. But there he was, hollering and cheering wildly. Every one of our squad knew it, and we played our hearts out. We won, 57-51, and later Jenks Simmons, the El Reno coach, protested, tongue in cheek, that Bud's proximity to our team gave us an unfair psychological advantage. I don't know if that was true, but I was proud to have him sitting close by, and I know he was proud of us.

It often surprises people to learn that Dad didn't spend much time throwing the football around with me or Pat. We talked sports instead. During my high school days as a quarterback, he took the time to explain his philosophy about moving the football. Dad believed the quarterback had a better feel for the game than the assistant coaches in the press box and that the quarterback could be programmed to call the proper call in any game situation.

As he did with his own players, he quizzed me about a variety of hypothetical game conditions. "Okay," he'd say, "you just got the ball on the 35-yard-line. It's first down. What do you call?" I'd respond, and he'd continue, "Second and seven on the 38-yard-line. What's your call?" As a result, football became a game of intelligence as well as stamina and conditioning. And today, as I watch televised games, I always know exactly what play Dad would call next.

During my senior year, 1960, Norman again played in a state championship game, this time against Northwest Classen in football—and this time, we were on the losing end—16-14. There was a controversial call that clearly affected the final score. Northwest Classen's quarterback, Mike Miller, lateraled to his fullback, Walt Lawson. When the ball hit the ground, some of the officials called it an incomplete pass, and both teams started back to their huddles. One official, who hearsay has it was Miller's uncle, hollered, "Pick up the ball, Walt. You can run. It's a lateral." Lawson scooped it up and ran 69 yards for a touchdown. Because both teams believed the ball was dead, the game cameras had been shut off, so there's no game film of this unusual play, but local sportswriters said it would be talked about for years, and it was.

I think losing the ball five times on fumbles might have had more to do with the outcome of the game than did this one play, but whatever the reason, we lost, and I was in tears as we left the field. The locker room was a shambles. Our backfield coach, Wray Littlejohn, was so angry about the controversial call he broke down the locker room door with a single forearm blow. Pat, who had come home from Stanford for the game, several times interrupted my interviews with the local sportswriters by hollering obscenities and demanding the game be forfeited. He finally was asked to excuse himself.

Then Dad came in. He quietly congratulated the team and coaches on a great season. And that was all. I've kidded Pat for years about the contrast between his style and Dad's. Neither of us has ever been able to emulate the equanimity Dad always demonstrated, no matter how difficult the circumstances.

ᏅᎯ

By the time I was a senior, it was evident I had the athletic skills to play for Oklahoma. Pat and I were reared believing we would go away to school, be on our own, and get out from under Dad's shadow. Pat enrolled at Stanford, but when it was time for me to choose a school, there was great speculation around the state about whether I'd decide to stay and play for Dad. One of Dad's assistant coaches, Bob Blaik, son of the revered Army coach, Colonel "Red" Blaik, had played for his father and convinced Dad there was no reason I couldn't play for Oklahoma if I wanted to. The decision was left up to me.

I visited five schools, dropping by Duke only because Carl James, then the assistant athletic director, asked me to make a swing through on my way to West Point. The one thing I knew about Duke was that Oklahoma had beaten them in the 1958 Orange Bowl, but once I got on campus, I was impressed with its academic excellence and religious atmosphere. I also learned they played a big-time football schedule. And Duke was far enough away from Oklahoma that I'd truly be on my own. In addition, I worried Dad might suffer a great deal of adverse publicity if I played for Oklahoma and the team suddenly began to lose.

One of Pat's friends, Chris Caudill, the center on Stanford's football team, told me during my visit there that all schools looked great while you were on campus; the only way to make a good decision was to go home, close the door to your room and think about it.

I did that, and after a few weeks of careful consideration, I decided I should move on to Duke. It was one of the most painful decisions I ever made, but, finally, I knew I had to tell Dad. After he returned home one evening, Mom sent him to my room. I was lying face down on my bed when he came in and put his arm across my shoulders. I burst into tears and said, "I think I should go to Duke. I really want to play for you, but I think it would be better for me to be on my own." I still remember his strong hands rubbing my back while I cried uncontrollably, and I remember how kind, comforting and supportive he was. Within a week, the *Daily Oklahoman* headlined its sports page: "Jay Wilkinson to go to Duke."

There were many more tears. The day before I left, I cried in Coach Littlejohn's arms. And I cried as I caught the plane to North Carolina. Dad told me later he and Mom sobbed their eyes out when the plane rolled down the runway for take-off. He kidded me that he cried because I wasn't going to play football at Oklahoma. I knew better.

On the plane ride to Durham, all I could think of were the words of a then-popular song, "Please, General Custer, I don't want to go . . . "

ð

Once I arrived at Duke, though, I began to realize that nothing was really going to separate me from Dad—that geography had nothing to do with how we felt about each other. Communication was always the backbone of our relationship, and our communication continued in letters. I didn't know until later how unusual Dad's letters were. I would guess most guys at Duke didn't get frequent seven-page letters from their fathers—letters packed with unabashed love, affection and concern. The letters Pat and I received during our college years are among our most cherished possessions. Those delivered to me filled me with confidence when I was low, assuaged the pain of separation, and assured me that no matter what, I was appreciated for who I was, not for what I accomplished. Many men can only dream of such affirmation from their fathers, but the evidence of Dad's and my closeness was in my mail box several times a month.

In the beginning, Duke was a foreign land. I was lonely, and it was difficult to become acclimated to Duke football. They wore high top football shoes; I was used to low cuts. They wore bulky, strap-on hip pads; I preferred the light, snap-in pads I'd worn at home. I wrote Dad to elicit some sympathy for the hardships I was being forced to endure. He wrote back:

> *I know things will get better because you are the kind of person who can adjust and find the good in all situations. When I read your letter, I recalled similar times in my life. When I left home to go to Shattuck, I was truly blue . . . . When I left you, Pat, and Mother to go to sea during the war, I was shaken. I loved you and wanted to watch you and help you as you grew up—and I was leaving not knowing if I would ever get back again. But . . . the experience and training I received more than compensated for the heartaches.*
>
> *One of the first things an education brings . . . is the realization that the world is a big place—full of many different ideas and ways of doing things. You have watched our team practice and naturally are attuned to our ways of doing things . . . . Bill Murray has been a fine coach for many years. Instead of wondering why they do things differently, you should be studying what they do so you will understand that their approach will get the job done more effectively, maybe more easily than we can.*
>
> *When any person leaves a pleasant situation to enter the "unknown," there is always the realization of how nice, good and comfortable things were before. Yet only by facing the future and accepting . . . progressively difficult challenges are we able to grow . . . . You have more total, all-around ability in all fields than anyone I have ever met. You will certainly be a great man and make a great contribution . . . but to do this you must take on . . . more difficult challenges. You will grow and develop in direct relationship to the way you meet and overcome what seem to be hard assignments. You will learn to love Duke and to take pride in the school and their football team. By developing as a student and an athlete, you will prepare*

*yourself to do bigger and better things . . . . Always remember, I believe in you no matter what. You must do what seems right to you. Don't ever be swayed by what "other people will think." My grandmother, a great lady, always told me to "dare to be a Daniel; dare to stand alone." It is the best advice one can have for happy, successful living . . . . Only in this way can you find peace of mind.*

Dad was right. I came to love Duke in only one semester, even though it was more intellectually rigorous than I'd expected. There was no separate, less strenuous academic curriculum for athletes, and during my first week of classes, my French professor called me aside, saying, "Mr. Wilkinson, I want to inform you that I have reviewed the freshmen test scores and you are in the lower two percent of the entering class. I don't know if you are academically capable of staying in my course." His remarks scared me to death, but gave impetus to my academic pursuits. By the end of the year, I was in the top ten percent of the class. And, of course, Dad had some thoughts on the subject.

*I brought your book,* Preface to Philosophy, *with me, and I'm enjoying it. One paragraph from William James' "Essay on Habits" should be of value to you. In case you haven't read it . . . "Let no youth have any anxiety about the upshot of his education . . . . If he keeps faithfully busy each hour of the working day, he may safely leave the final result to itself. He can . . . plan on waking up some fine morning, to find himself one of the competent ones of his generation in whatever pursuit he may have singled out."*

That quote was vintage Bud. Work hard. Try your best. Don't worry about the end product. Immerse yourself in the process and in the moment. He was equally adamant about these issues when I found myself on the seventh team in football.

*Don't be concerned about starting off on the seventh team or on what team you play. Simply do your best every day at whatever you're doing—be a leader and be tough. If you approach the game in this manner you can't miss.*

*We think of you often and are looking forward to Easter. You're the finest son a father ever had. I'm so proud of you.*

And sometimes, among the exhortations, I got coach to player information, too.

*The reason you practice every day is to improve—to learn to execute better . . . . It's a gradual development—hard to recognize from day to day but easy to see from week to week.*

*When you come up on defense, don't even think about playing off the blockers. Come up so fast, with so much determination to get to the ball carrier, that your speed and aggressiveness will carry you through or past the blockers. Try it and see how it works.*

At the beginning of my sophomore year, I was far down the line at quarterback. The week before the opening game, Ed Chestnutt, our excellent receiver, ripped up his knee—an injury that would keep him out for the season. I asked Coach Murray for the chance to try out for the lonesome end slot, and I made the team as third receiver. During the season, I also was used as a punt return specialist. I was finally seeing some real action.

But things weren't going so great for Dad. The previous year had been his only losing season at Oklahoma, and now his team was starting off even worse. I was very nervous for him. He was equally concerned about me.

*Please don't worry about our football team. You have enough problems of your own. We'll get along all right. Even if we don't do well this year, we have in the past and we will again.*

*We'll be pulling for you with all we have this week. I know Clemson is tough . . . but I believe you have what it takes to win.*

We lost and so did Oklahoma. They finished their first five games 0-5. It was the day following the last loss that Dad went on his Sunday television show and uncharacteristically predicted Oklahoma would win its next five games. Oklahoma won its next four games; the final game would be against Oklahoma State. Duke was playing Notre Dame the same day. Dad wrote to me:

*If we win Saturday, I'll consider this a most memorable year. Our team has shown great courage to come back. It would be a shame to lose now when we can finish so well.*

*I'll be listening for the Notre Dame score. You had a fine year—truly tremendous—and I hope you can climax it with another breakaway run. Christmas will be so much fun. It will be wonderful to see you again.*

The season end brought victories for both our teams, as Duke defeated a much more talented Notre Dame team, 37-13. Personally, it had been a fine year for me; I finished the season as the nation's second leading punt returner, behind the great Lance Alworth.

After Christmas break, I returned to face my dreaded final exams. I fretted about my grades and the lack of direction in my life. Dad's next letter showed me the depth of his understanding.

*I know that academic work is particularly difficult when goals and objectives are not clearly defined. Pat, wanting to study medicine, can see cause and purpose in the courses he is taking. You, not knowing what your goals are, find it . . . extremely difficult to see the validity in much of what you are asked to do.*

*Education in the final analysis is simply the development of self-discipline of the mind. James Conant, former president of Harvard, once said, "Your education is what you have left over when you have forgotten all that you have learned."*

*If you can bear down on your studies and do well in them, even though you do not have a great deal of interest in them, think how simple and easy it will be to do well when you are highly motivated and truly enjoy the work.*

*I know what a sense of commitment you have concerning your future life. I'm also convinced in due time your course will become clear. If you live each day well, the future will take care of itself.*

As my sophomore year ground on, my grade point began to dip, and I was distraught over my academic performance. Dad, in a series of his letters, continued to pound home his point:

*If you are doing the best you can, don't worry about what grades you make. There is a fine quote from Ralph Waldo Emerson, "When it is dark enough, men see the stars." I'm sure you will come out fine, and if you don't, you'll learn from the experience.*

*In making an effort to develop and realize your full capabilities by vocabulary growth, the speed reading, etc., you are showing great integrity of purpose. Time spent in such pursuits does not improve your grades at all, but you learn more than when you memorize to get grades. The fact that you realize this and work to satisfy your own convictions . . . is a sign of great maturity.*

*As you know, the Kennedys were average students. Admiral Halsey finished in the bottom quarter of his class. There are many similar examples. Remember you are in college to learn, which involves the development of proper values and the wisdom . . . that comes from a broad experience in many different subjects. The inter-relationships of facts and ideas— the understanding of why things happen as they do—plus the ability to project into the future are the essentials for any educated man. The ability to parrot back facts doesn't have any . . . lasting meaning.*

I survived the sophomore year, but just prior to my junior season, my face appeared on the cover of *Street and Smith*, a national sports magazine. Though I'd had an excellent year as a sophomore, I questioned whether most people would feel I deserved this kind of attention. Coach Murray told me it was an honor for Duke as well, which made me feel better, but I had left Oklahoma to get out of the limelight, and here it was again. Besides, I'd been shifted to halfback, and learning how to function in the new position was a real challenge. I wrote to Dad about my ongoing worry about the whole situation. He responded:

*The start of football season, and the first ten days are always tough, no matter how well prepared you are mentally and physically. The self-control and the ability to push your-self—to do your best when you don't feel much like it—are probably the greatest values you receive from playing the game. They will stand you in good stead all your life.*

*You have high ambitions. This is a totally necessary state of mind for excellence of performance, but you must not press or be impatient. Mickey Mantle is never sure which time . . . he'll hit the home run, but he goes to the plate each time set to do his best. This is the attitude you must strive to perfect. Do your total, all-out best, on every single play. Never be discouraged if you don't do too well nor overly elated when you make a good play. Simply do the best you have in you on the next down.*

*I know you are hot, tired, and probably sick of football and practice, but this discipline—putting up with a totally tough, unhappy situation is one of the great lessons of the game you'll appreciate as time goes on. No matter how tough things get in the future, it will never be worse. Life has some rugged hills for us all—and this training enables you to climb them— with a song in your heart.*

*We miss you and think of you each day. I pray for your happiness, growth, and development and love you with all my heart and soul.*

The opening of the season brought Duke a loss to eventual national champion, Southern Cal. Dad's opening game against Syracuse was a great victory for Oklahoma. Dad was heavily involved in both contests, as the Duke game was nationally televised.

*I was sorry about your game . . . . Your team moved the ball well. When in the fourth quarter you came back from second and 30, I was sure you'd carry it in, go for two points, and win. Speaking as an unbiased observer, I felt you were the best back on the field, both offensively and defensively.*

*This defeat can make your team. There's always a tendency to let down when you're beat, but you have the talent on your squad, and losing shakes out overconfidence. If everyone plays with dedication, you'll win the rest.*

*We won today, and I almost feel guilty about it. Syracuse was better in every phase of the game except heart, courage, and the will to win.*

*I hope you and your squad will rally and fight back. The fact that you made that fourth quarter drive should give you all confidence.*

*The vitally important factor in competition, Jay, is not the result of a single game or even the season's record . . . . Sacrifice of time and self in preparation—making a determined, all-out effort—and still falling short, can strengthen a man beyond any other experience if he can learn to go forward again with even greater determination to get the best out of himself in the most trying of circumstances. This I know you can and will do.*

*I love you, Jay. No father can ever be more fortunate than I in having sons like you and Pat.*

Duke went on to three consecutive victories, but I was depressed because I didn't feel I was playing well or contributing much to the team. Pat, who by then was studying at Johns Hopkins, came to one of the games and relayed my sense of failure to Dad, who wrote to me:

*Pat said he was concerned about you. I am too, Jay. I know you're doing a good job in football and your studies, but I don't think you are living happily. Many people go through their entire lives chasing a rainbow—never happy with their present circumstances—but in reflection realize the days gone by were great.*

*I feel sure in spite of your loneliness and longing, your lack of confidence in your grades, your fatigue at football practice, that in retrospect, this fall will have been a time when you truly "lived," because of the challenges involved, your adjustment, and your ability to meet them.*

*Abe Lincoln has been quoted on many aspects of the human condition, but my favorite of his quotes is, "People are about as happy as they make up their minds to be."*

*Each night after practice, I am sad and let down. Never have I had a team try as hard as they did against Texas, yet we lost. We lack skill and must make up for it with courage. Saturday is the key game. We'll do our best and I hope it will be enough . . . . I am more frustrated than I have ever been, but I am still trying to be as happy as I can.*

*I started out to give you a pep talk—and am winding up giving one to myself!!*

*Try hard to be happy, Jay, with the present, while still looking forward to the future. I love you and I'm still more proud of you than words can express.*

In 1962, suddenly and almost overnight, the Cuban missile crisis brought the reality of nuclear war home to everyone. I called Mom and mentioned that football just didn't seem very important any more. Within a few days, Dad sent his perspectives to me:

*I share your concern over the international situation but don't believe it is a bit different than it has been for the past eight to ten years.*

*The so-called "cold war" is an actual war in every way except there are no overt military actions .... Military actions haven't begun because the Russians know they can't win. As long as we maintain our ability in the literal sense to absolutely blast Russia and every living thing off the face of the earth, there will be no war.*

*For your generation it is a long, hard road of constant preparedness. In our Christian society, we earnestly strive for peace and freedom. But recorded history shows that man ... has [always] lived in war or threat of war. It is not pleasant, but unfortunately it has been a ... fact of life along with illness, hunger, privation, etc.*

*Mom said you told her football didn't seem important now. Actually, Jay, it never has been an end in itself. Although people distort the idea ... the game is fundamentally education for the participants. As Admiral Byrd said, "It isn't getting to the Pole that counts; it's what you learn on the way."*

*This is the best brief analysis of football. It isn't winning or losing that has lasting value or importance. The effort, dedication, and sacrifice you make for a cause—your team—the working with others toward a common, most demanding goal [is what matters]. The loyalty, the joys, the disappointments, and above all, learning to give your total best mentally, emotionally, and physically are the qualities that make a man, and there is no other place they are learned so well.*

*You will find as you grow older that your football experience will have given you an inner strength and discipline that will enable you to meet the vicissitudes of life and fortune with your head held high and your banners flying, because you will know what hard, demanding preparation really is and that life's challenges come not from outside events, but rather from your own self as you do the very best of which you are capable.*

*When you do this, as you always do, you have literally won, regardless of the score. I should add that it has been my experience that the score will be right, too (the personal or the business situation included), because most people are incapable of delivering their best in all situations.*

*This one learns to do in the field of competition. MacArthur said, "On these fields of friendly strife are born the seeds that on other fields in future years will bear the fruits of victory."*

The missile crisis was averted and tensions eased. Duke finished the season 8-2. We were very disappointed, having thought we'd be going to the Sugar or Orange Bowl. The team turned down a bid to the Gator Bowl. Oklahoma was going to the Orange Bowl, however, and Dad asked me and Pat to join him there. I wasn't sure what I wanted to do until I received the following letter:

*We've had a good year, and I would be mighty pleased if it were over and we didn't have to play a Bowl game. We simply aren't of Bowl caliber . . . and it seems too bad, after a much better season than anyone anticipated, to get waxed in a Bowl.*

*I want very much for you to come to the game and hope you'll decide to. I also understand your mixed emotions about the whole thing. First, not having Duke participating is a disappointment. Next, I know you'd still rather be playing for OU (even though, all things considered, I believe you have done the wise thing in going to Duke). To be in Miami, semi-around our team, makes the two [things] . . . constantly rub against each other, and the way to avoid that, obviously, would be not to go.*

*On the other hand, I'm sure you'd have a great time, and the vacation would do you a world of good physically and mentally . . . . If you'd like to work out with us, you could be Namath, the Alabama quarterback, in practice!! Since you're a better thrower than he is, it would be a big help!!!*

*Joking aside, whatever you decide will be fine with me. You can be as anonymous as you care to be.*

*Remember what Lincoln said. All of your life, in every circumstance, there will be elements you wish were different. But every situation can be enjoyable if approached with the correct mental attitude.*

*I'm proud of you, love you, and miss you.*

I did go to the game, but felt awkward sitting on the sidelines with the Oklahoma players. As Dad predicted, Oklahoma was defeated, and Namath threw spectacularly.

Right after the game, I returned to Duke, only to be hospitalized with bleeding ulcers. Apparently the pressure of being highlighted on the magazine cover, coupled with the stress of what I felt was a mediocre season and the pressure of final exams, had conspired to overcome my body. When spring practice rolled around, I wasn't ready to play, so I had time for some thoughtful reflection on my life and the importance of football in it. I visited the Episcopal Theological School in Cambridge, Massachusetts, and decided to take my graduate degree there.

My summer in Norman was followed by another hospitalization, this time at the Mayo Clinic, for yet another ulcer. I wasn't sure I'd be able to play football my senior year, but was finally given permission by my doctor at the Duke University Hospital. He concluded I'd spend more time biting my fingernails and worrying about not playing than I would under actual practice and game conditions.

One of the reasons I developed an ulcer was that I was trying to lose weight and didn't keep enough food in my stomach. Paradoxically, though I ate regularly in the hospital, the bland diet reduced my weight, and I returned to school weighing nineteen pounds less than the previous year. As a result, I had greater speed and quickness.

Duke opened the season with four victories and a tie, losing in the sixth game to North Carolina State. I was devastated by the loss. After I talked to Dad, he sent some thoughts:

*When I heard the score, I knew how disappointed you'd be. You must realize that times have changed, and if you have a schedule with comparable teams, you're just not going to win them all.*

*The only thing that concerns me about your situation is your continued deep concern with yourself and your attitudes. All of us must be analytical and honest with ourselves . . . but you can do this so much of the time that it becomes damaging . . . . You do need to prepare yourself mentally and physically for everything you do. When the time is over—a game, an examination, a speech, an interview, a business presentation, anything—you must analyze your performance and make note of what you could have done better. Resolve to do those things better . . . and then go on to the next of life's tests and problems.*

*The greatest thing you can do to clarify, help, and improve your own attitudes from being too self-centered is to do what I have said above and then literally lose yourself in helping others with their concerns and problems.*

*When Christ said, "You must lose yourself to find yourself," he was not speaking of material things—fasting, giving away all worldly goods, not caring about your appearance or abilities. On the contrary, he meant be as good, as capable as you can be; then use this talent for the benefit of others.*

*If you are not a talented, producing, capable man, you can't really do much for others. But with a degree of wisdom and great compassion, you can turn outward in love to help others.*

*Your concern for others, while trying to be honest with yourself, but not worrying about yourself beyond recognizing where, why, and how you can improve, is a real secret to a joyous, contributing life . . . . In your association with any group, your attitude is the key—"What can I contribute?" to the group as opposed to "What can I get out of it?"*

*You've always done these things, Jay, which is why you are such a wonderful person. I mention them only to help you reaffirm your own faith, belief, and understanding—not because I have even the slightest concern that you haven't already lived and practiced these precepts.*

*We had a remarkably fine sermon at early Communion this morning by the SMU Episcopal chaplain who was visiting. He pointed out that science has advanced so rapidly it has shattered our previous understanding of the world . . . . What we knew and thought about the world a century or even 50 years ago was vastly different from what we know to be true today.*

*In this shattering of these beliefs, many of us have made the fatal mistake of feeling there is nothing in which we can truly believe. But the guiding moral precepts and faiths which are the foundation of our society still are eternal.*

*He then pointed out that being human . . . we are unable to live up to our ideals. But he added this was the great gift of Christ. The honest effort, the falling short, the forgiveness, and once again, the effort. This is applicable to all of living, particularly football.*

*I've probably gone on longer than I should, but all I've said is so full in my heart, I wanted to share it with you. I love you deeply and I'm so proud of the man you've become.*

My final game was scheduled to be with the University of North Carolina. Mom arrived from Oklahoma to be with me. But the day before the game, one of my fraternity brothers broke the news that President Kennedy had been assassinated. The game was canceled and rescheduled for the following week. We lost in the last thirty seconds on a 47-yard field goal.

In spite of my frequent misgivings and the tension surrounding my football career, my senior year was the best season I ever had. I was voted the Atlantic Coast Conference Player of the Year and made first team on the American Football Coaches All-American Team, the UPI All-American Team, the Look All-American Team, and was eighth in the Heisman Trophy balloting. I also was presented with the Atlantic Coast Conference Scholar-Athlete Award. Dad was present for my introduction on two of the All-American teams, and they were two of the warmest, richest experiences of my life. I had accomplished my personal goals, and his constant encouragement and deep involvement in my life, even from a distance, had helped me weather the tough times.

I was proud of Dad because of his success and his absolute commitment to excellence, but I also was proud because he took the time to let me feel his love.

He was my father, but he was also, and remained until his death, my best friend.

# 6

# *In Washington with the Kennedys*

&

*"A sound mind in a sound body ..."*
—*Juvenal*

In late February, 1961, near the beginning of my second semester as a college freshman, I received an unexpected letter from Dad.

*Dear Jay,*
*I have a problem which is surprising and difficult. Yesterday a man named Ted Reardon called me from the White House and asked me, on behalf of the President, to become the Executive Director for Youth Fitness. This would be a presidential appointment.*
*There is no doubt that it is a fine opportunity to make a contribution for a cause in which I believe, but if I accept, I will probably have to give up my job at Oklahoma, move to Washington, make only one-third as much money while residing in a far more expensive place, and then be out of a job in four or eight years when we have a new President.*
*It is an honor even to be considered for such a position. I'm going to Washington ... to talk with Mr. Reardon about it. I'll call you when I know a little more, as I would like to know what you think before I accept or refuse. In the meantime, please don't tell anybody.*

It seemed that soon after his election in 1960, President Kennedy asked his aide, Ted Reardon, to find someone to lead the President's Council on Youth Fitness. In a memo to Kennedy, Reardon replied that the program needed a nationally prominent and popular sports figure to head it up. As an afterthought, he added, "—somebody like Bud Wilkinson." After reading the memo, Kennedy called Reardon and asked if he thought Dad would take the job.

I was excited and proud Dad was being thought about for this position and waited impatiently to hear about his Washington discussions. It wasn't too long a wait. Within a week, another letter arrived. Dad, with his customary efficiency, had been to Washington and

> . . . *drawn up a proposal for youth fitness and forwarded it to the White House. If Reardon, the president's aide, doesn't like it, I'll have no further problem. If he does, I may have to go to Washington part-time and get the program underway.*
>
> *I don't believe, after thinking the matter through, that I could do any more good full-time than part-time—and since Dr. Cross will give me the time off—the most difficult part of the problem appears to be solved. I'll let you know what Washington decides, as soon as I hear anything.*

Four days later, the White House called.

> *They read and liked my plan. They want me to take a year's leave of absence, but I don't see how I can. I think I can do the job part-time, but I doubt if this will be acceptable to them.*

The part-time/full-time dilemma was resolved in a conversation between Dad and the president himself, in which Dad convinced Kennedy that, "I can better attract the press if I remain a college football coach. If I accept this position [full-time], in another twelve months, I'll be considered just another minor bureaucrat." In his next letter, though, in spite of the fact that Kennedy and the University of Oklahoma were willing to make adjustments to allow Dad to accept the position, it was clear he was still wrestling with the decision.

*They apparently liked my proposal and it looks like they'll take me up on the offer. I will be serving without pay and will probably be gone from home a lot—especially during the summer—but if they want me, I guess I should give it a try.*

*I'm supposed to write a brief summary of my proposal which they will send to the President's Council, which is made up of six Cabinet members. If these men concur with the program—and will support it—I'm going to appear before them to briefly answer questions concerning it, at which time it will be announced that I'm the Advisor to the Council.*

*Actually, I'm torn about it. If they don't like my plan, I'm free to do my own job. If they do like it, I'm trapped for a whole lot of extra work—at which I may fail. We'll just have to wait and see how it comes out.*

Though he was coming closer to making the move, the major impediment to Dad's acceptance had yet to be dealt with. The President's Council on Youth Fitness had originated during the Eisenhower years and been inherited by the Kennedy administration. Dad was very concerned Kennedy might treat the council as an ornamental, symbolic collection of appointments, with no real power or influence. During a meeting he confronted the president directly.

"Mr. President," he said, "tell me honestly and frankly, how important is this physical fitness program to you?"

Kennedy responded, "We're in a war with two great nations. Not a shooting war, but we're at war with China and Russia. If we cannot do something to improve the physical fitness of Americans, then, as history has proven, in fifty years we will not be able to compete with these societies. I am really for it."

That was enough for Dad. He jumped aboard, ready to head the program, which Kennedy said was designed "to make the nation's youth fit to learn, fit to understand, fit to grow in grace and stature, and fit to fully live."

Dad's first priority was to develop a top-level staff. His first program administrator was Dean Markham, a friend of Bobby Kennedy's from Harvard. Dad's good friend from Kansas, sportswriter Dick Snider, was appointed to the public relations position. Simon McNeely came onto the staff on loan from the U.S. Office of Education and took over federal and state relations. Dr.

Ted Forbes was in charge of program development; C. Carson "Casey" Conrad, California's Director of Health, Physical Education and Recreation, was consultant to the group. After about six months, Snider replaced Markham as administrator, and V. L. "Nick" Nicholson took over public relations.

At the beginning, in spite of Kennedy's enthusiasm and commitment, there was no program to administer. As Snider remembers, "There was absolutely no direction from anywhere. The whole program was conceived by Bud, and then other things . . . started to fall in line."

The statistics that demonstrated the need for the program were alarming. University testing showed that incoming students were progressively less fit. At Yale University, for example, fifty-eight percent of the incoming freshmen passed their physical tests in 1950; by 1960, only thirty-eight percent could do so. The U.S. Army had to reduce its norms for physical abilities in the mid '50s, because performance levels were so much lower than scores made during World War II. A series of tests in Eastern cities demonstrated that active seventy-five-year-old women living in nursing homes were more fit than local schoolgirls. The nation was indeed becoming soft—a victim of its own technology.

In a speech before a group of newspaper editors, Dad made the point that even tasks requiring little effort, such as opening cans or sharpening pencils, were now done mechanically. In the '50s, he said, just the act of driving and parking a car three times a day, could maintain muscle tone in the arms, but by the '60s, "[driving] requires no effort at all. You can get into the smallest parking space by using one finger, and you don't have to shift gears . . . . And if your car isn't equipped with air conditioning, you adjust the window with another button."

With the daunting picture of a seriously out-of-shape America in front of them, Dad and his staff went to work, developing a program that would allow every child in America to improve his or her level of fitness. The program, which was applicable to any school, required no uniforms, no equipment, and no special knowledge on the part of the teacher. Dad knew the council had no power to tell school boards, parents, or teachers what to do; its role was simply to explain the reasons why the United States had to become more fit and what it was we needed to do to overcome our softness.

The program was not designed to create a muscle cult. Dad wasn't trying to develop a nation of gladiators, but, like Kennedy, he believed the survival of a nation depended on the fitness and vitality of its youth. At the outset of the program he said, "The Oklahoma football team, of which I am coach, opens the season against Notre Dame. Our fans hope we will be better than Notre Dame. But that's not what I'm hoping for at all. I want our team to be as good as it possibly can. We hope to develop all our capacities to the fullest possible degree. Our nation is like a football team with outstanding material. We can only be as good as we desire to be. For survival we must want to be the best in every area of life."

The centerpiece of the new program was activity, which Dad considered essential to fitness. He believed all children should be required to take part in fifteen minutes of vigorous physical exercise each day as part of the physical education or recess period, and that physical education should be based on a comprehensive testing program that measured fitness at the beginning and end of the school year.

All this emphasis on activity brought the program into conflict with the American Association for Health, Physical Education and Recreation (AAHPER). According to Snider, "The association felt the program was too simple. Professional physical education teachers, who believed strongly in theory rather than activity alone, opposed the plan. They liked to believe . . . theirs was a coat and tie profession, that you had to sit in classrooms to be a physical educator. At that time, for example, it was possible to get a physical education degree in North Carolina without ever taking your tie off.

"The association didn't want the image of the profession reduced to people running around in sweat suits blowing whistles . . . . It insisted there was more to physical fitness than exercise. Bud argued that without exercise there could be no physical improvement. He made tremendous progress with these people, but [today] the argument still goes on."

From 1961 to 1963, while I was in Norman working construction and conditioning for the Duke football season, Dad spent the summers in Washington, spending full time on the council, and those on his staff became aware of the seriousness with which he took his responsibilities. His top priority, he said, was "to get to the grass roots people and give them a plan. We can't just tell them to do it; we have to show them how to do it." He decided to produce an exercise booklet that could be used by any teacher in any setting to lead fitness activities. It would be a simple booklet, illustrated with matchstick figures.

As Snider remembers, "When he next came to Washington, Bud decided we needed a final push to get it finished and refined. He ordered all of us to my house, and we sat around the dining room table, writing and rewriting, all day and into the wee hours, but we got it done. We made it available to every school; we mailed hundreds of thousands of them and they were pretty well accepted.

"They were designed so even a fat woman in an elementary school in South Dakota, someone who'd never participated in an activity in her whole life, could use the book and put her class through a very meaningful physical education period."

All sorts of people wanted to jump on the fitness bandwagon. Meredith Willson, who wrote *The Music Man* and *The Unsinkable Molly Brown,* called, unsolicited, and wanted to write a fitness song. Snider says, "He asked that we send him an exercise expert so he could put words and music to the exercises; we sent Forbes. In less than a week, Willson came up with *Chicken Fat,* which had great music and such lyrics as 'give that chicken fat back to the chickens.' The song was featured on many TV shows, including Dinah Shore's.

"At a White House reception, Kennedy told us he liked the song, but every time he heard it he thought of 'chicken shit,' and he wondered if maybe we shouldn't change the title. We said we'd talk to Willson about it, but we never did."

Lee Iacocca, too, was interested in the fitness program, but for another reason. He dropped in one day with a group of automobile executives and representatives from Ford's advertising agency, to get Dad to endorse Ford's new Punt, Pass, and Kick contest. Though Iacocca was not yet the industrial titan and household name he later became, he was still a formidable force, used to getting his own way. Iacocca and his coterie probably expected easy acquiescence to their idea, given Dad's coaching background. They ran into a stone wall.

"Bud refused immediately," Snider remembers. "He said the contest catered to talented young athletes, most of whom were already fit, and that competing in this type of activity would do little or nothing to improve a young man's fitness. He explained our program was for the unfit, most of whom weren't gifted enough to participate in any kind of athletic competition.

"Iacocca's people were stunned; they left saying they had expected the government would support their worthwhile project."

One of the most valuable people to offer his help to Dad was Bill Colihan, a vice president of Young and Rubicam. He and a staff of associates visited the office one day, saying simply, "We think an advertising agency can help you, and we're a good one; we're volunteering." He assigned a full team to the effort, and was instrumental in getting Dad to appear before the Ad Council. The Ad Council took up the program and designed a full-scale campaign. Snider recalls, "Then it really got rolling, a national campaign, like Smokey the Bear. We were everywhere, with free ads in magazines, TV spots, radio spots, the works. The Ad Council was the best thing that ever happened to us."

Dad even got the original seven astronauts to participate by prevailing on Jim Webb, then head of NASA. "Bud called him up," Snider says. "We had the idea the astronauts would make great spokespersons for the fitness program. Obviously they were pretty fit. For the ads they weren't all dolled up in their uniforms or climbing in and out of the capsules. These were in casual situations, like on the golf course, and they'd interrupt their game to talk about fitness. Young and Rubicam produced those."

Without question, however, the most crucial support for the fitness program came from the Kennedys themselves, who were well known advocates of a fit and healthy lifestyle. "Oh, yes," Snider agrees. "One of the big things was Bobby Kennedy's fifty-mile walk. The president liked to needle Pierre Salinger; he noted one time that the Marines routinely took fifty-mile walks and wondered why Pierre didn't. Pierre's comment was, 'I may be plucky, but I'm not stupid,' so Bobby went out to the B&O canal towpath, which runs right through the District and forever up into Maryland, and walked fifty miles. Nobody knew about it. He just went out and did it, but it was publicized like mad afterward.

"After Bobby did it, Pierre used the excuse that we had talked him out of it—that we told him not to try. We told *everybody* not to try it unless they'd had a physical or were in shape to do it. It became a craze, just kind of overnight. Everybody was talking about walking fity miles.

"The networks did call, Bud wasn't in town, and I had to back Pierre up. He was taking a lot of heat from reporters putting the needle to him. He called me right quick and said, 'You have to get me off the hook. If anybody asks, you told me not to do it.' So that's what I said."

"One of the things that always bothered me," Snider continues, "is that I walked the fifty miles, too, and nobody ever asked me about it. I was sure as administrator of the program I was going to be asked; three Marines and guys I knew . . . went with me to carry me home. But, surprisingly, I made it, and nobody ever asked me. Bud never asked me.

"Anyway, Bobby's walk was probably one of the things that kicked off the explosion of walking, jogging and going to the gym."

And Bobby was there on other occasions, too, twice making speeches on behalf of the program to AAHPER conventions and serving as an example of the Council's belief that "you can't influence kids to be fit if you're not fit yourself."

Bernie Hillenbrand, former executive director of the National Association of Counties, who later knew Dad as a businessman, remembers him as a fitness role model. "You had a new administration and the first president born in this century . . . . It all seems commonplace now. But as a result of what Bud was doing and the general climate, you began to see people jogging and exercising . . . . It was the beginning of what we now call the health craze, things we just accept. I go out in the morning for my walk and see thirty or forty people, ranging in age from twenty to eighty out jogging . . . . At the time it was the first positive anti-couch potato thing people began to get into."

In short, Snider says, "It's unlikely any other administration ever did as much to make the public aware of the need to improve adults' and children's physical fitness. Bud practiced what he preached, too, running every day on the Georgetown University track."

Beyond their helpfulness to the cause, the Kennedys were friends as well. Mom and Dad were included in gatherings at the White House and at Hickory Hill, Bobby and Ethel's home. Though Dad was greatly affected by John Kennedy and revered him, he was particularly fond of Bobby. When they first met, Dad was impressed with his intensity regarding Jimmy Hoffa and believed Kennedy surely would bring him down.

On one occasion, Mom and Dad were at Hickory Hill with another couple. "We got to the house before Bobby and Ethel did," Mom says. "They had been to a cocktail party. When they got home, Ethel asked me if I would like to go up with her while she tucked all the children in. At this point they had about nine. She was really just dear with all the kids and they were so darling."

Dad saw another side of Ethel at a later party at the Kennedy home, a party at which Ethel stood on a table proposing a toast to the "second most powerful person in the world—my husband Robert," while Vice President Johnson was present. Dad said the incident made his blood turn to ice. But, in general, Dad loved being with the Kennedys and found the times at Hickory Hill exciting and lots of fun.

Snider remembers a more formal occasion in 1961. "It was one of Jacqueline Kennedy's most memorable parties and called for guests to drive to the Navy Yard, board the presidential yacht and cruise to a party at Mount Vernon.

"At the Navy Yard, there was this long stream of limousines, and in the middle, Bud and Mary in a yellow Volkswagen convertible."

Though the fitness program was having an impact nationwide, Dad was observing the workings of Washington up close, and he didn't like everything he saw. During his first year, the council didn't spend their entire budget. Therefore, Dad wanted to submit a smaller budget for the next fiscal year. His senior staff were appalled, arguing "if you don't spend this year's budget, we'll never to able to get more money for the council in coming years!" In spite of the staff's protests, Dad returned $49,000 of his $315,000 budget to the Treasury. His eyes were being opened to the fact that oftentimes budgets had less to do with programs than with self-aggrandizement. He began to believe neither Congress nor government agencies took any personal responsibility to be good stewards of the taxpayers' money.

And he felt there was some irresponsibility within his own support staff, as well. He noticed when the council invited outsiders to conferences, a few of the secretarial staff took sick leave because they didn't want to deal with registration and conference logistics.

He talked to Oklahoma Senator Mike Monroney about it. Monroney suggested he hire more people. Dad had a difficult time taking this advice, because he felt the present staff should accept the responsibilities for which they'd been hired. He wanted to get rid of those who wouldn't perform. Monroney replied, "You can't fire them. It'll take six to eight months to do it because of their civil service protection. If you want an active program, you'll have to hire more people." Dad was astounded, because he couldn't conceive of a situation in which people would not want to do the best job possible and also because he couldn't see running up more unnecessary expenses.

≥∙

During the time Dad spent the summers in Washington, his teams began to struggle. In 1960, the Sooners had a 3-6-1 season and finished fourth in the Big Eight. The next season began with five straight losses and concluded with five straight wins. He wrote to me:

*I hate to be discouraged about our team, but frankly, I am. We no longer have the real "Gung Ho" spirit, and without it the team can't do very well. I don't think I'm doing a decent job of coaching either—but I'm trying to. Somehow I feel I'm not getting through to the team like I should. Unless I can uncover the problem and correct it, we won't play well again.*

By 1962 and 1963, things were looking up, but in the off-season Dad was traveling constantly—recruiting, speaking, running Coach of the Year Clinics, and seeing to Council business. His letters from that period paint a picture of a tired, and at the same time, restless man.

Before long, the reason for his restlessness surfaced. Dad was thinking of running for office. He believed self-reliance and personal responsibility could not flourish when power was centralized in Washington at the expense of the states, counties and cities. He was also highly critical of the waste he'd seen in the capitol. He started to talk about running for the Senate. Of course, word got out, and Ted Reardon began to quiz Snider about Dad's plans. "I could tell him truthfully," says Snider, "that I didn't know, because I didn't."

As stories leaked out of Washington about an impending Senate run, Dad had to deal with rumors about his resigning from the University of Oklahoma, stating, "I can't control what is said in the newspapers . . . . The only thing I am interested in right now is OU's football schedule for the next season."

The 1963 season ended with Oklahoma taking second place in the conference and eighth place in the national standings. But the President's assassination near the end of the season appears to have been the final straw in Dad's decision-making process. "I know it wasn't until after the assassination that Bud seriously said to me, 'If I run, will you go out there?' " Snider says. "As I recall, the final decision was made in the Willard Hotel in Washington. Bud said he was going to run as a Republican and legally change his name to Bud. If I remember correctly, the only people there at the Willard were Bud, Mary, and me."

Unlike other universities around the country, Oklahoma played its game against Nebraska on the Saturday following the assassination. Rick McCurdy, who played for Oklahoma, recalls returning to Norman after the game. "I remember on the ride home Bud looked so weary and so tired. I knew he was a close friend of the president . . . .The next game we played was Oklahoma State, and before the game, he came before the team and said this was the most important game of his coaching career. I knew this might be his last game. I think ... with the president's death, he had a sense of responsibility not just to our football team or to our state, but actually to the country. Because he had been around the political scene enough, he felt a sense of the lack of leadership."

A few days after the season ended, Dad went to Dr. Cross' office and told him he had decided to resign from his coaching position. According to Cross' book, Dad told him he could "no longer get himself into a 'proper frame of mind' to prepare for a football game and therefore was unable to get his staff ready."

In January 1964, Dad tendered his resignation. A chapter was closed in his life, and in the life of the University of Oklahoma. He was ready to turn the next page.

# 7

## The Race for the Senate

ॐ

*"The time is out of joint . . . "*
—*Shakespeare*

In a 1955 article for *Sports Illustrated*, author Joan Flynn Dryspool stated, "If . . . Wilkinson were to run for political office in Oklahoma, he'd win by a landslide." But by 1964, when his race for the United States Senate ended in defeat, Dad agonized, "I can't believe more than fifty percent of the voters in Oklahoma came out against me." How could a candidate with ninety-five percent name recognition and nearly demi-god status lose the contest? How could Fred Harris, a less well-known state senator, have been elected when virtually all the pundits had conceded the election to Dad?

In the first place, Dad's timing was off. Everyone agrees that had he run again in 1966, he would have won in a walk, but in 1964 President Kennedy recently had been assassinated, and American voters, jolted by their president's death, were searching for stability and continuity. They were not about to vote Lyndon Johnson out of office, replacing him with the relatively unknown Barry Goldwater. Johnson's coattails were long. That fact, combined with the well-managed campaign run by Fred Harris and his advisors, swept Harris to victory.

Second, Dad ran as a Republican in a state that was 4-1 Democratic. According to Tony Calvert, who served as finance chairman of the campaign, "I personally admired him for deciding to be a Republican senatorial candidate . . . . I am sure he could have run on the Democratic ticket, but his political philosophy was conservative, and he wanted to run on that premise—not just run to win, but to win on his principles . . . . Power brokers from both parties tried to feel him out about running for governor or senator. I remember the statement he made to me after he chose to run. He said, 'I'd rather be a U.S. Senator deciding national and international needs and problems than sit in the governor's office handing out sewer contracts.' "

As a conservative, Dad was loyal to Goldwater—the real Goldwater, whose ideology Dad shared—not the wild-eyed extremist the Johnson forces later made Goldwater out to be. Dad, like Goldwater, was concerned about the intrusion of government into every aspect of American life. He also believed in the values of hard work, thrift, personal responsibility, and self-reliance—values on which the United States was built. Bringing those values back to the political scene was his primary motivation for running. He wanted to return the principles of team play, self-sacrifice, intense dedication to a common cause, and discipline—principles he thought were best developed in athletics—to their preeminent place in American life. Goldwater shared those ideals, so Dad stuck with him. All political observers believe, however, that fidelity to Goldwater cost him his own election.

Third, Dad and his supporters were somewhat naive about the political process. His campaign was guided not by professional politicians, but by good friends who were bright and capable, but not always politically savvy. In some cases, they—and Dad—misjudged the strength of the opposition and mishandled logistics.

Nonetheless, it was a well-fought campaign from the beginning, and at the end, though Johnson had carried the state by more than 100,000 ballots, Dad's race was decided by about 21,000 votes. He didn't win, but it was a credible showing by a first-time non-politician.

࿐

Dad's entry into politics was laden with controversy. Prior to the announcement of his candidacy, he resigned as football coach at Oklahoma, but maintained his position as athletic director and strongly recommended Gomer Jones be appointed head coach. Some of the regents felt Dad was using the A.D. position as a power base to get Jones selected, and he'd resign to make his Senate run as soon as Jones was installed. The majority of the regents were Democrats who wanted to delay a new coach's appointment until they figured out whether Dad was going to run. If they dallied long enough, he would be forced to signal his intentions because he would have to change his party affiliation.

In the meantime, a petition supporting Jones' appointment was signed by the members of the Sooner team and presented to the regents. The Alumni Association checked in, also in favor of Jones, but the regents stonewalled, saying they were going to wait a few weeks to select the new coach.

Dad was extremely concerned about the effects the delay would have on recruiting and upset that Jones was being made a pawn in a political battle. To put an end to the internecine warfare, on Saturday, January 18, 1964, he called a news conference and resigned the athletic directorship, saying:

It has become increasingly apparent that political maneuvering on the part of some regents has taken precedence over the early choice of a new coach.

So that these considerations can no longer play a part in the delay, I am resigning as athletic director. This action will free the regents from any further political involvement related to this selection . . . .

Jones was selected and Dad opened his campaign for the United States Senate.

ঌৡ

Henry Bellmon, the first Republican governor in Oklahoma since statehood, was there at the beginning.

"Shirley and I were invited to meet with Bud and Mary to talk about politics . . . . As I recall, Bud hadn't decided fully to run, but there were two things he wanted to be sure of—one, that he had the money to run with, and secondly, he wanted to be sure that Barry Goldwater was going to be the Republican nominee. He was delighted to find out, at least in my judgment, Goldwater would be nominated."

In the later meeting at the Willard Hotel in Washington, Dick Snider agreed to come to Oklahoma to coordinate Dad's campaign. Very shortly after Dad's resignation as Oklahoma A.D., both he and Snider resigned their positions with the President's Council on Physical Fitness and set out to campaign in earnest. Others who came aboard during the early days included Ed Turner, press secretary; Dick Taft, campaign treasurer; Tony Calvert, finance chair; Goodwin Broaddus, field coordinator; Dorothy Stanislaus, women's chair; Joan Hastings, youth leadership chair; Larry Goff, senior advance man; and Doc Jordan, whose agency ran the advertising campaign.

As the race geared up, Dad's first action was to change his name legally from "Charles Burnham" to "Bud" Wilkinson. It was, after all, the name people knew; many of his oldest friends never had even been aware his name was Charles.

"He got nailed on [the name change] the first month or so," says Larry Goff. "Some older people seemed to be offended by the fact that he would change the name his mother gave him."

With the name change out of the way, fund raising jumped to the top of the agenda. Early money was essential, as two other candidates, Tom Harris and Forest Beall, also were contending for the Republican nomination. Though the polls indicated the primary could be a walkover for Dad, nobody was going to hand him the nomination. There had to be a primary campaign. That and the general election would cost money.

"The first thing we did," Snider says, "was to go to Tulsa and have a meeting with the biggest of the big cigars, about twenty guys .... All of them were very positive and they were aggressive—'let's do this and let's do that' .... Bud made it clear to everybody all the way that he would run as hard as he possibly could and work as hard as he could, but he didn't want to spend time raising money. He never did have to."

Other members of the campaign staff also were in the quest for dollars. Goodwin Broaddus had come into the campaign somewhat innocently. "Jerry Peterson, who was sort of the Kay County Republican chairman at the time, was asked to represent Bud as the county chairman, but he was committed to Forest

Beall. Clyde Wheeler, [a Republican advisor], called me and asked me if I'd kind of put my name on the door for Bud .... He wanted me to come to the organizational meeting. I was so overwhelmed about it, I forgot to ask him where the meeting was .... I'd probably shaken hands with Bud once or twice at a Touchdown Club meeting, but I didn't know him. This was the first time I'd ever sat down with him .... I was overwhelmed and kept forgetting everything.

"Tony Calvert was there, and Clyde, and it was the first time I ever met Dick Snider," Broaddus says. "I went out of there scared to death. I thought, 'Here's this guy asking me to speak on his behalf, to represent him, and what if I screw up?' I never felt such a sense of responsibility in my life."

Broaddus turned out to be a strong representative and good fund raiser. "I was given a budget to raise for Bud's statewide campaign that was just unheard of .... Tony Calvert told me, 'We've got Kay County down for $10,000-$15,000.' It doesn't sound like much now, but in those days to get it out of Kay County was the pits. Kay County had a history of never really participating in any kind of statewide operation. The Republicans would contribute, but they would also contribute to the individual candidate, and usually the candidate had to come pick up the check himself, and usually it was for $25 .... You had to beat everybody over the head. I was trying to find someone who could put the hammer on them."

Broaddus found Harper Baughman. Baughman, however, was not an easy sell. "I don't like to get involved in things like this," he told Broaddus. "I might make somebody mad who buys lumber." But Baughman was a fan of Dad's and Broaddus arranged a meeting. "I had maybe six or seven of the movers and shakers and their wives at dinner. Harper was slobbering just as bad as I was slobbering about being in the same room with Bud. I got Harper over in a corner, and Bud came over and we all sat down and Bud got his recruiting face on .... Bud said, 'Harper, you're so good that you really need to handle this Kay County finance thing.' Harper says, 'I don't know.' Bud reached out and put his hand on Harper's knee and said, 'Harper, I really do need you on this.' Harper just melted. That was it. He went out and raised all the money. I was in some [of the meetings] where he really just hammered them. They were all wanting to wait until after the primaries to be sure their money wasn't wasted and all that kind of crap."

Tony Calvert, as state finance chairman, was on a different path. "I thought I would test the water at the top of the financial well in Oklahoma City," he remembers. "Charles Vose, chairman and president of the First National Bank, was as much a behind the scenes kingmaker as there was in Oklahoma City or maybe the state . . . . I decided to go see him on a cold turkey basis.

"Mr. Vose was easy to approach because he had the reputation that you didn't drop by to see him unless you were a good friend . . . . I went to his secretary and introduced myself and stated I would like to see him. She said, 'Go right in.' After opening with a few social amenities, telling Mr. Vose that I was going to be Bud's financial chairman and giving him a rough idea of our budget, I asked for the maximum $5,000 contribution. . . . He pushed his chair back and stood up. I don't remember his exact words, but they were similar to, 'Are you out of your simple mind?' I felt as if I'd pulled a real *faux pas*. I thanked him and left with my tail between my legs. But it was only a few days later either he or his secretary called and said to come by his office. Much to my surprise, there was a check waiting, payable to Bud's campaign, for $5,000."

Calvert continues, "Mr. Vose always had lunch at what the other members of the Beacon Club described as the Round Table, a table you didn't sit at unless you were . . . one of the so-called "godfathers" of the city. All these people were friends of Bud's and admired him and contributed to his campaign when asked. I figured between my visit and the time he gave me his contribution there had been considerable conversation about Bud at the Round Table. Later, I knew the product I was selling—Bud—was so appealing that he overrode the ineptness of my approach to Mr. Vose."

Calvert also raised funds in other than one-to-one sales calls. "Jim Hewgley and Mac McClintock agreed to be the financial chairmen for Tulsa. We agreed the quicker we contacted big givers the better. I arranged a 4:00 p.m. to 6:00 p.m cocktail party for 25-30 businessmen in Oklahoma City . . . . The party was to be held at the Beacon Club. Hewgley and McClintock were to have a similar party from 6:00 p.m. to 7:00 p.m. at the exclusive Southern Hills Country Club in Tulsa.

"In Tulsa," Calvert says, "with all its inherited and established wealth, it was much easier to raise money for conservative programs and candidates than in Oklahoma City. Tulsa had always been considered statewide as a metropolitan city, whereas Oklahoma City, with the seat of government and the stockyards, was a . . . cowtown."

With the givers in the room in Oklahoma City, Calvert used time-honored fund-raising techniques. "After a drink or so, I advised the Beacon group what the campaign goals were and asked the invitees to consider either giving or pledging to raise a certain amount. This approach is usually better because the contributor will give more by figuring he can raise part of his pledge by soliciting a friend. As it usually turns out, the contributor waits too long or finds out the friend has already given. So the contributor usually ends up contributing the entire amount. The party went off smooth as silk. By 6:00 p.m. I had raised $75,000 given or pledged."

Excited by his results, Calvert phoned McClintock at Southern Hills. " 'You raised how much?' he said. I could tell by the inflection in his voice that he couldn't believe his country cousins would contribute that amount on such short notice."

The total raised by the cocktail parties was about $125,000, a large sum of money in those days. "There is an old adage about raising money. You go where it is. Yet regardless of the amount given, every contributor received an acknowledgment from Bud."

Calvert decided an out-of-state fund search might prove fruitful. A breakfast meeting held in New York yielded some assistance, but it was a trip to Texas that handed Dad's campaign one of its biggest surprises.

"Bud was to give an endorsement speech at the Texas Republican convention on behalf of George Bush, who was running for the U.S. Senate," Calvert recalls. "He gave an applause-drenched speech . . . . Then either Dick Snider or Ed Turner got the word out that people were invited to drop by Bud's suite after the convention. The big surprise was that H. L. Hunt himself came by. At that time, Mr. Hunt was reportedly the richest man in the United States, if not the world. On top of that, if there ever was a 'Mr. Conservative,' he was it.

"After a short period of time, I noticed he and Bud were engaged in conversation in the corner of the room. Bud was attentively hanging on his every word . . . . After a while, Mr. Hunt went over to the *hors d'oeuvre* table and Bud came over to me. He had a pleased as punch look on his face. He reached into his inside coat pocket and handed me a bulging white envelope and said, 'Wait until everybody leaves before opening it.' "

When the last guest had left, Dad and Calvert were nearly beside themselves with anticipation. How much was in the envelope? What would they do if there were more cash than the legal limit? Maybe it was filled with contributions from all the Hunt family or Hunt executives. They locked the door and popped open the envelope. "None of us could believe our eyes," says Calvert. "It was filled full of pamphlets on an ultra-conservative Washington D.C. radio station Mr. Hunt sponsored. There was not one red cent in that envelope . . . . We all just shook our heads in disbelief."

In spite of the dearth of Hunt money, Dad's campaign war chest was healthy. "Lack of money wasn't the reason for our defeat," says Dick Snider.

❧

Other highly placed Republicans were confident about Dad's ability to pull off a win. He and Dick Snider had an early meeting with Senator Goldwater. "Bud and I saw him in his office in Washington. As soon as we were seated, he reached in the bottom drawer and pulled out three old, dirty—not dusty, but dirty—restaurant tumblers, set them on the desk and pulled out a bottle of bourbon and poured all three about half full. There was enough booze in there to choke an elephant.

"He said, 'My mother always warned me about tobacco and evil people, but thank God, she never got around to whiskey.' So we sat and sipped that bourbon and . . . he told Bud to go for it."

"It was a big surprise when Bud ran, frankly," Goldwater says today. "The first thing we heard was that he was running. He didn't snoop around and ask questions. He just ran. I like that better than trying to run polls. I spent a lot of money on him. I didn't see how the hell he could ever lose a campaign."

Former President Eisenhower agreed. Ike was living in Gettysburg when Bryce Harlow, an Oklahoman and Procter and

Gamble executive who had been Eisenhower's chief speech writer, arranged for Dad to meet with the former president.

Ike greeted them and the three men spent hours together, with Eisenhower telling stories about Winston Churchill and the paintings they'd exchanged. As the afternoon wore on, Eisenhower said to Dad, "I wonder if you've had any second thoughts now that you've decided to run."

"Mr. President," Dad replied, "I've got two boys in college. If I don't win, I'm unemployed."

Eisenhower chuckled and then told him that when he'd retired from the Army, he'd decided to forego his military pension, feeling it might create the appearance of impropriety should he decide to run for office. "I had a warrant officer," Eisenhower said, "who'd been my valet for my entire career as a senior officer. I assured my aide I didn't expect him to turn down his pension out of misguided loyalty to me. 'General,' he told me, 'I reckon you and I can always make a living.' Coach Wilkinson, I suspect you won't have much problem either."

ૐ

Dad was true to his word to run hard, and his primary campaign was as well organized as his football practices had been. He said that primary campaigning is like using a rifle; general campaigning requires a shotgun. In the primary, he needed to approach only those who could vote for him— Oklahoma's registered Republicans. To reach them, the campaign staff decided to count the number of days from the end of the state convention to the primary, relate that number to the number of registered Republicans within any given county, and spend a proportionate amount of time in each county, with major concentration given to those counties with the highest registration.

Though Dad was a newcomer to politics, his name recognition was so high and his campaigning so intense he swept to an easy victory over Beall, the former Oklahoma GOP Chairman, and Tom Harris, an Oklahoma City businessman. Final tallies were Wilkinson, 100,544; Harris, 19,170; and Beall, 7,211.

On the Democratic side, the picture was a little murkier. The previous year, on January 1, 1963, the Democratic senator,

Bob Kerr, died. It fell to the then-governor, J. Howard Edmondson, to appoint a successor. Since Edmondson's term was to expire January 14, 1963, and his replacement, Henry Bellmon, would surely send a Republican to Washington, the choice had to be made quickly. Edmondson, therefore, resigned from the governorship and Lieutenant Governor George Nigh appointed him to the vacant Senate seat. Edmondson could serve only until 1964 before he had to run again to complete the remaining two years of Senator Kerr's term, and if he wanted the next full term, he would have to run once more in 1966.

Thus, Edmondson had been in office nearly two years when he stood for election to complete the remaining two years of Senator Kerr's term. He was joined by former governor Raymond Gary and state senator Fred Harris.

As Harris remembers it, "I had planned to run for governor again. I'd run the preceding time .... I'd been in the state senate for some time, so I thought state government was what I knew. I thought the U.S. Senate was somewhere way off in the future.

"But then Bob Kerr died. I was going to support Bob Kerr, Jr., but the lieutenant governor appointed Edmondson. Somehow that offended the Kerr people—I don't know if they thought about it as Bob Kerr's seat and they should have been consulted or what .... Raymond Gary and Howard Edmondson wound up very much polarizing things.

"At the last, Bob Kerr, Jr. decided not to run, and people who had been going to support him and didn't want to support the other two wound up talking to me. I was really sort of talked into running for the Senate without having planned on it. I think an early poll showed Gary and Edmondson had about thirty-three percent and I think I was fourteen percent. I thought that was pretty good because they were very well known and I was not."

Harris' optimism wasn't universally shared. He ran into many who asked him how he expected to beat Dad when Dad was so well known.

"I thought it was an advantage for our campaign that I had primary opposition .... If I could go through a primary and a runoff with these two former governors—one of whom was a senator—by the time I got to the general election, I'd be as well-known as Wilkinson was. That's the way it turned out."

Following a runoff election against Senator Edmondson, Harris entered the campaign as Dad's Democratic opponent.

ॐ

To win the general election, Dad would have to garner the Republican vote and pick up 300,000 Democratic votes. With the 4-1 Democratic registration in Oklahoma, wresting that many votes away from Harris, particularly in Southern Oklahoma—"Little Dixie"—would be a formidable task. I have personal memories of having doors slammed in my face and being subjected to vicious verbal abuse as I canvassed Little Dixie neighborhoods for Dad.

The rest of the campaign staff was experiencing tough sledding, too. There were Wilkinson supporters in Southern Oklahoma, but they didn't feel free to express their opinions. "Somebody tipped me to a fellow down in Wilburton," Goodwin Broaddus says. "I went down there. He wouldn't talk to me on his phone. He would not talk to me at the office. We had little codes, and I'd have to phone and use the code that meant I was to meet him at such and such a place. I couldn't believe all this really existed. He said, 'I'll lose my job if my boss finds out that I'm talking to you. I want to help Bud.' He was scared to death. He told me the telephone operators listened in on calls. It was fierce."

Broaddus recalls his favorite story from the entire campaign. "We went over to a barbecue [in Southern Oklahoma]. Bud came down and was speaking . . . . You could see where the cars were coming in along this county road, which was surface dirt. The dust was just hanging . . . . All of a sudden the dust was settling and nobody was coming. I said, 'Bullshit.' It was probably half a mile to where the traffic stopped, and I trotted down there sweating like a pig. There's this huge deputy standing there, and he wouldn't let anybody cross the bridge unless they paid a dollar. He had traffic all backed up and nobody could turn around. Everybody was just stopped. I said, 'You can't do this.' He said, 'It's my bridge.' I had to give him $100 to go home. That's what we got into down there."

One of Dad's campaign strategies was to use television as much as possible. His televised coach's program had made him very familiar with the medium, and his quiet, articulate style was well suited to the intimacy of television. Of course, he would press the flesh all the way across the state as well, but the campaign leaned heavily on media.

There were a couple of secondary reasons for using television. Paradoxical as it sounds, television often gave people more real access to the candidate than they would have if he came to their home town.

Doc Jordan handled much of the campaign strategy, including the TV coverage. "Bud's supporters would be so excited about being part of the Bud Wilkinson effort and to be recognized by Bud. When he would come to Enid, Altus, Ardmore, Bartlesville and other cities, they wanted to keep him away from the common man. They didn't want him down on Main Street going into the café to have coffee; they wanted to take him to their country club to have lunch . . . . He became a symbol of their importance and they liked to display him and liked to tell everybody that 'I am Bud's coordinator,' or 'I'm Bud's good friend here, and if you're real nice to me, I'll let you meet Bud at my house for cocktails at 5:00 p.m., and we're not going to let any of the great unwashed in.' That was a constant battle. These people were damned serious. They paid their bucks and they wanted their trophy, and their trophy was Bud knowing their names.

"Bud Wilkinson," Jordan continues, "was the closest thing Oklahoma had to a genuine celebrity . . . . He was everything you wanted a celebrity to be—handsome, poised, masculine without being macho, very well-spoken—he was a winner who coached winners and gave Oklahoma a chance to forget its inferiority complex over the Okie stigma."

Jordan tried to get Dad to be more assertive with those who were impeding his access to the rest of the electorate. "We'd say, 'Bud, when they try to do that to you, you've just got to walk away and go downtown.' He'd say, 'You can't do that. If somebody says they have a check for $2,000 for you, you've got to have lunch with the guy. You've got to take the money and do what he wants you to do.' There were sometimes disagreements about what we thought he should do and what he thought he should do. He, of course, had gotten to where he was by using his own judgment, and he was prone to use his judgment in matters like the country club/café thing."

Combined with the "country club" attitude of some of his supporters was Dad's own discomfort with small talk. Dad was not a "hail fellow, well met" type. Though he was a consummate communicator and loved being with people, his innate sense of reserve and reticence meant he was not as comfortable mixing and mingling with crowds as he was in one-on-one situations. Therefore, small tables at country clubs often were more attractive to him than larger, more crowded settings.

Advance man Larry Goff also served as a sounding board for Dad. "When we first began, and he got up to talk to people, he had to work at it. He had a hard time at first asking people to vote for him. That was something he had never experienced and that politicians had to do. He got to where he would say, 'I hope I can count on your vote,' and wait for an answer, which is the important thing."

Governor Bellmon remembers "a meeting or two we attended. My plan was always to be early and stay late . . . . Bud never seemed to have the warmth most candidates showed. He tended to be a little stiff and proper. I spoke to him about it once or twice. He always said, 'I know how to get along with football families, and I can certainly get along with political people.' He probably could, but it never seemed like he came across as if he was enjoying himself or he was glad to meet these folks."

Perhaps even more telling was an incident involving an early political appearance Bellmon and Dad made. "Over at Locust Grove, we . . . dedicated the Marcum Ferry Dam. We invited John Love, the governor of Colorado, to be the main speaker . . . . When it was over, I stayed there and shook hands and talked to some people as you always do. We looked for Bud, and we didn't know where he was. It turned out that as soon as his speaking was over, he had left the scene of the event and gone over to Dorothy Stanislaus' house to listen to the OU/KU football game. He was a candidate, but he still had more interest in football than he did in campaigning."

Dorothy Stanislaus, who organized Bud's Brigadiers, the women's arm of the campaign, noticed a characteristic of some of the crowds who came out to rallies and campaign stops. "The problem," she says, "was that everyone was so awed by him, you had a hard time getting them to move up to him because they just wanted to stand back and look at him."

All these circumstances, taken together, made television very attractive. Jordan says, "One of the ways we devised to give the people more access to him was the television coffees. We had those in Tulsa, Oklahoma City, Ada, and Lawton, four out of the five weekdays. We'd set it up with the women's organization; [women would have coffees in their homes and call in their questions from those gatherings]. Bud would be on the phone . . . and one of us would screen the calls . . . . Bud would pick up a slip of paper and say, 'Here's a question from Mrs. John Doe, who wants to know what I would do about such and such.' Then he would answer it, of course. Bud was so photogenic and so telegenic . . . we tried to keep him on TV.

"He was already comfortable on television . . . . He was very good on his feet, very poised, very polished, very sincere; he was beautiful to work with on TV."

≈

The message of Dad's campaign, on television and in person, was that he had a vision for the United States that included a balanced budget, deficit reduction, a strong national defense and a decentralization of governmental powers. He was lukewarm on the Civil Rights Act, not because he didn't believe in equal rights, but because he was opposed to trying to legislate them. He was in favor of the oil depletion allowance so important to the oil industry in Oklahoma, against federal aid to education, and he believed in the right-to-work laws that were being hotly debated at that time.

Dad was, in fact, a Goldwater Republican, and it was at the beginning of his campaign that he publicly aligned himself with Goldwater and refused to back off from that position. Unfortunately Goldwater also attracted a fringe element of radical right-ists. By tying himself so closely to Goldwater, Dad found it hard to disassociate himself from those who were adulterating Goldwater's philosophy and misrepresenting his positions. Had

Dad listened to his advisors and taken a more moderate stance regarding Goldwater, he might have won the election. Some Republicans who distanced themselves from Goldwater were able to resist the Johnson onslaught; those bound up with Goldwater sank with him. Today Goldwater himself says, "I knew I couldn't beat Johnson. We knew that the day I made my acceptance speech." Dad, however, didn't know, and it cost him dearly.

"A key moment in the campaign was the kickoff," says Dick Snider. "We had the buses from every county in Oklahoma . . . . We had Henry Bellmon on the stage and a lot of dignitaries. Bud made the best speech of the campaign and the most forceful, but he embraced Goldwater 1000 percent—the next President of the United States and so on. The next day I got a hell of a lot of phone calls. But Bud was locked onto that from the word go. I don't think he mulled it over."

Dorothy Stanislaus was a veteran political organizer who clearly saw the danger. "Some of us tried to convince him not to tie himself too tight to Goldwater. That was strange in view of the fact that I had been a strong Goldwater delegate that year. I had been on the platform committee, and yet, I just felt like it was a mistake for Bud to tie in with him. Bud said he wasn't going to upset the ticket. I know the day the campaign kicked off in Oklahoma City . . . right up to the time he made his speech, some of us were trying to convince him not to do it, but he did. Dick Snider and Ed Turner were on the same side I was. In fact I really don't remember anyone being on the other side but Bud."

Once Dad was on the Goldwater bandwagon, some of Goldwater's supporters thought they could dictate Dad's actions. Youth leadership chair Joan Hastings dealt with a few of the repercussions.

"The Young Republicans were gung ho for Goldwater and also gung ho for Bud Wilkinson. But a time came in the campaign when they felt that Goldwater was not doing as well in Oklahoma as he should, and they needed even more emphasis on the support of Bud Wilkinson.

"I'm probably a purist in political life," Hastings explains. "One candidate does not go out on a limb for another candidate when they are in a race. It's wrong—and it's wrong to ask it.

"Bud was supporting Goldwater very strongly. All of his advisors, not just me, had said, 'You work on your own campaign and stay in it. Don't get into the other because that's just very poor campaigning.' "

At a Young Republican meeting in Muskogee, the Goldwater faction decided they were going to insist Dad sign certain endorsement papers as a litmus test of his loyalty to the head of the ticket.

Hastings says, "I will never forget it. I stood up and told them I would resign as Young Republican National Committee-woman and as National Chair, and that they were very poor politicians. Bud Wilkinson's campaign was too important to Oklahoma to even ask such a thing.

"It created a problem for all the people involved. I supported Goldwater. As a matter of fact, after he was nominated I became an advance person for him for a while. But [the Goldwater faction] was harmful to Bud's campaign .... They were like the religious zealots of today. If you're not totally in agreement with every single thing they want to do, they're not going to support you. I think it cost us the race. I really do."

இ

The Democrats were having trouble with the top of their ticket, too, Fred Harris recalls. "I think what Johnson had in mind was almost a kind of coronation. He didn't want to get involved in Democratic races, particularly where there was a doubt about the outcome. We couldn't get him to do anything for us.

"Then he had an appearance scheduled at the State Fair. There was a small Democratic fund raising reception in a room under the stadium, and of course, I was invited to that. It was closed to the press.

"My television advertising guy had a lot of guts, and I don't know yet how he did it, but he got himself and a sound and film crew into that room. To show you how hard it was to do that, Tom Steed was kept out of that room, and he was a member of Congress."

Johnson went around shaking hands, finally coming to greet Harris. "When he did that, my television guy stuck a microphone in his face and signaled his camera crew, and he said, 'Mr. President, would you say a word about Fred Harris?'

"Well," Harris goes on, "you could see Johnson was just livid, but he was also aware the camera was rolling. You could see his face just kind of change, he turned to me again formally and shook hands with me, then he looked straight into the camera, and here's word for word what he said. 'I need Fred Harris in Washington. Send me old Fred and together we'll charge Hell with a bucket of water. Old Fred will bring home the bacon and tack the coon skin on the barn door.' "

&

Though Johnson painted him in country-esque language, Harris was no yokel. He was a Phi Beta Kappa with a law degree from the University of Oklahoma, and at the age of thirty-three was already an eight-year veteran of the Oklahoma state senate. He had knocked off two former governors to get to the general election, and he wanted to win. He couldn't attack his opponent personally, as at that point Dad was a virtual icon around the state, so his strategy was to point up his own governmental experience.

"In the general election, our slogan was 'Prepared for the Job,' Harris says. "It intended to say that Bud was not prepared. It was a high road campaign on the issues and on that basic theme."

As opposed to Dad's use of media, Harris ran what he says "was the most personal campaign anybody had ever run .... I had studied two or three campaigns—Birch Bayh's in Indiana, for example, and I knew that in order to win we had to look at Bud almost like an incumbent. He was so well known and such a strong figure in Oklahoma that the only way we could win was by really working terribly hard in organizing almost block by block and a lot of personal campaigning."

Harris, a populist and liberal Democratic, came down on the opposite side of most issues from Dad. The battle lines were clearly drawn. To highlight the differences between the two men, Dad now pressed for a televised debate.

In hindsight, the debate was a coffin nail in Dad's campaign, but at the time, it seemed to be a terrific tactic. And for a while, the Harris people played right into Dad's hands. They didn't want the debate, and Dad was able to capitalize on their ducking the face-to-face meeting.

"I was thinking that Bud was already so well known and he'd been on television forever," says Harris, "and people would expect me to be a debater since I was in politics. If he just did fairly well, he'd be the winner, so I didn't want to do that."

"Bud really wanted the debate badly," says Dick Snider. "He thought he would cut Harris up. He thought the comparison on TV would be like Kennedy and Nixon. He sent me and Ed Turner over to the enemy camp and his only instructions were to 'concede whatever you have to, do whatever you have to do, but get the debate . . . . Don't blow it. Get the debate.' "

Harris continued to backpedal from the idea, until Bill Carmack, an OU professor and political consultant to the Harris campaign, convinced him he could no longer evade the challenge.

"I got a call that Fred wouldn't debate Bud, and Bud was really making mileage out of that. He was using it everywhere . . . . Fred was just plain flat-out scared of him and you can quote me. He said, 'That man is on television with one of the most popular shows in the state every week. I have never been on television, and he'll make me look like a total amateur. I will not expose myself to that.'

"I went up to Fred's office that day and got Fred. I walked right into his office and I said, 'Fred, let's go for a ride.' He said, 'I'm too busy.' I said, 'My business is the most important business of the day.' "

Harris and Carmack drove to the downtown airport and parked the car, as Carmack worked Harris over to get him to change his mind. "I said, 'Fred, you're going to lose this damned election because your fear shows. If you won't debate Bud Wilkinson to win the Senate seat, why would a voter think you'll debate Everett Dirksen in the Senate? You're running for an office that lives and dies by debate, and you're running by explaining that you're afraid to debate the man you're running against. How do we know you wouldn't get up to Washington and decide not to go to the floor for fear you'd be exposed in a debate?'

"That hit him right in the gut," Carmack says. "He said, 'But what will I do?' I said, 'What Bud's got on you is years and years of speaking publicly and using television. What you've got on Bud is seven years of knowing state issues intimately.' "

Harris decided to accept the debate. Carmack determined the rules. "[I told Fred], 'Bud will kill you if it's one of these so-called political debates where the questioners get to question each other. Bud has poise and natural charm and experience . . . but if we can get a college-type debate where you get two full ten-minute slots to explain in detail your positions, you'll look good.' So that's what they did."

Following Dad's instructions to get the debate at any price, his team agreed to the format that hurt him the most. "I decided early in the debate," says Harris, "to take positions on as many issues as I could rapidly and challenge Bud to do the same, and I was also going to say that I was for Johnson and Humphrey and challenge him to say if he was for Goldwater and Miller. The Goldwater thing was particularly helpful."

Most people agree the debate was a draw, and a draw was a win for Harris. "What we did," said Carmack, "was what the OU team did on Saturdays. The debate showed we could play with the big boys. Everybody knew Bud was a consummate performer in public—probably the best in the state. The question was, would Fred be effective representing us or is he too much the hick lawyer from a small town?"

"I'll tell you," says Snider, "Harris surprised most of us. Ed Turner wasn't surprised because he said all along Harris was no dummy. He shocked the hell out of me. I thought he was a country bumpkin."

The polls showed Harris had drawn blood. "Early in the campaign," he says, "the black vote was going about 5-4 for me. After the debate, it was going about 7-3. When Strom Thurmond came into Oklahoma to campaign for Bud, it went to 9-1. Bud was just a likable person, a real Oklahoma hero, and all of that appealed to black people as well as white people. Early on, I thought if the [black vote] didn't change it would be fatal. But I think the Goldwater thing was harmful to Bud and so was Thurmond coming into the campaign."

ॐ

The debate behind them, the candidates turned to the grueling work of meeting the people.

"Bud was a great candidate," says Dick Snider. "He worked like hell. Not ever at any time in the campaign did he say, 'Aw, the hell with it, I'm going to relax the rest of the day, or I'm going to take the afternoon off, or I'm not going to show at that last coffee.' Now, he got trapped occasionally spending too much time with people who were already going to vote for him. You had to go to the damn country club or the boardroom at the bank."

The pace was grueling, according to Larry Goff, and sometimes the logistical wires got crossed. "We'd get into places at 11:00 p.m. or midnight or 1:00 a.m. and get up at 6:00 and start again for the entire day. One of the hardest things was to get people to leave him alone . . . and give him an afternoon off sometime during the week. The other thing they wanted to do was pop up in different places. Rather than leaving from Oklahoma City to Norman to Ardmore, they went from Oklahoma City to Miami and then down to Altus. They jumped him all over the state. The idea was to be in a lot of different places—lots of visibility—but I don't know if it was a good idea or not. It seems like it took a lot of energy. It was tiring. I was tired and I wasn't the guy giving the speeches and having to be on stage all the time."

In addition, Dad answered every question voters brought to him. Those who were present at Dad's campaign stops often handed staff members slips of paper with questions or personal concerns written on them. The staff would collect them, and each week Dad would dictate individual responses to each person's query. It took hours.

Looking back, says Goff, "I would do some things differently. I wouldn't hop back and forth across the state. I wouldn't do that to any candidate . . . . It's really easy for a candidate to become tired and punchy—where you're not really coherent. Bud had major issues stands, but it hurts when you're not real alert and real sharp.

"Sometimes [to relax], he'd play golf. I remember one town we were in where they must have had a 15-some; some guy had gotten all his buddies. It wasn't fun or relaxing. It was just an extension of the campaign."

One of the campaign swings brought some extra excitement. "Bud and the governor were coming into Shawnee late one night and all the lights on the airport were out. They had to park cars along the runway so we could get in. Mary just had a fit. It was pretty wild," recalls Goff.

In some places Dad and Goff created their own media events. "We were in some little town, and the local radio station was willing to give us air time, but they didn't have an announcer. I became the local announcer, and Bud and I went in and did a half hour show with me interviewing him. He'd be writing down and handing to me the stuff he wanted to talk about."

Just as during the football season, Dad often had trouble sleeping during the campaign. "We'd get into a town," Goff says, "and he'd come down to my room and we'd talk or play gin rummy or drink a beer or something like that. He'd just talk about what was going on for thirty minutes to an hour until he wound down and could go to sleep."

The Harris campaign was also on the road, even more extensively than Dad and his staff. While Dad, with this well-financed war chest, could make TV commercials to reach the public, Harris was shorter of funds. Therefore, he made, announced—and kept—his promise to visit every town in Oklahoma. Duke and McQueen, which were ghost towns, received a visit, as did every other tiny hamlet or crossroads. According to Bill Carmack, "Fred slept in his own bed four times in seven months."

The campaigns ground on, and sometimes tempers frayed. "A couple of times," says Dorothy Stanislaus, "I mentioned to Ed and Dick that I was concerned. Here was this popular guy running around with Goldwater and things just weren't jelling the way they should."

The staff chalked up Stanislaus' instincts to pessimism. "I'm not a pessimist at all," she says, "but shortly before the election, we had a rally and it just didn't turn out like it should have. I thought people were backing away from us. Again, they told me it was all in my mind. That was part of the problem. Even the campaign staff felt like it was won. You just can't do that. I don't care who you are. Bud never did, but his staff gave that impression a lot."

Dick Snider disagrees with Stanislaus' assessment. "There was never a day Turner and I thought we had it won. Polls never showed that, and feedback from the boonies never suggested it. Bud kept saying, 'When they see my name on the ballot, they'll vote for me.' And I remember election eve when we were at Bellmon's house talking about who should be on Bud's staff in Washington. I asked, 'What makes you think we're going to win?' Both Bud and Bellmon smiled and Bud said, 'Oh, ye of little faith.' "

&

Stanislaus, Turner and Snider turned out to be right. Yet the night before the election, though Dad was exhausted, he was confident. He and I sat together in our bathrobes on the patio, talking long into the night—a starry night with a soft breeze from the south. Dad went to bed truly believing he would win. He knew it would be close, he told me, but all of his life, he had remained optimistic and positive. He was no Pollyanna, but he had built his life on the idea that success was possible if you prepared, played the game hard, and believed in your ability to win.

He knew the majority of the people of Oklahoma revered him, and he disagreed with his advisors who said if Johnson beat Goldwater by more than 100,000 votes, Dad probably could not win. His teams had won against bigger odds than that, and he thought no matter what the outcome of the presidential election, more than half the voters surely would pull the lever for him.

He was very tired, he said, but poised and ready for the challenge of the Senate seat. Surprisingly, for one so often afflicted with insomnia, he slept well, as he always did the night before a game when he knew he had prepared and done his level best.

The day of the election, Dad and Mom voted early, and Dad went briefly to his Oklahoma City headquarters. After the polls closed, the end of his dreams came quickly. We heard the first returns as we drove from Norman to Oklahoma City. By the time we arrived, we knew things were heading downhill.

Even as the sobering results were filtering into Oklahoma City, Dad greeted cheering partisans, telling them, "Regardless of the outcome, I'd like to make this observation: A candidate is one who represents the composite philosophies and political beliefs of those who support him. Ultimately, we will triumph." He conceded in Oklahoma City before flying on to the Tulsa headquarters. Snider composed the concession telegram, read it on live television and sent it over to Harris' headquarters.

As the family flew to the Tulsa headquarters with Dick Taft, Jack Ging, and other supporters, it began to rain. "We got to Tulsa," says Taft, "and it was raining like hell, and Louise and Mary both fell down on the slick sidewalk."

After visiting with the Tulsa contingent, "Bud and Mary brought us home about 4:00 a.m.," Taft recalls.

It had been a tough, nose-to-nose, clean campaign, free of the usual political mudslinging. The end was a terrible, humiliating disappointment.

Harris' "visit every town" strategy had worked. As the *Daily Oklahoman* reported the day after the election, "Support in the metropolitan counties of Tulsa and Oklahoma failed to come up to the amount needed to offset the Harris margins elsewhere." The final tally was Harris 466,782, Wilkinson 445,392.

&

I've always felt the death of his mother and the senatorial defeat were the two things that caused Dad the greatest sorrow. He was bewildered and hurt by the election results, but as his father had taught him at the time his mother died, when a door is closed, it's closed. Look ahead, not backward. And that's what he did.

Early on the morning after the election, Snider recalls, Dad came over, and they had a cup of coffee and a couple of milk punches. Dad decided to call a press conference for 11:00 a.m., where he announced he would never again run for public office. Pressed to discuss his losing campaign, Dad said, "Defeated generals do not discuss the arts of war."

On the day after the election in 1964, Dad was just what he told President Eisenhower he'd be if he didn't win. He was unemployed.

# 8

---

## *From the Broadcast Booth*

---

ಸಾ

*"Seize the day . . . "*

—*Horace*

Dad's unemployment was of very short duration. He and Mom took a few weeks off to recover from the campaign, but on New Year's Day, 1965, Dad found himself in the NBC broadcasting booth, providing analysis for Jim Simpson's coverage of the Orange Bowl. His association with NBC would last until 1966, when ABC won the rights to the college football broadcasts.

Though this was Dad's first exposure as a national commentator, he was not a media novice. He'd been in TV since the early '50s, first with his coach's program, and then as host of the first nationally syndicated sports program, *Sports For the Family*. The coach's show, which was broadcast live each Sunday afternoon, was Dad and Howard Neumann's idea.

"We were just hashing it around," Neumann says, "with Cheba Graham, who was the head of the Oklahoma Milk Producer's Association. Cheba thought it was a great idea. He said, 'I think we should sponsor it. Put something together.' He said he had a board of directors he had to get it by, but he ran what he called a guided democracy. I thought it was a wonderful term. Bud often used it, too."

The show, later sponsored by Kerr McGee, went on live every week, and as with every other aspect of his life, Dad prepared rigorously for each program.

"We would meet every Thursday," says Neumann. "Bud always said he wasn't superstitious. He didn't believe in stepping on the sideline, of course, and he always wore the same suit and hat to games. But I didn't challenge him on it. So every Thursday noon we met at the same restaurant—a barbecue over on old Route 77. We'd meet on Thursday, because by Thursday, everything was done as far as the game was concerned except his meeting with the quarterbacks. Now, no superstition here, but we would always have the same thing. Barbecued beef and a big hot fudge sundae and coffee. Every week, there was no looking at the menu. No alteration. That was it."

With no concern about food choices, Dad and Neumann could get right down to business. "We'd plan what we were going to do, any graphics or title cards, and so on. He would give me alternate plans depending on win or lose. Of course, for the first three years, there were no losses," says Neumann.

"On Sundays we'd get up early and go and time the show," Neumann continues. "He was so specific in the timing of a live show. We would time every segment. We would sit across the desk for the show and talk it. He never failed to come out right on time, and he always covered everything he wanted to cover."

That isn't to say the shows were flawless. There were mistakes, and somehow Neumann always seemed to end up paying for them. "He liked to have demonstrations," Neumann recalls. "One day, he and the trainer, Ken Rawlinson, were demonstrating the muscle stimulator—the electrical impulses— and he had the dial set wrong and my wrist came up and almost hit me in the head. It was live, of course, and you had to keep smiling."

It was harder to smile the day Dad demonstrated Absorblo®, a new filler for injury hip pads. "He was explaining the pads," says Neumann. "He put them on me and said, 'What this does is diffuse the blow, so that a previous injury is protected. Instead of taking the force of the blow on the injury, it diffuses out over the entire pad. I'll show you with this baseball bat, and I'll try to have really good aim.' " After three good hits to the pad, Dad cranked up the bat and caught Neumann square on the leg. "He took the bat and swung it, but he looked at the camera instead and he missed the pad," Neumann says. On the tape, you see Dad's eyes widen as he realizes what's happened and you see Neumann support himself on the desk for the rest of the interview, but neither of them gave away the secret at the time.

In spite of the mishaps that accompany live television, Neumann says, "One of the things that made the show stand out was the fact that there weren't too many people who were very good on camera back then. Television was only a few years old. Bud got on and looked at the camera and was an absolute natural. You didn't have to tell him twice how to do it. He was just a natural—he communicated with the audience. He did one thing that even today people have to remember. He didn't talk to the camera; he talked to one person."

One of the high points of each show was a discussion of strategy, usually illustrated by Dad's famous "little men." Instead of drawing two-dimensional X's and O's, Dad pushed magnetized figures around a tilted board painted like a football field, as he slowly and patiently explained the tactics of the game. Viewers learned why football often changes to a running game inside the 10-yard line, and about the importance of the defense's angles of pursuit. They studied the option play, the belly series, punt returns, and more. By watching Dad's little men every Sunday afternoon, any Oklahoman could become a much more knowledgeable and sophisticated fan.

Neumann was instrumental because he acted the part of Everyfan. "That's one of the reasons he liked doing the show with me instead of a sportscaster," says Neumann. "He said a sportscaster has to let the audience know that he's an expert, too, but I played the average fan who didn't know anything .... This big, good-looking, strong guy was able to explain everything so simply anyone could understand it .... I'd never run into any coach who was so uncoachlike, who was such a great teacher."

꙳

Given the success of their first venture, Dad, Neumann, Ned Hockman, and Lowe Runkle formed Bud Wilkinson Productions and began work on *Sports for the Family*. Sponsored by Meadow Gold, the idea of the show was to make all kinds of sports more enjoyable for the fan, the weekend athlete, or the serious student of various games, by providing information, tips for better play, and behind the scenes glimpses into coaches' offices and locker rooms.

"When we finally got the go-ahead for the first show," Neumann remembers, "Bud asked me to write down the names of people that meant something to me in each sport. I wrote some and he wrote some. He had the flu at the time, so I went over to his house, and . . . we lined up all the guests—Gene Littler, the upcoming hero in golf; Doak Walker; Kyle Rote; Wes Santee, who'd nearly run the four-minute mile; Patty Berg; Allie Reynolds—all in one afternoon."

Ned Hockman, who produced and photographed the shows, recalls, "We would set up Bud's schedule and my schedule and travel wherever it was necessary to shoot the person we were featuring. We covered all the sports—basketball, diving, golf, hockey, ice skating, football, baseball—and we'd have the big names in the sport.

"We did three thirteen-weeks series with Meadow Gold Milk and Ice Cream. After that the show was renamed *Inside Sports* and sponsored by the National Guard for a year. Then we recycled those and resold them to individual markets. They were fifteen minutes shows. If we'd made the things thirty minutes and shot them in color, we could probably still be selling them now."

One famous non-sports figure made an impromptu visit to the program. "We were on our set," says Hockman, "and that weekend Bob Hope came in to do a show at the Municipal Auditorium. We thought it would be good if we could get him to do a little segment with us. There was a door between the major stage in the auditorium and our little theater stage. We all went over there, and they were rehearsing and Bud went up and introduced himself . . . and they talked, and Bud said, 'I have a little show here that I'm doing. I wonder if I could get you to be on it?' Hope said, 'Oh, yeah, I'll be on your show and you can be on mine.' So that was the deal.

"We did the show," Hockman goes on, "and Bob was real good, and then Hope did his show and introduced Bud, and the whole audience gave him a standing ovation. Howard and I were standing there with Jerry Colonna, and Howard says, 'You know, the agency is going to want a release' . . . and he asked Jerry whether we should get a release and how much we should pay

Hope. Colonna said, 'Now, boys, you couldn't afford him. If he said Wilkinson is on his show and he's on Wilkinson's, that's all you need.' "

When the Hope show was completed, the team shot two more and, excited about what they had in the can, sent the films to Chicago for distribution. "In those days," says Hockman, "we always shipped everything with a 'Hold at Airport' provision. The person receiving it would send a runner down and pick up the film at the airport. That way, there was no way it would get lost. With this shipment, somehow that order got mixed up. We were waiting for the phone call Monday night or Tuesday, because we were proud of the fact that we were going to surprise our ad agency with Bob Hope being on one of the shows.

"I got the phone call, and the ad agency representative on the other end says, 'Ned, where's the film?' I told them what we'd done and they said, 'We can't pick it up. The airport is twenty-five miles away.' I said, 'Hold it a minute. I've worked all over the world and twenty-five miles don't mean a damn thing to somebody who wants something at a certain time and wants to be sure it doesn't get lost. Get off your ass and go get the damned film out at the airport.' The guy was real mad and hung up."

Hockman told the story to Dad. "Bud looked up and said, 'Call him back and tell him the deal is off. Tell him to send the films back to us.' I said, 'Are you kidding, Bud?' He said, 'No, tell them. You're the producer/director. Just tell them to send all the film back and that we're canceling the series.' "

After Hockman did what Dad suggested, the ad agency backed down. "We knew they had bought time all over the United States . . . . The point is that even though we were struggling along, Bud Wilkinson Productions didn't have to take any guff from anybody. The ad agency didn't send the film back, and they were real thrilled when they finally went out to get it."

One of Dad's favorite interviews was with the great New York Yankees pitcher, Allie Reynolds, and he frequently told the story as an example of sports psychology.

As Hockman remembers, "We were up at Yankee Stadium discussing what we were going to do . . . and Bud says, 'When ole Case calls you to come in, tell us what you're thinking.' Reynolds says, 'You really want to know?

'When I step out, I see the stadium and all the people, and then I see the batter reaching for the bat. He picks up the bat, and then he takes his hand and dips it in the dirt. He rubs the dirt into the bat. I'm walking in all this time. I see him swing the bat. I see my wife and the white dress she's in. I walk a little bit more and I see the batter swinging. I'm getting closer and closer. Then I see my little boy, with his white shirt and his little black bow tie, and my wife and her beautiful hair. I see the batter again. Then I see my home, my Cadillac, my wife, the guy swinging the bat. That batter is trying to take away everything I have—my family, my home, my car, the food off my table. By the time I get to the pitcher's mound I'm ready to go.' "

Dad also interviewed a famous ice skater. At the end of filming, he asked her if she had any particular words of inspiration she'd like to share with the audience. "Why, yes," she said. "My daddy always used to tell me it didn't matter if you won or lost but how you played the game." When they returned home and viewed the film Neumann remembers Dad laughing and calling out, "Cut, cut. I can't show that to my players. It's too important to win!"

At the end of every filming session, Dad would drop in a little sermonette tied to the content of the show. On the program that dealt with sports officiating, for example, Dad mentioned that though we might like to "boo those who give us bad calls in life, it's better to take personal responsibility for our mistakes." On the diving show, he talked about how divers compete against themselves, and how we must do the same in all of life, defeating ourselves before we worry about the other guy. He often quoted poetry or military history to make his philosophical points. It was basic Bud, and as a teacher, he couldn't resist the opportunity to insert his own viewpoints into the broadcasts.

੨ఎ

Of course, Dad also had a great deal of experience on the other side of the microphone. He'd been interviewed continually for the seventeen years of his coaching career and had good instincts about what reporters and sportscasters needed to write great stories or to shoot impressive video. There were some broadcasters he trusted implicitly. One of them was Curt Gowdy.

"We started out together," says Gowdy. "I was just a young announcer in Oklahoma City in 1946 when he came in as assistant to Jim Tatum. It was my first year as a broadcaster for the Oklahoma games. WKY bought the exclusive rights to the games—the first time it had ever been exclusive. Then they were sold to KOMA and I was the voice of the Sooners.

"Bud was way ahead of everybody," Gowdy goes on. "He always had something surprising and new. He was just a very, very bright, innovative coach who was sort of born to coach."

During Dad's 5-5 season, when Oklahoma was playing Army in Yankee Stadium, Gowdy, accompanied by Roone Arledge, went to visit Dad in his hotel room.

"We talked a while," Gowdy says, "and then Bud said, 'Listen, we're going to pull a surprise play . . . . When Army's in their huddle, we'll quickly line up and snap the ball and then lateral out to the back.' As I recall, the guy went about 70-80 yards for the touchdown. On the way down the sideline, he hit the ABC camera man and cut his lip. The camera flew out of his hands.

"Roone could never understand Bud's telling me their strategy. 'Jesus,' he said, 'that guy told you everything.' I said, 'He trusts me. He knows he can trust me.' "

Jim Simpson also had an inkling of what was going to happen in that famous game. "The first time I really talked to Bud happened only because I was with Curt Gowdy. He called us together and said, 'Look, between plays when we have the ball, don't take pictures of cheerleaders or people in the stands eating hot dogs, because we may go.' "

His wide knowledge of television made it easy for Dad to slip quickly into big time sports commentary and to become a valuable asset in the broadcast booth.

Dad's first broadcast, the Orange Bowl, says Jim Simpson, "was Alabama-Texas, and because Bud was such a good friend of Bear Bryant's and had coached Darrell Royal, the Texas coach, through Bud I knew everything that was going to take place in that ball game—the offensive plan and the defensive plan."

As always, Dad tried to be completely prepared for each game. "Bud was in very good spirits," says Simpson, "because he was really back into football after the Senate race. One day he got a little nervous, though, and he said, 'Let's make sure we know how to get to the Orange Bowl. That's the only thing that could go wrong.' We drove from the hotel to the Orange Bowl, with Bud taking notes; we made a few bad turns but we got the whole plan exactly laid out. Now, it was New Year's Day and time to go down to the Orange Bowl to do the game. Bud got out his notes for the game and how to get there, and we got into the car and drove straight there, showed our credentials, went right inside— and then got lost under the Orange Bowl. The workmen had to direct us back to the elevator to get to the press box, so we could get to the game."

Simpson and Dad became fast friends and much later reteamed to broadcast games on ESPN.

Until 1966, Dad stayed with NBC, providing analysis for NCAA football. That year, he jumped to ABC when they acquired the rights, and he stayed with the network until 1978.

ی

The broadcast team in 1966 was Chris Schenkel, Bill Flemming, and Dad.

"When Roone Arledge decided to form a team," says Flemming, "I was a logical choice since I'd worked for ABC when they had the games in '60 and '61. Chris had always been a favorite of Roone's, and Bud was an absolute choice."

"I was totally ensconced at CBS and loved it," Schenkel says. "Roone was a Giants fan and I was the voice of the Giants. Roone decided since he was starting the sports department at ABC . . . he would try to switch me over. At that time I was doing the Giants and other NFL things, the Triple Crown, the Masters—all the big events . . . I said, 'Roone, you don't have football and you don't have golf.' He said, 'I promise you we'll get golf and I promise you that you'll be in football within a year. When we get football, I'll make sure you have the No. 1 man to work with.' He lived up to that promise and that promise was Bud Wilkinson."

Chuck Howard produced the ABC coverage of college ball. It was a tough job. "As head of production," he says, "I had to coordinate the production of the studio show . . . . We had thirty-five minutes most of the time, and I had to decide what elements would be in those minutes—who was in the studio, who did we have as a guest, what games did we want to emphasize . . . in effect we structured the format for the first thirty-five minutes of the show, minute by minute. Then we had to format the halftime show. We were very much involved, as opposed to today where they go back to the studio and the site of the game is hardly involved at the half. We also didn't have satellites and highlights from other games at that time.

"In addition," says Howard, "I had to decide who would produce the four regional games and who the announcing teams would be for the other three games. I had to coordinate a lot of details with the sports information directors, the band directors, players and coaches we wanted to interview, and so on.

"The real thrust was being basically in charge of the live broadcast .... Andy Sidaris selected and directed the cameras, but I had to be aware of the situation if I thought [Andy wasn't getting the shots]."

Howard also served as a catalyst to the broadcast team. "I didn't talk much to Chris, because Chris was a very good technician, as far as yardage, downs, time left and things like that were concerned.

"But you have to keep the audience updated," Howard says. "For instance, maybe we'd mentioned at the top of the telecast that Oklahoma had lost both their offensive tackles and this was going to be a problem. There's a tendency to assume everybody's heard that, but that obviously isn't true. People pick up the telecast in progress. So I'd mention that to Chris. Or maybe the weather had changed, and I'd want Chris to talk about that.

"With Bud," Howard continues, "I'd say—and he would be the only one who could hear me—'Bud, I don't understand why Kansas continues to try to run into a stacked front. They have to throw the ball or screen or something.' If Bud thought I was off base or the comment didn't warrant anything, he'd just forget about it. But if it did warrant something, he'd pick it up in his own words .... Sometimes we'd talk during the commercials. I'd say something like, 'What could Woody Hayes be thinking of in this situation?' and he'd pick it up."

Howard worked closely with director Sidaris. "The producer helped me a lot," Sidaris says, "because we would sit down and discuss who we wanted to isolate on each play, especially in college football, because it moves so fast, about 170 plays per game .... The producer has the overall concept of the telecast and deals with commercial placement. The director makes it happen, close-ups, and the flow, pace, and tempo of the game."

Sidaris is a creative director credited with a variety of innovations, including what he calls "honey shots,"—attractive women in the stands— camera placements, and microphones and handheld cameras on the sidelines.

Dad, too, was preparing carefully for every game. "We often had adjoining rooms and would prepare together," says Schenkel. "He did wonderful charts and things, so everything was right there in front of him. I can still see him with that cigar, just working his head off."

ta.

NCAA football, because it was the only game in town, had a huge following. Obviously, the producer, director, and broadcast team were under a considerable amount of pressure, moving from city to city, broadcast to broadcast. There were deadlines, tension and jumpy nerves. But there was also fun—lots of different kinds of fun.

Andy Sidaris recalls, "It was nice for Bud to go out and not have to worry about the coaching and truly enjoy a ball game and watch some great football—to be able to get the rewards from having done all that coaching and sweating bullets every week, and to have some laughs and to really enjoy the people around it."

Dad surely was enjoying seeing his old coaching pals in a different role, and his familiarity with them made for great broadcasts. Sometimes he'd get more inside information on a game than even he expected.

"Woody Hayes really admired Bud," Chris Schenkel says, "and at one Ohio State-Purdue game, we were staying at the same hotel as Ohio State. Bud and I arrived about the same time Woody did. Woody just handed him his game plan right there in the lobby. He said, 'Here, Bud, here's what we're going to do.'

"We went to our rooms and Bud was looking the plan over and trying to explain it to me. About an hour later, there's a knock on the door and it's Woody. He said, 'Bud, we're about the same age, and you know my mind slips from time to time and yours probably does, too. I'm just a little afraid you might leave that game plan on your desk when you and Chris go out for dinner. Do you mind if I take it back?'

"I told Bud later, 'It's got nothing to do with your memory. Woody just remembered I'm a Purdue grad.' "

Dad also had a wonderful relationship with Bear Bryant. "Bear just kind of worshipped Bud," says Bill Flemming. "He told me once, 'He's the finest football mind I've ever run across,' so when the two of them would get together it was fun. The Auburn-Alabama game was always played in Birmingham. We'd go down to the game, and Bear would stay at the Bankhead Hotel, and he'd always invite Chris and Bud and me to dinner Friday night.

"It was kind of strange, though, because Bear always ordered two tables. Bear and Bud would sit at one and Chris and I at the other . . . . I would say to Chris, 'Listen to this,' . . . and we would hear these arcane conversations about football. Chris and I would talk about girls and things like that."

Flemming continues, "Bear would be into the Scotch really good and he would rarely eat . . . . But Bud and Bear could really speak the same language. Rarely, as I recall, did they discuss a whole hell of a lot about the game coming up; it was mostly just theory . . . . I think Bear was always testing Bud's brain about how he could do things better, and Bud was a genius on defense . . . . We were supposed to be getting information about the game and Bear used the opportunity to pick Bud's brain.

"I'd see Bear leaning against the goal post the next day, his hat kind of pulled down, and he'd say, 'Hi, Bill, did you have a good dinner last night?' I'd say, 'Thanks very much; it was very nice of you.' This would repeat itself every year."

Younger coaches had much the same reaction to Dad that Bryant did. Keith Jackson says, "Let's say we walked into the locker room to interview any young coach who'd been a player or a youngster when Bud was building his legend.There were times I preferred to do the interview myself rather than have Bud there, because the younger coaches wound up trying to pick Bud's mind instead of me being able to find out what they were going to do."

Fans also remembered Dad. Schenkel broadcast the classic Oklahoma-Nebraska game with him in 1971, seven years after Dad retired from coaching. "We were in the booth before the game, and Bud said, 'Let's check the condition of the field,' which is something we often did. He wanted to get back on that turf. I could tell he was champing at the bit.

"We just barely got within sight and the stadium erupted for Bud. I get goose bumps and almost a tear in my eye now talking about it—it was that awesome. I've never heard anything like it. It sustained until he got out where everybody could see him with both arms waving. That might have been his biggest thrill. He had tears coming down his cheeks."

The broadcast teams often went out together the night before games.

"We'd go out at nights and we'd sing," says Andy Sidaris. "We'd get a little too much to drink . . . . Honest to God, we didn't put away all that much booze, but we'd be tired the next day, because Bud would sing all night—every damn college song ever written."

According to Chuck Howard, on one occasion, the ABC team even supplanted the bar band. "We're in Lincoln, Nebraska, and we're staying in a Holiday Inn or Howard Johnson's, and they have this singing group there on Friday nights. The bar is jammed. We go out to eat at some steak place and get back about 11:00 p.m., basically ready to go to bed. But we hear the music from the bar, and Bud says, 'Let's go have a beer or two.'

"Flemming takes one look at this scene and says, 'You guys are headed for trouble.' We had the early game of a double header, which means we went on the air about 11:00 a.m. For everybody, that's a fairly early day. Flemming says, 'Adios, guys, I'm out of here. This has trouble written all over it.' When the crowd saw Bud, everybody was screaming and yelling."

Soon after the ABC team arrived, the band took a break. "So," Howard goes on, "Jerry Kapstein says, 'I can play the piano . . . I can play some fight songs if you guys will come up.' I said, 'Jerry, this is ludicrous,' but we were half tanked . . . No pain. A couple of Scotches at dinner and now we're working on Drambuie or beer. Bud was just like a dog with a bone. 'This is terrific,' he says. I say, 'Bud, no.' But he says, 'Yes, yes, yes,' and sure enough, Jerry started playing and Bud says, 'We can't leave Jerry up there all by himself.'

"So we get up there and do 10-15 minutes of fight songs and it was great. Everybody loved it . . . . Bud could really sing. He knew those songs, not just humming them—he knew all the words. When the band came back, they liked what we were doing . . . . They watched us for thirty seconds to a minute before we relinquished . . . . We wanted to stay and watch them do another set."

The next morning at 7:30 breakfast, says Howard, "We were all screwed up. Flemming says, 'I knew it, I knew it. You guys really look beat up.' He was getting on our case."

Dad stepped up to address the issue. He said, "I'll tell you . . . my version of what happened last night. You went to bed and got a good night's sleep. Fine. We stayed up and didn't get a good night's sleep, but you know what we did? We had one of the greatest times. We had a good time, and that's what life is about. We seized the opportunity. We will have something to remember long after our headaches are gone. We'll remember this evening. You blew it by not being a part of it."

As Howard says, "Bud was a 'seize the day' guy. When I first met him, here was this tall distinguished man, well-dressed and all, and I had no idea how much fun he was to be with. He wanted to do his job; he wasn't a shirker, but he wanted to have a good time in life. That was an occasion where he did and we all did. If it hadn't been for Jerry and then for Bud, we'd have never gotten our asses up there. No two ways about it, Bud was the ball carrier on that."

Some Friday evenings, however, Dad was with his old coaching buddies, visiting their locker rooms and firing up their teams.

Terry Jastrow, now the senior producer of ABC's golf coverage, was a production assistant to Howard. "I loved the games when Bud was really close to the other coaches. In those days, the Duffy Daugherty, John McKay, the Darrell Royal or the Frank Broyles games were great, because Bud would take Schenkel and Howard and me to meetings or dinners; he saw we were included. You really got to know the big coaches like Bear Bryant. You were calling him Bear ten minutes into the event because that's what Bud called him."

"Sometimes," Jastrow says, "coaches like Daugherty or Woody Hayes would gather their teams at the end of practice and they'd get Bud to say a word. I'll tell you, it was Knute Rockne returned. He was quiet, powerful and direct, and those guys were jumping through their uniforms when he got done. He'd say stuff like, 'This is the opportunity you live your life for, this is what you play a sport for, this is what athletics is all about. It's a question of being a man, being all you can be, focusing on the positive.' You were ready to suit up and go play yourself by the time he got done with one of those speeches."

࣮࣪

The entire ABC team talks about the one event they recall as the most fun they ever had as a group. "We challenged the Monday night football guys to a touch football game," says Andy Sidaris.

"There was a lot of competition between the two groups," adds Chuck Howard, "mainly who could put on a better telecast and so on. We started talking about playing one fall, but the schedules were bad. It took us literally a year to put the thing together. Finally Frank Gifford got Yankee Stadium. They had some real good athletes—Gifford, Chet Forte, Bobby Goodrich, who'd been a starting wide receiver at SMU."

"From the moment this thing came about, Bud was all fired up about it—sort of 'God damn, we gotta play these guys; we're going to kick their asses'—that kind of thing. We finally got a date in November. Not only did we have Yankee Stadium, but we were going to play cross-field, fifty-five yards or whatever it was. We had it lined, and we had uniforms. The rules had been set up. It was supposed to be a fast rush."

"Bud's whole concept," Howard says, "was to beat the rush with reverses and laterals—dazzle 'em with footwork. No matter how fast they'd rush us we'd just lateral the ball around a couple of times, and the rush wouldn't bother us."

Dad's schedule then came unraveled and the game was put off a week. "Then he started dancing around again. I kind of figured he wasn't going to make it," recalls Howard.

"It was a weekday game," he says, "and it was cold as a bitch, but not a cloud in the sky. We had to play at 11:00 a.m ... and the only way Bud could get there was to come from Tulsa through Chicago, and he had to charter a plane to get to Tulsa. As late as the night before, we weren't sure he was going to make it."

Game Day, says Sidaris, brought the whole team to LaGuardia to meet Dad's plane. "He arrived at 9:00 a.m., and his plane was a little late, and we were all screaming because we had to have Bud; he was the one who worked out the plays.

"When he got off, all the people thought we were nuts. We were right there in the hallway screaming, 'Let's go get those bastards.' We were running down the hallway like we were coming out of a stadium tunnel."

"We went out to the field and worked out," Howard recalls. "People were there from the office. Gifford had brought Ethel Kennedy and everything.

"Before the game, we warmed up and then went back into the locker room, just like what happened in a real football game," he continues. "Bud is kind of like fire and brimstone, but more than that, he says we're going to try an on-side kick. We had lost the toss, so we were kicking off. Everybody said, 'Bud, it's a touch football game. You can't on-side kick in a touch football game. What are you talking about?' He said, 'These are football rules, aren't they? Then who said we can't on-side kick? That's the last thing they will ever think of. It will do two things. First, we will recover the ball, but just as important as that, they'll be all pissed off. They'll be pissed off at each other. This is what we're going to do.'

"Sure enough," Howard concludes, "not only did we on-side kick, we recovered and went right in to score."

The game got even more exciting. "I was hitting some passes," says Sidaris, "but we couldn't quite make it happen. Finally I said, 'Let's try something different.' I lateraled out to Bud and he fired the football at me about 200 miles an hour.

"I was running toward Frank about the time Bud was throwing and I spun around. I was looking over my left shoulder and the ball was coming over my right shoulder. It stuck in the right side of my neck. I grabbed it with my right arm. I said, 'Frank, take that, you son of a bitch.' It was one of the funniest things ever. Bud and I rolled around on the grass and laughed forever because I caught the ball on my neck."

The game ended 19-18 in favor of the Monday Night Football team. "After that, we went into town and got plastered," says Sidaris. "We ate all night and got bombed and had a great time. Everybody stayed downtown."

&

At broadcast time, everyone was all business. Dad was learning the big league broadcasting game, and in his quiet way, he was teaching some of the sportscasters a little bit more about the game of football.

"He gave me so many good tips to look for," says Bill Flemming. "For instance, I'd ask him how he knew a certain thing was going to happen. He'd say, 'Because I never watch the ball.' I said, 'What? You never watch the ball?' and he told me he always watched the interior linemen instead. 'You can learn to do that, too,' he said."

Flemming did learn. "It was amazing how it changed my perspective as a play-by-play announcer. Unlike radio, you don't have to be talking every second. You can be looking. I could see the flow, the way things were going to go. He gave me a better overview . . . . It carried over into basketball, too."

Flemming was returning the favor, helping Dad with his broadcast technique. "Bud got into a habit of saying, 'Bill,' after he'd make some observation on the game. I said to him one time, 'Look, you're talking to the audience, not to me.' One of my pet peeves is that the color guys talk to each other instead of just coming out and saying what's going on. It's kind of a crutch. Bud took it up right away. 'Boy,' he said, 'you're absolutely right. It is a crutch.' So it was kind of a two-way thing. I was bringing him some expertise and he was giving me some football stuff. I think anytime you have a marriage like that it really makes for a good team."

Dad had one habit no one could break. Chuck Howard and others felt Dad was too much of a gentleman in the booth. If a bonehead play was made, he refrained from jumping down the coaches' or players' throats, at least while he was on the air. But during the commercial, says Andy Sidaris, "Bud would say, 'I can't believe that son of a bitch would run off-tackle' or some bullshit like that. Of course, he'd be right, and Chuck wanted him to rip them up, but Bud wouldn't do that."

Dad was also reluctant to praise a player inordinately—to build him up at the expense of others. But in the commercial break he'd share his opinions.

"I remember," Flemming says, "we were doing a game at Stanford and during a break Bud said Jim Plunkett had the best vision of any quarterback he'd ever seen. Chuck Howard came on and said, 'God damn it, Bud, why don't you say that on the air?

You always save your best stuff for the commercials.' Bud never wanted to criticize anyone, to step on anyone's toes. Chuck was always riding him about it. He'd say, 'Be more forceful; come out and say if you think Plunkett's the best quarterback you've ever seen. Go ahead and say it!' Bud was reluctant to do that."

To some fans, however, Dad didn't seem all that kind and gentlemanly. Ara Parseghian, who was then coaching at Notre Dame and later followed Dad into broadcasting, says, "I can't remember what year it was, but many Notre Dame fans had written in and called, complaining about Bud and his biased comments for the opposition. Moose Krause came to me and said, 'Let's go over to the studio during the week and look at the telecast so we're better informed when we respond.'

"Moose and I sat down at WNDU and listened to the whole tape, and we both looked at each other and said, 'Where are these fans coming from?' We shook our heads and walked out of there . . . . There was nothing partisan or critical, at least in our view. [When I went into broadcasting], I had the same problem with Alabama. People wrote to ABC and said they had to get rid of me because I was anti-Alabama."

࿇

One of the most exciting games Dad worked as a broad-caster was Arkansas-Texas in 1969. By this time Dad also was working as Special Consultant to President Nixon, and the president decided to attend the game. Billy Graham was in town and came to give the invocation. The game was between the No. 1 and No. 2 teams in the nation. Texas took the contest by a score of 15-14.

"I don't think I've ever gone to a game," says Bill Flemming, "where you had so many features surrounding a regular season college game. It was a national championship game. Not only did we have Billy Graham, but we had the president.

"We stayed at a place called Cherokee Village, which was about twenty miles out. In order to avoid the tremendous crush of traffic, we ordered a chopper. When we got up, the weather was so bad you could hardly see the cars in the parking lot; I was really concerned about it. We got on board the chopper and just sailed over the treetops all the way over, and at the stadium the weather was worse. Everybody was wondering if the president would really get there."

President Nixon arrived safely and took a large role in the day's activities. At halftime,he was interviewed by Chris Schenkel in the booth. "That's a famous interview because Bud primed him," says Schenkel. "Before we went on, the president asked Bud what was going to happen in the second half, and Bud told him—got all the ducks lined up for him. So we went on and I said, 'Well, Mr. President, what do you think is going to happen in the second half?' and he repeated exactly what Bud had told him—boom, boom, boom—he remembered everything word for word. The newspapers all said Mr. Nixon really knew football."

After the game, says Flemming, the president visited the locker rooms. "Since we didn't know what the outcome would be, we had to have cameras and microphones in both dressing rooms. The president went to the Texas locker room first. I just accompanied him, and he kind of took the interview from me . . . . The guys were yelling and screaming and it was a pretty big thing.

"It was the president who suggested we visit the losers' dressing room," Flemming remembers. "When we'd finished the interview with Darrell, the president said, 'Let's go see Arkansas.' I had a floor manager with me and I said, 'Tell Roone the president wants to go the other dressing room. Is it okay?' It came back immediately that we were 'hot' in both places—'hot' meaning we had the equipment set up. The mood in that dressing room was pretty funereal. But Broyles was just first class. No excuses. He was just very gracious."

ঽৡ

When each collegiate game was over, the broadcast team's primary concern was always the getaway. Many had to be in other cities for other broadcasts; Dad would return home or to other business ventures. Getting away from the stadiums fast enough to make split-second connections was essential. "It seemed like the last plane out was always ten minutes after we got off the air," says Bill Flemming. Some of the methods used to depart were unconventional, to say the least.

Flemming, who was a pilot, often scouted the best escape routes from the air. He and Terry Jastrow remember the one getaway that was foiled. "I gave everyone a map of how we could get out," says Flemming, "but we got out on the road and were hopelessly lost. My plane is sitting in Columbia, Missouri, and Chuck has to catch a plane so he can get to the Giants or Jets game the next day. So we're out in the country and everybody's saying, 'God damn it, Flemming, the map isn't right.' I'm driving and Bud is sitting over on the right hand side."

"Finally we come to a farmhouse," adds Jastrow, "and Bud says, 'Pull over by that farmer.' We pull over and this old farmer is on the tractor. It has to be the first tractor ever made. Bud jumps out and says, 'Excuse me, sir, but can you give us directions to the airport?' That farmer looks at Bud, and his jaw drops, and he gets down off that tractor like in triple slow motion, and walks up to Bud and says, 'You're Bu, Bu, Bud, Wilk, Wilki, Wilkinson' . . . the worst stutter you ever heard  . . . . He told Bud what a great coach he was. Bud was desperate to get information for the airport, I was laughing, and Bud was so polite with this guy. He [recapped] Bud's entire coaching career."

Flemming says, "Chuck is sitting in the back seat screaming, 'Forget this guy . . . he's wasting more time,' but Bud didn't have the heart. We must have been there five minutes, and those five minutes killed Chuck. He missed the flight to Chicago by five minutes."

Other getaways were more successful, though sometimes they relied on alternate methods of transportation.

Chuck Howard took part in an elaborate leave taking after a game at Stanford. "Palo Alto is some distance from the San Francisco airport and the stadium is huge. There were about 85,000 people there that day . . . . The problem was magnified by the fact that Stanford . . . would not offer us any kind of police escort . . . . The only way we had a shot was by helicopter."

The helicopter the team needed was the one used by the Stanford hospital. After coordinating with the helicopter crew, there was one further problem. The helicopter pad was located several miles from the stadium. How to get from the stadium to the helipad? Jastrow came up with the idea of using motorcycles.

"Bud was really charged up about it," says Howard. "He always liked the whole scheme—the challenge of whether you were really going to make it. The tighter, the more the thing was in doubt, the better he liked it. If the chances were 80-20 you were going to make the flight, that really wasn't what Bud wanted. He wanted a 60-40 or 50-50 shot.

"This was the first time we'd done motorcycles," Howard continues. "Bud was concerned about whether the Stanford students and their bikes would show up exactly where and when we needed them .... The game was over and Bud came dashing down. The motorcycles were all there, and the guy Bud had drawn had hair down to his waist. He said, 'Hey, man, like, what do you say, dude?' He was a real hippie. First of all, the joy that came into Bud's eyes when he saw that the motorcycle was there was one thing, but it was tempered by the sight of this guy.

"I was the last one riding on a motorcycle, and there were Bud and this hippie, both of them with their helmets on ... Bud, with this smile of joy on his face—the whole helicopter ride, it was all he could talk about."

Terry Jastrow had set up the motorcycle brigade, but it wasn't the most convoluted scheme he devised. "At Boulder, Colorado," he says, "Bud and Chris were flung on the backs of two horses and ridden to the police escort that was going to take them to the helicopter in Boulder, so they could make a flight to Denver that we had held for 15-20 minutes for them to catch it. It was amazingly elaborate. It took all week for me to set it up."

Jastrow concurs with Howard's assessment of Dad's liking for the getaway plans. "He had a really positive attitude—'We'll get this done. This is no problem.' He really believed he was going to win and he made you believe it, too."

è●

After twelve years with ABC, Dad hung up his earphones to concentrate more on his business interests and later to coach the St. Louis Cardinals football team. But in 1980, after his dismissal from the Cardinals, he returned to commentary with Jim Simpson at ESPN. They were together for three years.

"I said," says Simpson, " 'Bud, I'll tell you what. As in the past, I don't know how much money they'll pay you ... but I guarantee we'll have fun.' He said, 'Let's do it.' "

At ESPN, there wasn't the kind of logistical support that characterized the network broadcasts and Dad set up appointments with coaches and made travel arrangements by himself.

Simpson says, "Knowing his background, my biggest shock was when some of the college coaches who did not, have not, and never will approach his achievements in football would give him two minutes to visit and then say they had to go to a meeting. Bud never said anything except, 'Well, he had to prepare.' Whatever personal disappointment or affront he took from it, I never knew."

"One time," Simpson goes on, "we were doing a game in Norman, and we were standing down in the runway near the press box, and it was so damn cold you couldn't believe it. The crew was trying to change lenses and it didn't work. We were there for more than an hour. Bud, being Bud, wasn't complaining, but he was being besieged by people. I went back to the truck and raised hell. He was a legend and they were treating him like that while they fixed their damn lens."

At ABC, one of the things Terry Jastrow noticed about Dad was that he functioned well in chaos. "I noticed early on that the bigger the moment, the more tension filled, the cooler, calmer, and more direct he became . . . . You wanted to be around him because he was cool. He had the thing well in hand."

Nowhere was this more clearly shown than when Dad and Simpson were scheduled to do a Missouri game for ESPN. "We were finally in the area of St. Louis," Simpson remembers. "He wanted me to see his home and meet his friends. He had a friend who had a helicopter; we had it all set up so that person would meet us with the helicopter. We'd be there in time for the party, even though we got off the air at 5:00 p.m.

"Then somebody told us we might not do the Missouri game after all. I said, 'Good God, Bud has all this stuff planned—caterers and everything—we're going to go back there by helicopter.' So I went to him and said, 'Bud, what will happen if we don't do the Missouri game?' He said, 'We'll adjust.' Most people would have hollered, 'God damn it, you can't do that. I have a big party planned.' Not Bud. He taught me so much. I think I've always been a gentleman, but he kind of refined me; I took things from watching his demeanor."

Simpson indirectly learned a little bit more about football from Dad, too, he says. "We were doing a Florida State-Pittsburgh game—sitting with Bobby Bowden, one of the nicest men in football, and he said, 'Bud, you're the one who told me to throw out the X's and O's. I said, 'Excuse me, throw out the X's and O's?' Bobby said, "Yes, put down names. Because if X weighs 155 and O weighs 275, you knew who's going to win that battle. So when I prepare for a big game, I put down the names of the people we're going against.'

"I told that story to [former Dolphins quarterback] Bob Griese once," Simpson says, "and he said, 'If that isn't right. They'll send in a 185-pound halfback to replace a fullback who weighs 235 on a third and long—and have him block. The X's and O's are the same, but I get creamed.' "

&

Dad's last foray into sports broadcasting was the short-lived Freedom Network, where he teamed once again with Bill Flemming. The network broadcast games from the service academies. It had good support but got lost in the mire of politics.

It was while working with the Freedom Network Flemming first noticed Dad's health was failing. "We had our production meeting in the afternoon . . . . When I saw him the next day, we met at the truck and then started to walk up to the press box. I remember he stopped and looked back at the field once and said, 'Boy, I don't know what it is—probably just the cold air—but I'm going to have to rest a minute.' Then we got to the press box and had to climb another flight of stairs. By the time we got to the booth . . . he was kind of gray and didn't look all that good. He sat down and didn't say much. He was very, very quiet."

After a dry run, the color seemed to come back to Dad's face. He had a cup of coffee, and "when we finally did it, he was terrific," says Flemming, "right on top of it." But that episode was the beginning of the congestive heart failure that resulted in his death eight years later.

&

Dad loved the world of broadcasting—the camaraderie, the fun, the escapes, the games. And the other sportscasters held him in high esteem, recalling his combination of discipline and warmth.

Terry Jastrow says, "He was so polite and such a gentleman to everyone. There was absolutely no reason he should have taken the time and care to look an eighteen-year-old college kid like me in the eye and be gracious and warm and polite. But he was. He made you feel like you were important and you mattered to him. You figured he'd do it with Roone Arledge and Chris and Darrell Royal, but he treated everybody the same."

"Bud was good on television," says Keith Jackson, "because he was soft spoken; his initial impression was one that was low key, even though sometimes his intensity would burn through and you'd realize he wasn't low key at all."

Chris Schenkel says, "He had a wonderful sense of values—all kinds of values. I think they probably came from the way he grew up. He had a lot of admiration for the people who surrounded him. He talked about his family all the time. And he had a lot of compassion. My God, he'd see a wounded bird in the form of a person, a wounded sparrow I call them, and he'd stop and talk to them and never look down on them. I never saw him look down on anyone."

One of his strongest values, of course, was that you had to earn what you had—to work for it and not have it handed to you. First generation stuff. Schenkel remembers a time Dad pounded that lesson home. They had worked a Sugar Bowl together and received Sugar Bowl watches. "Bud knew and liked [my son], Teddy. Teddy had come to a Notre Dame game when he was about ten and Bud, kiddingly, was trying to tell him never to go to that school . . . . It was wonderful.

"Anyway, I said, 'Oh, Bud, holy mackerel, won't this be a great watch for Ted?' He grabbed my arm and put a grip on it and said, 'Don't you ever give that watch to Ted. He's got to earn it. Do you hear me? He's got to earn it.' For Bud, that watch, which was from the Alabama-Notre Dame game, really symbolized this great era of football—and I was going to give it to a ten-year-old kid."

Jim Simpson adds, "When I told my sister-in-law about Bud's illness, I said, 'Bud is the only man I know that when he sees you or leaves you has the capability to throw his arms around you, with tears in his eyes, and say to another man, "Do you know how much I love you?"' That's not supposed to be the macho thing to do, but this guy doesn't have to prove anything as a football player, as a coach, or as a man. "

That's not such a bad legacy.

# 9

## Back to Washington: The Years with Nixon

🐟

*"So many men, so many opinions  . . ."*
                                        *—Terence*

Dad and Richard Nixon shared a similar political philosophy and a love of sports. The two men met when Nixon was vice president of the United States and Dad was serving a term as vice president of the American Football Coaches Association. At one of the association's national meetings, Nixon was the featured speaker; Dad was assigned to meet the vice president at the airport. They chatted in the limousine going to and from the airport, and Dad was impressed with Nixon's intelligence and confidence.

Dad became fond of Nixon for another reason best illustrated by a story the president once told him. Nixon had played football at Whittier College, but the next year was concentrating on his studies in order to win a scholarship to law school. The coach called Nixon at home and urged him to return to the team, saying, "Nixon, you are never going to play if the game is in doubt. If we are so far behind we can't win you may play, and if we're far ahead, you might get in because the result is in the books anyway. But you are the kind of guy we need because you try on every play. Our team isn't going to develop without people like you. We need you to go out for football." As Nixon said to Dad, "What could I do? The man said he needed me."

Dad felt this story said more about Nixon than all the Watergate tapes, and he respected the president as a man who understood the value of discipline and preparation.

When Dad ran for the Senate in 1964, Nixon, by then the former vice president, campaigned on Dad's behalf on several occasions. After Dad lost, he and Nixon kept in contact, and as Nixon warmed up for his presidential bid, he and Dad continued to correspond. At one point, as Nixon grappled with the "loser" image that had dogged him since the Kennedy defeat and the California gubernatorial race, Dad sent him a chronology of Abraham Lincoln's political career, replete with losses and defeats. Nixon replied:

*It is a pretty devastating answer to the "loser" argument. I hope we can find a way to get some distribution on it among opinion leaders on whom it should make some impression.*

As Nixon framed his campaign strategy, it became clear that this run at the presidency would depend heavily on television. Largely undone by television in the 1960 campaign, Nixon understood the power of the medium, and this time he wanted to use it to his advantage. He surrounded himself with media-savvy people—Roger Ailes, the twenty-six-year-old executive producer of the *Mike Douglas Show*; Frank Shakespeare, who came from CBS; Harry Treleaven, the creative director of advertising who developed the "Nixon's the One!" theme; Leonard Garment, a lawyer in Nixon's firm; Paul Keyes and others.

Dad was instrumental in bringing Treleaven into the campaign. In late summer, 1967, Dad arranged a meeting that included Nixon and Danny Seymour, an executive with the J. Walter Thompson advertising agency. During the course of the meeting, Nixon asked Seymour who he thought was the best PR person he could hire for the campaign. Seymour named Treleaven, but said he'd be impossible to get. By October, however, Len Garment had prevailed on Treleaven to join Nixon's campaign team.

Another member of the staff was Bill Gavin, an English teacher who had written Nixon a letter in 1967 urging him to run and to go live on television, taking questions from the public. Out of this idea arose the "Man in the Arena" concept, a series of carefully controlled live broadcasts held in ten cities throughout the country. Panels of citizens were selected to ask the candidate any questions they wished; a live audience of 300 Republican partisans was present to cheer the answers at each broadcast.

Ailes says, "I actually conceived the whole project and took it to Nixon and said, 'I have an idea.' They had ... wanted to go about this in some other way. I said, 'Look, the best thing the guy does is stand on his feet and answer questions. We ought to put him in that circumstance where he doesn't have any notes. You'll need someone to moderate it ... and feed the questions or move on to the next question.' That's where Bud came in."

Dad moderated the Man in the Arena telecasts, because, as Ailes says, "Nixon trusted him. He admired him and liked him and, most of all, he trusted him. He knew he was stable and wasn't going to do anything crazy. Bud handled the introduction of the panelists and [when questioning began], he would sort of watch Nixon and try to figure out when it was time to move on. He was more of a safety valve once the show started.

"Nixon liked to have Bud around," Ailes continues, "because ... as you come around the last turn in a presidential election, everybody gets a little bit scared and hysterical. Bud had been through that ... in games and so on; he was always cool, and I think that had a calming effect on Nixon .... In the meetings, Bud was so cool, so professional ... he was a one-take guy in a room full of egos, opinions and all kinds of crap. I learned from him in that circumstance, although I'd been through some high-pressure situations."

"Bud was wonderful," says Leonard Garment. "It was sort of a mark of Nixon's view of Bud that he would lend by his presence an air of legitimacy, credibility, warmth, sportsmanship and fair play by being the one who was the intermediary. He made the president feel relaxed."

The campaign was bitterly contested and in doubt nearly to the end. With Humphrey closing rapidly, the Nixon forces decided to produce an election eve telethon, with Nixon again taking questions, this time on the telephone, from voters throughout the country. Beamed from Los Angeles, one telethon was for the East Coast, and after an hour break, another was put on for voters in the west.

Dad's role in the telethons was to relay questions that were called in to the candidate. In actuality, the questions were prewritten, and when a caller phoned with a similar question, the pre-written question was credited to the caller and handed to Dad, who read it to the candidate. Julie and Tricia Nixon were members of the phone bank, and during the evening, Dad spent some time on camera with them, asking them what they thought were the major issues, based on their callers' questions.

"When I was talking to Julie and Tricia recently," the president recalled just a month before his death, "they agreed Bud was the best interviewer I ever had in forty-seven years in the political arena. He had an ability to ask hard questions in a soft way."

From his own experience with call-in shows during his Senate campaign, Dad knew it was important for Nixon to be relaxed on the telecasts. He used to jokingly say he was Nixon's stable pony, using the metaphor of the calming effect some thoroughbred horses receive from having a companion horse close by before the start of a big race.

ᴈ●

Dad served as part of the president's transition team and kept in close personal contact with the new chief executive. They attended the Rose Bowl together, and Dad visited with Nixon in Key Biscayne. Mom and Dad were frequently included in Nixon family gatherings, such as Pat Nixon's birthday dinner.

Outside the whirl of activities that accompany the transfer of governmental power, the mood of the country was ominous. The Chicago riots had been captured in ugly detail on television, major cities had been torched, the war protest was in full swing. The country was torn asunder along lines of race, class and age. The new president's plate was indeed full. To deal with the morass of issues facing him, he needed staff people he could depend on and trust. One of those people was Dad.

In January, 1969, Dad was appointed Special Consultant to the President; his charge was to evaluate the massive number of federal boards and commissions and to make judgments regarding their use and effectiveness. The special consultant status was devised so Dad could continue broadcasting for ABC without conflict of interest or the appearance of impropriety. As a consultant, he was not a government employee, and since he was paid only for the days he actually worked, he never took taxpayers' money when he was not working on the taxpayers' behalf.

In his new position, Dad was an ex-officio member of both the Cabinet and the Council on Urban Affairs. Though Nixon today is remembered chiefly as an architect of foreign policy, his domestic agenda, largely created by the council, was dynamic and progressive, according to Tom Cochran, executive director of the United States Conference of Mayors.

"There were a number of major initiatives that came out of the Nixon administration," says Cochran. "It was a time when elected officials were included in the policy discussions at an early stage . . . . In some administrations, they cooked the meal and served it up for you to serve to other people, [but] early in Nixon's first term, mayors were called in to work with Ehrlichman, Bud and Pat Moynihan. It was sort of a golden age for elected government."

Former HEW Secretary Robert Finch adds, "We learned some valuable lessons and . . . it was really the first time anybody had tried to reorganize and get across federal programs and dollars in terms of the cities. Bud was very helpful in that regard."

Cochran mentions Nixon's New Federalism, revenue sharing, local block grants, the Environmental Protection Agency, the Comprehensive Employment Training Act (CETA) and a variety of other urban initiatives as examples of the administration's commitment to domestic issues. Dad was there at the beginning of all that.

"[Bud made two contributions]," says John Ehrlichman, Nixon's assistant to the president for domestic affairs. "One was symbolic. He had an absolutely wonderful image . . . . Just having him associated with the White House activities was a big net plus for Richard Nixon because of that clean, upstanding and admirable image. Secondly, however, he had a lot of experience. He had run things. He had been in university politics, so to speak, and he knew a lot . . . so his advice was heeded by those of us he worked with."

Once in the White House, his duties extended far beyond the task for which he was hired. Almost immediately, the president asked Dad to provide a weekly television news analysis and interpretive report. According to a memo from Nixon, he was looking for a new perspective. The two men who were providing news analysis, he said, "are excellent men, but both tend to be advocates rather than being objective, as each would be the first to admit. Another weakness is that neither is particularly interested in television, and the television news summaries do not yet get quite the attention they deserve . . . . They [tend] because of their innate conservatism, to approach subjects somewhat negatively . . . . We need to get the balance somebody like Wilkinson might provide."

In one of the news summaries before Neil Armstrong's historic walk on the moon, Dad suggested the president go on live television to speak to the astronauts after they landed on the moon's surface. Surely, he said, it would be more dramatic than simply calling them or inviting them to the White House after they returned to Earth. Dad recommended a split-screen technique, and the recommendation was adopted. H.R. Haldeman's diary entry from July 20, 1969, indicates the president was elated by the broadcast, for which he wrote his own remarks.

Within a very short time, Dad also was involved in substantive work on three closely linked areas of the president's domestic policy—drug abuse, youth affairs, and volunteerism. His office was next door to the president's "working" office in the Executive Office Building, and Dad frequently was found in conference with the president and often sent Nixon memoranda on such things as ways to make speeches more visually interesting to the television audience—methods Ross Perot used with great success in 1992. He also advised the president to make sure the administration spoke with one voice on matters of national policy and brought "beyond the Beltway" concerns of ordinary citizens to Nixon's attention.

Dad also was assigned the task of coordinating all the White House officials' speaking engagements, making sure the administration was not over-represented in some areas of the country and under-represented in others, and keeping in touch with GOP state headquarters regarding what officials were scheduled for appearances in their states.

Some of the speeches he coordinated were his own, as Dad was one of Nixon's favorite surrogate speakers. Articulate and well-informed on domestic issues because of his close ties to the president and the Cabinet, Dad was an impressive presidential representative.

ﾟ▲

Though the administration's primary concern was ending the conflict in Vietnam, drug abuse was its No. 1 domestic priority. Dad was in the thick of the battle against drugs.

"One of the main contributions Bud made," recalls Egil (Bud) Krogh, deputy counsel to the president, "was to really perceive that we had to address what we called the demand side—in other words, the propensity to use drugs—which had to do with education and treatment, rather than just focusing on prevention by police or by Customs at the border . . . . His contribution was in charting the original course of moving from the emphasis on the supply side and focusing on young people."

As Dad and Jim Atwater, a special assistant to the president who reported to Dad, found out, the nation's drug policy was hopelessly confused. "We discovered to our horror," says Atwater, "that the whole thing was totally uncoordinated . . . . The Justice Department had its own program, HEW had its own particular program, the armed services had their own program . . . and they were all saying different things . . . . Bud and I organized an interagency committee with representatives from all the departments that were involved . . . and began to work together. I literally introduced people in my office who had been working in drugs for twenty years and had never come in contact with each other. Not only that, but I introduced people in HEW who had been working on drug programs for ten years and who didn't know each other."

One thing all the agencies needed was an elementary manual on drug abuse. "The simplest kind of thing," says Atwater, "starting with A and building to Z. What are the dangers? How do you approach the problem? We got some money, we had somebody write it, and then I rewrote it almost word by word, because we didn't get what we wanted . . . . It had a title like *Answers to the Most Frequently Asked Questions About Drugs*, and it had quite a sale, if I remember correctly."

Dad hated waste and inefficiency, and "when he discovered every agency in town was putting out its own drug information, he got a little teed off," says Atwater. "What happened was, we set up a computer program that even in those days enabled you to get a whole list of programs that were viable around the country. If you were interested in starting a program to reach junior high schools in the inner city, you could contact us and we would turn out the four programs that looked like what you wanted, and you wouldn't have to start from scratch. Bud hated to reinvent the wheel .... I think it was the start of the drug clearinghouse I read about in the papers every day."

Dad also set up teachers' seminars, training teachers to instruct other teachers in drug abuse issues. "It was a worthwhile idea," concludes Atwater, "and it worked."

In addition, Dad helped the administration save money on anti-drug commercials. "Somehow we heard the White House was going to spend some money for a series of TV commercials," Atwater says. "That got Bud's attention because of his experience [with advertising]. He said we could get the Ad Council in there and get the ads done for free .... That's precisely what happened."

Jeff Donfeld, one of Dad's assistants, adds, "We also got involved with trying to identify heroin users in Vietnam, because it became politically correct to try to stop the war by the allegation that heroin-dependent soldiers would be coming back to the United States as trained killers ... so I was involved in setting up a urinalysis identification program in Vietnam and getting drug-dependent soldiers into treatment programs.

"So much of the perception of the Nixon administration was hard-ass law enforcement," says Donfeld, "but in my judgment, it was a brilliant, conservative, compassionate effort to do something positive about the drug problem."

"The Nixon administration's focus on drug abuse was unprecedented," Donfeld continues. "People talk about Bill Bennett being the first drug czar. What's astonishing to me is that the institutional memory of the federal government is exactly zero. In 1971, I was told to go out and find the best man in the United States on the subject of drug abuse, and I did. His name was Jerome Jaffe, and he was both a pharmacologist and a psychiatrist .... I brought him into the Oval Office and he became the first drug czar. All this was connected to the Special Action Office for Drug Abuse Prevention, which was the first piece of administration legislation that was passed unanimously in Congress."

ã

Probably the most inventive anti-drug activity Dad introduced involved recruiting disc jockeys from around the nation to
help spread the word. Dad always understood the power of radio
and television, and he knew young people were influenced by
the DJs. The actual idea for including the radio personalities came
from columnist Art Buchwald, but once Dad had the bit in his
teeth, he ran with it.

Tom Campbell, the top-rated San Francisco DJ, was instrumental in the anti-drug movement. "I was broadcasting for KYA
and also writing an entertainment column for the San Francisco
*Examiner*. I became so concerned with drug abuse in the city,
especially in Haight-Ashbury . . . I wrote a letter to President
Nixon. A number of people chuckled and said I'd never hear a
thing. But, sure enough, the president called me back and said he
was sending his youth advisor out to visit with me."

Dad went on a two-day odyssey with Campbell. "I took
him to the Fillmore West . . . just to see what the street scene was
and what was happening in San Francisco."

On his return to Washington, Dad set up a meeting of the
influential DJs, such as Murray the K and Cousin Brucie. "We
discussed trying to use alternative values," says Campbell. "We
came up with the idea of an Ad Hoc Committee on Youth that
basically would be the top disc jockeys from the various major
markets who really reached youth . . . . We had all the heads of
the various agencies there at the White House . . . and we came
up with ways of designing public service announcements and
other things to try to fight . . . narcotics. Later we had the station
managers come in."

The station managers and disc jockeys cooperated on many
anti-drug initiatives throughout the United States. "One of the
events we did," says Campbell, "was what we called the KYA
Drug Rap. . . . Coca Cola underwrote it. We had over 1,000 editors
and reporters from the high school newspapers in northern
California; we had people from the White House there, as well as
a few people . . . like Timothy Leary. It was like a debate . . . . The
students were invited to write an editorial based on the debate,
and we gave a scholarship. We tried to go beyond saying, 'Don't
do it; it's against the law.' We tried to educate and reach out to
people . . . . 'Just say no' doesn't work. What do you do instead?"

୧ଈ

Because most of Dad's life had been spent with college students, he was a natural as the president's youth advisor. Campuses were besieged, students had taken to the streets, and the administration needed someone who understood young people. Dad's job was to try to open the dialogue between Washington and the country's youth.

His view of students never varied throughout this period. He believed this was the first generation of students whose basic needs—food, shelter, and health—were generally being met. Not having to scratch out their living, these young people could have chosen a life of hedonism, and some did. The vast majority, however, in Dad's view at least, were looking outward, trying to make a contribution to the fabric of American life. He recognized the campus unrest for what it was—frustration with the systems that dehumanized and divided people—though he didn't countenance flouting the law and wreaking destruction. He thought lawbreakers should be punished.

As upset as he was by rioting and unrest, whether on the campus or in the inner city, he was equally disturbed by the establishment types who wouldn't listen to youth concerns—those who wanted to keep young people quiet and in their place. He understood the students' anger and said there was a great deal to protest about. "Young people seem to feel that they are shut out of the decision-making process, unable to open channels of communication . . . . They want the opportunity to express themselves to the people who make decisions . . . . But if the door is closed and they are locked out, then there's a rub," he said.

Dad began to formulate the administration's approach to youth programs. He discovered there were four basic types of programs: those concerned with educating and training minority and disadvantaged youth, those that developed opportunities for service among idealistic youth, programs designed to train young professionals, and those concerned with opening the channels of communication between the government and young people. He recommended an immediate evaluation of all these programs and the development of a "coherent policy, with clear priorities and strategies for the whole process of youth development." He also stated in a memo to H. R. Haldeman, Nixon's chief of staff, that "in the participatory politics of 1969, the *process* of developing new programs and evaluating old ones may be just as important as the ... substance of the programs themselves .... Programs designed within the inner recesses of government will be ... pure rhetoric, signifying nothing .... The staff plans to conduct a series of meetings in the coming weeks with a variety of young people to solicit their ideas, feelings, hopes and criticisms."

Dad made many recommendations, including a council to coordinate the multitude of youth programs and a youth advocate in each major government department, but change was slow. Ehrlichman recalls, "It was reactive. It was a time when there was great ferment in the land. A lot of what we did was day-to-day reaction .... On any given day what we were doing was not part of any grand strategy; it was much more trying to adapt to whatever the crisis of the day was .... The pressures were from all sides .... There were just some programs we were stuck with. Some worked well, some didn't work well. But being realistic about it, we had to live with them. Basically we were up against a fence like Kent State. After Kent State [lots of] kids came to Washington and we made a great effort to meet with them and talk with them and explain the president's policies, and a certain number of them saw the president. They saw Henry [Kissinger]. They saw [HEW Secretary Robert] Finch. Bud was very active in that."

A Washington summer internship for hundreds of college students was a major success, says Jim Atwater. "They put students with high-level executives in various departments—people who were really doing things. It involved a lot of planning and a lot of agonizing, trying to get something rolling with a number of departments in government. But with Bud's name and the White House, we were able to do it .... His name was magic in Washington."

Even with the successes he was having, Dad was becoming frustrated by the lack of action on issues he considered important. "You simply don't evaluate all the youth programs in the country in a few weeks with inexperienced people," says Atwater. "The White House pushed us to do this kind of thing, and we did do three or four of them, and some of the things later came true."

ə.

In 1961 President Kennedy appointed Dad to head the President's Council on Youth Fitness. Kennedy convinced Dad to accept the position by stressing how important it was to his administration.

Dad and Dick Snider take some time out of their busy schedules to play a round of golf at Burning Tree in Washington D.C. Snider, a sportswriter from Kansas, was one of Dad's closest friends and played a big part in many areas of his life.

Bobby Kennedy and Dad converse at an AAHPER convention. Dad was always impressed with Bobby's intensity and liked him very much.

In 1964 Dad ran for the United States Senate. He also endorsed Goldwater, which turned out to be a tactical error for his own campaign.

Dad records a television commercial. TV was a cornerstone of his campaign.

*photo by Ned Hockman*

Dad and former president Eisenhower met for several hours to discuss the senate campaign.

*photo by Dick Cobb*

Dad at one of the hundreds of stops he made during the campaign.

Mom and Dad on Election Day, 1964.

Mom and Dad watch the results of the primary race come in.

The unhappy end of a long, grueling campaign. Dad lost the election to Senator Fred Harris by approximately 21,000 votes.

Dad with his good friend Ned Hockman, professor emeritus of journalism and mass communications at OU. Hockman photographed all the Oklahoma football games and was a partner in Bud Wilkinson Enterprises, producers of *Sports for the Family.*

*photo by Ned Hockman*

Bob Hope and Dad traded visits to one another's shows, Hope appearing on *Sports for the Family* and Dad being introduced on Hope's live show at the Oklahoma City Municipal Auditorium.

*photo by Ned Hockman*

*photo by ABC Sports*

Dad joined ABC's college football broadcast team in 1966. Here, he and Chris Schenkel call a game. With his early years of television experience, Dad easily made the switch to network broadcasting.

A later ABC broadcast
team: Dad, Chuck
Howard, Andy Sidaris
and Keith Jackson.

In 1980, Dad teamed
with Jim Simpson to
broadcast collegiate
football for ESPN.

Dad was appointed Special
Consultant to the President in
1969, working closely with
the Nixon administration to
formulate domestic policy
regarding youth affairs, drug
abuse and volunteerism. In
this picture he appears in the
Oval Office with (left to right)
Arnold Palmer, President
Nixon, Al Kaline, Bart Starr
and Chris Schenkel.

Dad with Henry Kissinger
and Bob Hope.

The President, Dad, and Health Education and Welfare Secretary, Robert Finch, in the Oval Office.

*photo by White House*

Dad addresses the White House Fellows, a group of business people who also spent a year in government service.

*photo by White House*

*photo by White House*

Dad meets with Henry Ford II, chairman of the Center for Voluntary Action.

President Gerald Ford, Dad's old gridiron opponent from the University of Michigan, appointed him to the United States Olympic Committee.

Dad's friend from Texas, President George Bush, throws out the first ball. Dad can be seen to the right of the president.

Dad and Donna O'Donnohue were married in 1976, and they worked and traveled together until he became seriously ill.

Dad returned to coaching in 1978, taking over the reins of the St. Louis Cardinals. After eight straight losses, he celebrates the team's first win.

An enormous testimonial dinner was held for Dad at the University of Oklahoma in September, 1991. Master of Cer-emonies Curt Gowdy is at Dad's right. Dr. George Lynn Cross, president emeritus of the university, is on his left.

The day after the testimonial dinner, Dad was honored at halftime of the Okla-homa game. It was one of the most memorable moments of his life.

Dad's next major assignment was to be president of the Center for Voluntary Action, a non-profit, non-partisan organization brought into being by executive order. HUD Secretary George Romney, formerly the governor of Michigan, chaired the cabinet committee from which the organization grew. "The three ways we have of solving problems in this country are government, economic systems and volunteerism," Romney says. "The least recognized and the least organized was volunteerism."

Romney had run against Nixon in the early part of the primary season, but had dropped out. "Nixon came to see me in the winter of 1968 . . . to get my support," Romney says. "I had visited seventeen ghettos from Harlem to Watts following the riots in Detroit; I saw volunteer programs in those ghettos that were superior in most instances to government programs. I told him about them and asked if he'd like to visit with some of the people running those programs during the campaign. He said he'd like to, so I arranged for some of the people . . . to be here in Detroit. When he visited, he talked with them. He didn't know much about volunteer activities before that . . . and that's why he looked to me."

Though Dad was not eager to take on the presidency of the new center, many of his youth recommendations had a voluntary component, so he came to the job with that bias already in place. "He was very instrumental in determining the course we took," says Romney. "The most significant thing he did was to say, 'Before we go out to enlist people to volunteer, we've got to be sure that they're placed in a meaningful role or they won't continue.' "

Romney goes on, "We had a woman on our board by the name of Joyce Black. She had been president of the Junior League . . . . She persuaded Mayor John Lindsay of New York to support her in setting up a strong volunteer action center with a paid administrator and so on . . . . It was called the Mayor's Volunteer Action Center. Using that as a model, we secured $1 million from the Ford Foundation and $1 million from the government, and Bud began to encourage these local volunteer centers."

According to Romney, four things are necessary for successful volunteerism: leadership, people, media support and money. The money part has been well organized; the people part still needs work. "The National Center for Voluntary Action was the first national organization whose purpose was to strengthen the people part of volunteerism," he says. "There are now almost 500 of these local volunteer centers across the country, but there ought to be five times that many. The National Center was later merged with an organization in Denver .... Then when George Bush was running, he started talking about the Points of Light."

President Bush later created the Points of Light Foundation, which was merged with the National VOLUNTEER Center in Denver. "The principal purpose of the Points of Light Foundation is to build these local volunteer centers and to strengthen volunteering at the local level, where the problems are," says Romney. "So what Bud was involved in ... is now the Points of Light Foundation."

Romney indicates that local voluntary programs are most effective when they are locally managed. John Ehrlichman seems to support that position. Even with the powerful Henry Ford II as its chairman, "The Center for Voluntary Action was not a conspicuous success," Ehrlichman says. "It had worked extremely well in Michigan; we were never successful in replicating it on a national scale ..... I'm inclined to think from that experience ... that there are just a lot of things that succeed locally or statewide that you can't reproduce nationally."

≥≈

About a year into Dad's tenure in the White House, he began to feel as if his inner circle status was being undermined. Atwater confirms what was happening. "The first disappointment was Bud's lack of access to the president. He simply could not get through the Haldeman barrier. They put us in a corner as time went on .... They weren't quite certain what to do with us. Things were tossed our way that nobody knew what to do with ... for example, Denver's bid to get the Olympic Games."

The president obviously still regarded Dad as a friend, according to a story told by John Ehrlichman. "There was a time during the campus riots when we brought in the Vanderbilt chancellor and the president of Howard University .... They were supposed to be the president's experts on the campus situation. The fact is, there was no acceptance on Nixon's part. He accepted Bud, listened to him, took his advice. They were peers. He never had that kind of rapport with these experts. They sat there and cobwebs grew on them, and I'd say they saw the president twice in all the time they were there. Bud was in and out all the time."

But the time between meetings was growing. Bud Krogh attributes Dad's waning influence to an administration now more concerned with implementation and legislation than policy development. "Bud came in and was close to the president and worked during the transition with him. Arthur Burns was brought in . . . and Pat Moynihan. Principally what you had were idea people who were very, very knowledgeable about government theory and programs but were not necessarily the most gifted in terms of . . . running the government machinery.

"During the first year," says Krogh, "the president wanted to focus a great deal more on international affairs—foreign policy, the war, China—and I think what he wanted was a structure that would enable domestic policy to be carried out without a lot of internecine conflict . . . . You saw the transfer of responsibility from Burns, Moynihan and Bud to Haldeman and Ehrlichman . . . . They could run it much more efficiently . . . . It was something the president felt was a good idea; he didn't want to be bothered with a lot of the policy discussions that were taking place during the initial months.

"I don't really think there was a conscious effort to exclude Bud or Burns or Moynihan," Krogh says. "I think it was a recognition that they could make contributions in other ways but not in actually running programs."

"That could be," Atwater responds, "but if so, they never came around and shook our hands and said, 'Good job, lads.' . . . From our side of the fence, it looked like we were being picked up, shuffled and moved around."

Ehrlichman, however, seems to concur with Krogh's view, adding that the Nixon administration was one of the most active ever in terms of domestic policy. "Nixon was not a passive president," he says. "He was very activist, and we were sending legislation to the Hill every other week . . . transportation, welfare reform, tax reform. We had a very active health reorganization study, not dissimilar to what's going on [today], but obviously taking a considerably different direction. It was extraordinary. We had both houses of Congress of the opposite party, but we got a very high percentage of legislation through by building coalitions. We like to think a lot of that was the result of good staff work in the departments and in the White House."

Additionally, Nixon's image was becoming more presidential in its own right. "Bud helped Nixon establish his persona in 1968," says Dwight Chapin, special assistant to the president. "It wouldn't have worked in 1972, because Nixon had established his own persona by that time." Whatever the reason, Dad's access was cut off, his office was given away and he became more and more dissatisfied.

With the National Center struggling, his office moved, and his access to the president denied, Dad began to chafe at the lack of substance in his role at the White House. He continued to plan the White House Sunday prayer services, the activities of the Bicentennial Commission and attended to other duties, but he was restive. In December, 1970, he sent a memo to Robert Finch, who had left HEW and come to the White House staff, saying, "The assignments which I currently fill are not demanding, since I am not engaged in particularly meaningful activities. If I am not able to make a significant contribution, I prefer to resign and return to private life."

He was prevailed upon to stay, but things didn't get much better. He finally resigned on January 26, 1971.

In retrospect, Nixon said, "We were so busy in those first two years trying to wind down the war in Vietnam and opening the Chinese and Soviet initiatives, I was unable to spend the time with Bud that I would have liked .... We did not adequately use Bud's enormous talents during the White House years .... I believe he would have made an outstanding ambassador. I discussed the possibility with him on occasion, but we never found a post in which he was interested."

"He was always so positive," says Jim Atwater. "I remember Bud saying, when we were all becoming conscious of the territorial fights in the White House, that if we just stick to our own game plan and do as well as we can, things are going to go fine."

᠈᠊

Dad was very surprised, early in his association with the president's transition team, to hear that the president's first priority was his re-election four years hence. Nixon's program was so ambitious he felt the full eight years were critical. It was, of course, that priority that led some members of the staff into the Watergate debacle.

"I knew something was going to go. I knew they were going to screw up," says Atwater, "but I didn't have any idea they were going to do it as badly as they did."

As Jeff Donfeld says, "I always felt Bud was a gentle gentleman, and that the shark-infested environment of the White House was not an environment in which he could flourish. It was so punitive. There was no tolerance for independent thought. You were either the carrier of the party line or you were out. Those were the people who were successful within ... the White House in terms of privileges and acknowledgment. Those were the people who got in trouble, too."

"Bud was a wonderful man," says Dwight Chapin, "and there were just certain aspects of how things were going to be run that he didn't agree with. [The White House] was just a lot different from what people thought it was going to be. Some people could handle that and adjust to it and some people were principled enough that they couldn't."

So the White House years came to a close. Dad remained Richard Nixon's friend and continued to respect the president's accomplishments. He grieved over Watergate and the destruction of many of Nixon's forward-thinking policies. He stayed close to other presidents, being appointed by Gerald Ford to the United States Commission on Olympic Sports and by Ronald Reagan to the Board of Visitors of the United States Air Force Academy. In the 1980 campaign, he served as state chairman of the Bush campaign and maintained a close personal relationship with President Bush. But after 1971, politics as a profession never appealed to him again.

# 10

## *Bud the Businessman*

&

*"To business that we love, we rise betime . . ."*
*—Shakespeare*

If there was one constant in Dad's multi-dimensional life, it was his interest in business. He had, after all, spent part of his youth working for his father at the Wilkinson Home Finance Company, where he had come to understand economics, money and credit. All of this served him well when he went to Oklahoma, where he was athletic director as well as head football coach. As A.D., he was responsible for the administration of all aspects of the university's entire sports program, and he honed his ability to delegate and manage his time. He was already a strong coach, communicator and motivator, and with a little on-the-job seasoning, he developed all the skills necessary to become a strong and effective business leader.

Dad had some very specific ideas about what was required to be a success—in business, athletics, government and in life. His philosophy of success in business was contained in a series of handwritten notes he used as an outline when he spoke to business groups. He believed to succeed you must:

- Know yourself and your potentials. See yourself without illusion. Learn what is important to you. Discover what gives you pleasure and satisfaction.
- Choose as your lifework that which you enjoy. Joy in your work is essential to business and personal success.

- Resolve to give your clients, employers or employees your best at all times, and apply the Golden Rule to every business situation. Only when you know you are fulfilling your potentials and acting honorably can you find peace of mind in your work. Have the courage to do what is right.
- Believe in what you represent and help others discover how your product or service can assist them in attaining *their* goals, not yours.
- Take pride in how you do your job. See how your contribution affects the whole. Strive for consistent improvement. Walk the extra mile. Make the extra call. Make sure the competition gives up before you do.
- Help your client, employer or employee any way you can. It's intrinsically good to do so, it boosts your self-esteem, and it puts you ahead of the competition, most of whom are looking out for themselves instead of others.
- Delegate authority along with responsibility. Find the best people for the jobs and then let them get the work done without interference.
- Don't be afraid to start small. The worth of an enterprise is not determined by its size.

At no time were Dad's business principles more visible than during his tenure as co-owner of the Coach of the Year Clinics. As did a number of other coaches, Dad provided coaching clinics for high school coaches. His were confined to Oklahoma and Texas. The purpose, of course, was to get to know those coaches and thus make recruiting easier. Duffy Daugherty was running similar clinics in Michigan. Both Dad and Daugherty were also in incredible demand as speakers at other regional clinics.

The two coaches, who were good friends, were spending tremendous amounts of time on the road with their clinic engagements. They came to an agreement that instead of traveling every weekend for months on end, without a plan and without organization, they themselves would set up a series of weekend clinics, running two or three clinics a weekend for a specified period of time each year.

The Coach of the Year Clinics—three per weekend on four successive weekends in January and February—were intensive presentations for high school and college coaches and were designed to teach innovations in the game to coaches throughout the country. They were sponsored at various times in their history by Kellogg, Kodak and Champion. Presenters always included Dad and Daugherty; the American Football Coaches Association's Coach of the Year; outstanding college coaches, such as Darrell Royal, Joe Paterno, Barry Switzer and Lou Holtz; and some coaches from the areas where the clinics were being held.

For Dad, Daugherty, the Coach of the Year and some other popular speakers, the travel was daunting. As Ara Parseghian remembers, "They were difficult to do, I'll be honest with you. It was very time consuming and, of course, you had the fact that Notre Dame was very demanding . . . . I remember the year we were involved in it and were traveling all over . . . and trying to do recruiting at the same time. I look back on it now and I don't know how the hell I did it."

Johnny Majors made many clinic appearances. "Normally, I would make three or four a year. I started in 1974 and I could never turn them down. In 1976 I did all twelve . . . . I drove all night a couple of times and made all twelve from coast to coast."

Dad and Daugherty knew they couldn't handle everything by themselves, so they hired clinic managers in major cities. To these managers, they delegated the logistics of running the clinics. "The initial program was held in Grand Rapids," recalls Earl Browning, Louisville clinic manager. "Then they expanded to different cities. They started out in Pittsburgh, Dallas and Santa Monica. Then they went to Memphis first, and after one year, the Memphis clinic moved to Louisville. They added Atlanta and over the years Denver and Minneapolis." Additional clinics were held in Seattle, Boston and Washington, D.C.

The clinic managers' jobs were difficult. They arranged for exhibit space, handled reservations, and most nerve wracking, they dealt with the split-second travel plans necessary to move various coaches from city to city in the span of three days. Bill Russell, Santa Monica manager, says, "We had to time everything to the airline schedules, but in Santa Monica in the wintertime . . . occasionally we had fog in the mornings and evenings, and we'd have the airport fogged in, and we couldn't get people in the air. Here we'd advertised for a month to all the coaches coming in that so-and-so was going to speak, and his time and topic, and then we'd get a call saying he couldn't get in. We'd have to scramble and get one of the other coaches who'd already arrived to pinch hit."

In spite of the logistical nightmares, Browning says, "The Coach of the Year Clinic was no doubt the most successful clinic ever undertaken. A lot of people have tried to copy them since then, but they were probably the most instrumental in getting new information ... to other coaches. They had a significant place in the history of football and in disseminating information . . . . Football coaches were willing to share their information, and it was very successful in upgrading the game."

One of the key ingredients in the success of the clinics, according to Browning, was that "we had two influential people who took part in every clinic, and they would mix with the people and would discuss football with them."

Dad and Daugherty were a potent combination. Daugherty was the entertainer who could warm up the crowd. He had stories galore in his repertoire and he was a delightful *raconteur*. Dad was more serious and reserved. "They were a tremendous pair," says Bill Russell. "They were so different, yet so compatible. They'd come out and Duffy would start talking at point one and then he would hit a tangent that would stimulate his mind to talk about something else. He'd talk about five or six things before he finished, but he always got back to his original point. Bud would hit points one, two, three, four, five and his conclusion. He'd sit there and smile at Duffy while Duffy was on. It was really fun to see them. They were very close and had great admiration for each other."

After the formal presentations were over, Dad and Daugherty made themselves available to the attendees. On one occasion, Browning says, "Bud and Duffy had done their spiel, and I said, 'Before we go upstairs to talk business, I've got a favor to ask. We have about forty youth league coaches here . . . and they've got two rooms where they're having a party, and they never get to see any celebrities up there. Let's go see them.' I had told the guys I was going to bring Bud and Duffy, and they said, 'Oh, yeah, sure.' We went up to the hotel room and two or three of them were standing out in the hall, and one of them yells, 'Damn, they're here.' They ran in and got everybody and we walked in and I said, 'Hi, gang, say hello to Bud and Duffy.'

"We had a drink and Duffy was telling jokes and Bud was talking football. He was sitting on the bed with a beer in his hand, just part of the group. That's the way he was. He drew people to him. When he walked into a room it was just amazing."

Another key to success was that both Dad and Daugherty understood that people came to the clinics for different reasons, and the two did their best to meet the needs of all their constituencies. The coaches came to learn, and learn they did.

Florida State coach Bobby Bowden recalls his first clinic in 1955. "I was twenty-six years of age. Bud would have been about thirty-nine. He lectured on the option. That was kind of a new offense back then. I just salivated. I'll never forget—Bud demonstrated how the quarterback ran the option as I sat in the stands with the other high school and college coaches. That will always be one of my great memories. And I've told my coaches quite a few times abut how he said, 'I don't coach X's and O's; I coach people.' I can look back on forty years of coaching and so much of it originated with Bud."

"The best instructional programs came when the head coach brought a couple of his assistant coaches with him," says Russell. "I think the best one we ever had was when Duffy brought two of his assistants and had them on the platform with him for almost two hours. They got coaches up from the auditorium and demonstrated with them. All the coaches left that day talking about it, that's for sure."

Even when he wasn't Coach of the Year, Ara Parseghian often participated in the clinics. "They were great celebrations," he says. "Coaches getting together exchanging ideas. I always looked forward to them because I thought if I could just grasp one idea that might make our team a little bit better the following year, then it was worth attending."

If the coaches came to learn, the exhibitors came to sell, and Dad viewed the exhibitors, such as Wilson, Spaulding, and Riddell, as important clients. He and Daugherty made sure the exhibitors had plenty of time to rub shoulders with the attendees.

Bob Troppmann managed the San Francisco clinic. "There were about sixty exhibitors," he says. "It was great for them because they could visit with thousands of coaches; it would take them a long time to get out on the road and see that many."

Browning recalls, "Bud and Duffy insisted that the exhibits get some play . . . that you run the coaches through there. We would maze the coaches through the exhibits to the speaker, so they could see the displays . . . . The coaches were able to come in, see the newest equipment, find out what other people were buying, make their orders for the next year and get ready for the next football season."

The exhibitors responded, says Russell. "At one time, the Santa Monica clinic drew as many as 2,200 in paid attendance. There was such a demand for exhibit space that we had to put them at the far reaches of the auditorium and hope they got some traffic, which they did. We even had some exhibitor spaces behind the stage."

Another important constituency were the clinic managers themselves. Dad and Daugherty believed the managers would be most happy and productive if they had some ownership in the success of the program, so they were cut in for a share of the registration fees. "The way Bud and Duffy discussed it with each clinic manager," says Browning, "was, 'Look, you're not going to be able to quit teaching school on this. On the other hand, it's really going to supplement your income and give you an additional income you can do some extra things on. You can keep your job as a coach, teacher, or whatever you're doing and still make a significant amount of money.' Everybody looked at it as a second job."

Russell recalls, "The national sponsor fee went to Bud and Duffy. At the clinics, the net profit of each operation went one-third to the clinic manager, one-third to Duffy, and one-third to Bud. I think the largest net the three of us ever split was $45,000 out of the Santa Monica clinic."

Speakers themselves were compensated either with cash or travel. As Johnny Majors remembers, "The money was decent, but the friendship and the trips were a lot more important. Most of the coaches took money, but several of us took trips. One time Vince Dooley and I went to the Far East. We went to Scotland four times, to Ireland a couple of times, to Hawaii six or seven times. My wife and I loved to travel. She told me, 'Don't you ever lose contact with Bud and Duffy.' "

Dad probably would have said that the clinics were successful because he and Daugherty were doing what they loved, serving the needs of their clients—coaches, exhibitors, speakers, and clinic managers—and helping those clients achieve their personal goals.

Browning agrees. "It was a business, but I don't think Bud and Duffy were as serious about the business part when they started. It was a good way of getting information to the people and it was good contact with other coaches . . . . They were doing it to promote football. The money just happened to come."

"You just had this good feeling about the clinics," says Troppmann. "Bud and Duffy made sure they talked to all the exhibitors, and they were in the hallways talking to coaches and anyone they could touch. They always had the top football coaches as the clinicians. Our programs were always very solid. When coaches would go to the Coach of the Year Clinic, it was like Christmas and Easter."

After Dad's health began to fail and he could no longer keep up the pace, he sold his interest in the clinics to Daugherty, and within a few years of Daugherty's death, his widow, Francine, sold them to Johnny Majors and George Perles, who still own them today. Kodak and Kellogg, the original sponsors, have been supplanted by Toyota.

Dad always had a warm spot in his heart for the clinics, because they were Christmas and Easter for him, too. I think they are also superb demonstrations of the business growth that can occur when Dad's simple principles are observed.

ช่

Dad's second sports-related business was the Lifetime Sports Foundation. After his service to President Kennedy and his Senate run, the bowling industry, which was dominated by AMF and Brunswick, was searching for a spokesperson to promote bowling as a lifetime activity. Dad, says Dick Snider, who worked with him to set up the foundation, wasn't interested in promoting just bowling, but said if the focus could be expanded to include tennis, golf and other lifetime sports, he would head it up and do what he could to promote the organization.

The Lifetime Sports Foundation, according to a speech Dad gave in 1965, was "dedicated to the fitness of youth and sports that last a lifetime. To fulfill this defined role, the foundation will assist appropriate educational and recreational organizations, schools, and youth-serving agencies to broaden and improve their programs and services." In this speech, Dad also was very frank about the profit-making possibilities for the two companies—Brunswick and AMF—who were underwriting the foundation. He saw the organization's primary role as supplementing the efforts of the President's Council on Physical Fitness.

The headquarters eventually were located in Washington, D.C. "We wanted to work with the President's Council and also with the American Association for Health, Physical Education and Recreation," says Snider, "because we wanted to get the lifetime sports concept into the schools."

Dad thought lifetime sports were important because competitive sports could, by definition, involve only a few talented athletes. "One of his favorite speeches," says Snider, "was about how he had coached some of the greatest athletes that ever lived, but when they got to be forty years old, they couldn't break 120 in golf." Since they were no longer playing their competitive sport, even these elite athletes were missing the fitness benefits of lifetime sports. For the entire nation to be healthy and competitive, Dad wanted to create more opportunities for people to develop competence in a sport they could enjoy forever.

"The biggest step we took," Snider says, "was to create a pilot project in the El Paso, Texas school system. They regularly bused their people to bowling centers, golf courses, and tennis courts, and they made lifetime sports a very integral part of their physical education program."

The foundation lasted only a brief time. The schools generally were unwilling to make the kind of monetary and time commitment necessary to assure the program's success. As Snider says, "We were talking budget dollars and a commitment that a school board or parents might frown on.

"Bud was available to promote the project anywhere, anytime. We conducted clinics in major school districts around the country. They were well attended and very successful, and the thing was on a roll. It could have gone on and on, but it kind of died when Bud left. He was tied up in a lot of things—TV and the Coach of the Year Clinics; he had a lot of irons in the fire."

And only so much energy. Over the next few years, he concentrated that energy on clinics, television and politics. It would be a while before he returned to other types of business activities.

❧

It was his close friendship with Chris Schenkel that led Dad to one of his most interesting business ventures. Schenkel was also a close friend of Stuart Hunt and Hunt's brother-in-law, John Murchison, well-known Texans with a far-flung network of business interests, one of which was Silco, a holding company in Dallas. Silco comprised a variety of financial and insurance interests, including a company called Total Insurance Planning Systems (TIPS).

Because Schenkel and Hunt were friends, "Chris introduced us," says Hunt. "I went to a lot of football games and sat in the booth and really learned about football from Bud. I thought he was a great commentator."

At that time, Dad still was working as a consultant to the White House, but he was becoming disillusioned with his role there. "I said," remembers Hunt, "'Well, if you ever want to leave, I have something . . . .' "

Hunt then told his friend, Walter Hailey, president of Total Insurance Planning Systems, of Dad's dissatisfaction with Washington, and Hailey began to pursue Dad to join his team. "Bud's availability excited me very much," says Hailey, "and I started chasing him around the country. Wherever his plane would land, I would always be there to talk to him about joining us."

Dad was lukewarm. "The first thing he said to me, early in the game," says Hailey, "was 'Walter, I don't believe I have any interest in selling insurance.' Eventually, I was able to convince him."

What intrigued Dad about Hailey's operation was the way insurance was sold. TIPS' focus was an innovative method of selling multi-line insurance to retail grocers. General agencies were set up in grocery wholesale warehouses. Since the retailers had to go to the warehouses to make food purchases, it was a great convenience for them to be able to buy all their business and personal insurance—property and casualty, life, health, and disability products—at the same time in the same place, and volume buying kept premiums reasonable. Hailey called the concept NEER (Naturally Existing Economic Relationship) marketing. "It means to put your niche, your expertise, under the umbrella of something larger," says Hailey. "You put your office inside a wholesale office, and then when the grocer got his statement, it was for beans, peas, carrots and insurance. Just the way the wholesaler did, we fit right in there." Hailey's partner, David Keener, was general manager of Affiliated Foods in Dallas, a major grocery wholesaler. Keener's connections inside the industry helped the TIPS program establish a foothold.

Within a few months of Dad's joining the company, a series of stock transfers and spinoffs resulted in the creation of a new holding company—Planned Marketing Associates (PMA)—and Dad was selected as board chairman. Planned Marketing Associates was poised for tremendous growth, and Dad led the way.

"He ... set the goals for us," says Hailey, who remained as president of the TIPS General Agency. "He blazed the trail, and provided much of the leadership he had provided in football, which was recruiting, training, and motivating."

Dad fully embraced the PMA-TIPS concept, which fit in perfectly with his belief in doing all you can for the customer. "[When I was first approached to get into the insurance business]," he said, "I never felt that the products varied enough for this to be something I should do. However, the more I looked into ... TIPS ... the more I recognized that this ... meets the needs of the people we serve, delivers high-quality products to them at a lower cost, and at the same time assures full business and personal insurance coverage . . . . Food prices today are the biggest bargain the consumer buys. It stands to reason that by distributing insurance products in the same manner, we are providing them with the same bargain for their dollar."

Dad now set to work, using his considerable persuasive skills, to land major clients. "He could open any door anywhere," says Hunt. "A lot of sales people just don't have credibility, and people think, 'Oh, no, here's another salesman,' but with Bud, it wasn't that way at all."

"Having him was a great blessing for me," says Hailey, "because I always had a fear of rejection, and I never had to worry about getting appointments or being rejected when I had Bud with me. With Bud, we were able to develop some really big national accounts that we would have been unable to develop otherwise, because of his great charisma.

"The biggest problem you have in selling an intangible is credibility . . . . I have never, ever worked with anyone in my life that created the believability, trust and credibility Bud Wilkinson did.

"Bud and I would go around the country together and call on wholesale houses and go to conventions, and all the grocers would want to meet him. They would come to the booth or the room, and Bud would always be the speaker at the whole convention. This gave us a great, great image . . . . Bud was beyond being a good businessman and a great football player and a great coach. He was more of a statesman."

With Dad at the helm, growth was explosive. Vice president and controller Ted Eubank recalls, "It was the most exciting time in my business career, because it was such a dramatic growth period—taking that small company from a local Texas insurance group to a nationwide organization with 200 offices . . . . The people growth at the company and the financial growth were so exciting."

"People growth" was, of course, Dad's long suit. Eubank says, "Bud was such a great people motivator. . . . He liked getting out with the regional managers and working with those guys. On a number of occasions, we would have employee meetings and Bud would talk to the home office employees. It was so great to have him stand up right in front of you, training and motivating 300 or so people. He would come in three or four times a year and talk about teamwork. His motivation to home office people, to me, and certainly to our clerical people was very important."

If he could work a room, Dad also could motivate an audience of one. Vice president of commercial lines Andy Duvall was personally recruited by Dad to join PMA. "I was working for another insurance company, and PMA was courting me. I was very, very leery because it was much faster company than the conservative type of operation I was used to, much more entrepreneurial than what you find in large corporations. But my company was talking about moving me from Tulsa and I just didn't want to move my youngsters at that time. It was a drug time, and we weren't having any trouble with our kids. We wanted to stay where we were."

Walter Hailey called Duvall and asked him to meet with Dad at the airport in Tulsa on a brief layover Dad would have there. "I thought that was great; I'd get to meet Bud Wilkinson," Duvall says. "I went out and introduced myself and Bud and I had a twenty-five minute chat over coffee in the airport, and I agreed to go to work for him."

After the meeting Duvall phoned his wife. "She said, 'Okay, you're changing jobs. How much are they going to pay you?' I had to say I didn't know. He was so good at recruiting it didn't seem to matter at the time. I just needed to get with that bunch so we could make happen all the things he was talking about. The PMA thing turned out so well for me, and I can't tell you how many times I've tried to use his nuance in business—his great grace and dignity."

Duvall was with Dad at many of his motivational presentations. "He talked about rejection. Most of [the sales] business is rejection. Bud could invigorate those people who were down from hearing 'no' so often. He could kick your butt but still leave it attached. You never lost your dignity or felt like you had been chewed out, but you also felt you should do things differently."

è&

As the company grew, management decided to issue additional shares of stock. Goldman Sachs financial guru, Gus Levy, took the lead position in the public offering. "Levy never took an interest in a company as small as ours, but he decided to do that because of Murchison and Hunt and Wilkinson, and he liked our NEER marketing approach," says Walter Hailey.

Goldman Sachs attempted to bring other brokers to the table. Hailey went to New York to discuss PMA's conceptual and operational aspects, growth and financing with analysts from other brokerage houses. "The first time I went to Wall Street, I went by myself. There was a party for me at the Wall Street Club and seven people showed up. They had two bars and seven people. I told them obviously I had planned on a few more, but I had a little session with those seven."

The next time Hailey returned to Wall Street, he took along Murchison, Hunt, Schenkel and Dad. "This time we had a room that held 300 people, and they were standing out in the halls. I said, 'I believe there's something a little different about my meeting this time.' "

After the initial public offering, Dad traveled to various regions of the country, educating potential stock purchasers about PMA's strengths. It was a young, rapidly growing company, and it was important to show investors that it was a sound, well-run operation.

"I made a lot of those trips with Bud," says Royce Hunter, now chairman of Lone Star Life Insurance Company. "We would go talk with stock brokers across the country and tell them the PMA story about natural existing economic relationships and the three-legged stool—influence, money and marketing. He was very influential and helpful."

"He was fascinated by the numbers," says Duvall. "It was amazing how quickly he could assimilate the things we were doing, some of which were fairly original. And then he would say it his way—not quite the way we would say it, but other people would understand it better."

The road trips revealed some other aspects of Dad's character. "He and I were walking through a bank lobby in Minneapolis," says Hunter, "and we were in a hurry to make a meeting . . . and there was this elderly black gentleman standing by the doors. You could tell that he recognized Bud and wanted to go over to him, but he just inched out a little bit. Bud noticed that, and he stopped and put down his briefcase and walked over and said, 'Hi, I'm Bud Wilkinson.' You could see it just made that guy's day. That's where I got my first indication that there was a lot more to Bud than what you saw on television."

Andy Duvall went with Dad on a trip to Michigan. "One thing I remember about that trip was how people just melted. Opening a door was unbelievably easy if you used his name. The other thing I recall is that we got hooked up with Duffy Daugherty. It went on until 1:00 in the morning, and I had to almost crawl back to my hotel room, I was so drunk. Those two just continued on. Bud and I had an early flight the next morning. I got up and felt like death warmed over and I must have looked that way, too. I went down to the lobby, checked out, and here was Bud sitting in the restaurant having a cup of coffee, and he'd already run a mile. He was twenty years older than me."

Under Dad's leadership, PMA rose like a helium balloon. "When we first issued shares of Lone Star," says Hunter, "it was trading around $10-$12 per share, sometimes as low as $8. In the two years between the time they put all the companies together into PMA and the time PMA went public, the stock jumped from $10 to $42 per share. The public offering was $34."

The year after PMA went public, it was the most actively traded over-the-counter stock in the country. The 1972 annual report indicated a thirty-three percent increase in total revenue. Naturally, this growth attracted potential suitors for the company, and in 1973, the S.S. Kresge Company, with its K-Mart, Kresge and Jupiter stores, came to the front. By 1974, Kresge and PMA were merged, with Kresge exchanging 9/10 of a share of its stock for each of PMA's 2,110,000 shares.

It appeared to be a perfect match. K-Mart's chief retailing rival, Sears, had purchased Allstate and begun to retail insurance products. PMA's business philosophy was similar to Kresge's. As Walter Hailey reported to the employees, "We're discounters and mass marketers of insurance; they're discounters and mass marketers of merchandise. We think alike. We're expense conscious. Our management philosophy is very conservative . . . ."

Walter Teninga, Kresge vice president and chief financial officer, was equally upbeat. Quoted in the TIPS newsletter, Teninga said, "[Kresge] started our studies of insurance for diversification back in 1962. We could have bought a number of companies considerably larger . . . but we did not see in other companies the people we saw in PMA. And people is what it is all about." One of the people K-Mart saw was Dad.

"Bud was a super salesman," says Hunt. "He was solely the one who sold Planned Marketing to K-Mart."

Of course, Hunt's statement is not entirely accurate. The sales process was complex and included numbers of financial and business people from both sides, but Dad certainly was involved from the beginning.

When the afterglow of the merger began to wear off, it became clear that perhaps this deal had not been made in heaven, after all. "If I had it to do over again," says Bernard Carrico, Walter Teninga's assistant, "I would like to have spent a lot more time prepping the K-Mart group about all the nuances of insurance accounting and product profitability, because had the benefit of all that knowledge been well cemented, the communications problems that began to occur . . . probably would have been handled in a different fashion. To get everything done in a ninety-day period is, in fact, too quick. You need to do things a little slower."

"Retailing," Carrico continues, "is pretty much retailing, but this was so foreign, it was difficult. [I think PMA got into the deal] to latch onto the premier retail distribution company in the United States. PMA had a unique distribution system, and to be in line with a company that was distribution oriented made sense."

But, adds Eubank, "Retailer mentality is really totally different from insurance."

"K-Mart, for what they wanted to do with it, in retrospect, bought the wrong company," says Hunter. "They should have bought a much bigger company, probably one with a bigger field force .... They bought a specialty company with a specialty field force."

Whatever the reasons for the problems with the merger, the dreams of the parties involved were not realized, and the insurance companies eventually were sold back.

By this time, however, Dad had moved on to other ventures.

ﻉﻟ

Throughout his association with PMA, Dad was still in broadcasting as well, and it was on a broadcasting trip that his life took a most unexpected turn. In East Lansing for a Michigan State game, he met Donna O'Donnohue. An active alumna of MSU, she had once run for the board of trustees, a race she did not win, but one that brought her to the attention of the Michigan Secretary of State, Richard Austin. He appointed her his assistant, the first woman to hold such a position in the state of Michigan.

With their mutual interest in politics, she and Dad hit it off immediately. Two weeks later, the broadcast team returned to Michigan, and Dad met Donna again. It was the beginning of the relationship that would lead to my parents' divorce and Dad's marriage to Donna.

The divorce was out of character for Dad and a shock to everyone, including Dad and Mom's most intimate friends. In hindsight, however, it is evident Dad was changing. He had lost the Senate race and his inner circle status in Washington. He had begun a new career in business. Pat and I were grown and on our own. Dad had the freedom to choose a new path without consideration for younger children.

The choice, however, was agonizing for everyone. There was a vast age difference between Dad and Donna, and Dad knew what a divorce would do to his image and reputation as a family man and national exemplar. He was grieved, felt guilty and was very concerned about Mom. On a few occasions he and I spent time sitting together in the car, while he sobbed out his remorse and pain about what he was doing.

There was no denying the attraction Donna held for him, however. Her youth, her intellectual curiosity, her energy and vitality were what he wanted, and so, thirty-seven years to the day after their marriage, Dad and Mom were divorced, and in 1976, slightly more than a year after the divorce, Dad and Donna were married. From that time until he became seriously ill, they worked and traveled together, both nationally and internationally.

ta.

With the PMA sale completed, Dad had more time to devote to broadcasting and clinics—and to Donna—but another business opportunity came his way, and once again, boldly moving into a leadership position with a small business, he helped propel the company from relative obscurity to predominance in its field. The company was Public Employees Benefit Services Corporation (PEBSCO), founded by David Davenport. PEBSCO specialized in deferred compensation products for public employees, who until the '70s had been unable to avail themselves of retirement programs such as IRAs and 401(k) or 403(b) plans. In the early part of the decade, a few political jurisdictions petitioned the IRS for approval of such plans for their public employees. Other states, counties and cities jumped aboard, and by the mid-'70s, public employees began to have access to voluntary, supplemental, tax-deferred pension plans.

"I first met Bud in 1970 or 1971 when I was traveling back from Detroit to Washington," says Davenport. "He'd been with Duffy at one of the Coach of the Year Clinics. I had just set up a company that manufactured blazers we were selling to universities. That year, Chuck Fairbanks was head coach at Oklahoma, and we had just sold the University of Oklahoma's team an entire outfit of blazers and slacks. The year before, we'd had a blazer sales program with the OU Alumni Association . . . . I was telling Bud about it on the plane, and he said we should try to sell them through the Coach of the Year clinics. He immediately saw the marketing potential."

Dad, Daugherty and Davenport became partners in Sports Marketing Associates, Davenport's sports attire company. "We became very successful," says Davenport. "One year later, however, the NCAA issued a ruling that universities could not buy travel outfits for their teams, because the rich university had an advantage over the poor, and it was intimidation . . . . Bud was furious."

Some years later, Davenport moved to Oklahoma City. "Bud was active with PMA at the time," Davenport recalls. "I began PEBSCO in 1973, and I had finally gotten it going about 1974. For some reason, Bud and I began talking . . . . PEBSCO was not a reality by a long shot when I first started talking with him about it. There were a lot of legal and regulatory headaches. Sometimes I was really down and had a negative attitude about it. It was going well enough that I wanted to do it, but I wasn't really sure I was doing the right thing."

Dad and Davenport talked often. "As we became friends, I was less awed by him, but he still really gave me a lot of inspiration and confidence to go forward despite the problems. I don't think there would have been a PEBSCO without Bud . . . . I was many times in the state of mind to say the hell with it. The price is too great, the pain is too intense, the odds are too great. He was my inspiration and kept me going when I did not want to go on . . . . He was so very, very positive about it."

Dad came on the PEBSCO board as chairman. "Bud believed deeply in the fundamental idea behind PEBSCO, which was to give public employees the same kinds of investment benefits private industry provided for its corporate executives. It allowed hard-working public employees to take personal responsibility for their own financial futures."

In addition, Davenport says, "I felt that Bud more than anybody I've ever known just radiated personal integrity. His integrity and reputation were unquestioned. I thought if I could get Bud involved . . . it would enhance PEBSCO's corporate reputation."

It worked. "Every place we went," Davenport remembers, "he was always met and respected." That respect went both ways. "I never heard him say a bad word about anybody. When we got the short end of a business deal, he didn't have any problem telling me someone was a dumb SOB, but on a personal basis, we'd be somewhere, and people would come up and want his autograph or to talk about football, I never saw him anything but gracious, and I never saw him anything but genuine . . . . He never put on a public performance. He was genuine with everyone, and that was one of the things that made him the great leader he was. People could sense that he had a genuine respect for everybody—cab driver, waitress, or whatever."

Dad's reputation and people sense became critical to PEBSCO's success, because in 1977, the IRS, which was having trouble coping with the sheer volume of governmental voluntary supplemental plans they were being asked to approve, put an indefinite hold on all further approvals of such plans.

With PEBSCO's ability to expand sidetracked, Dad left the day-to-day world of business to take a position as head coach of the St. Louis Cardinals. But, says Davenport, Dad was available whenever the company needed his help. "He was always willing to take his one day off and go help me do something," Davenport says, "especially when we were working on the Tax Act of 1978 and trying to get the bill approved. Being a tax bill, it had to originate in the House Ways and Means Committee. There was a young congressman from St. Louis named Dick Gephardt, a Democrat, on the Ways and Means Committee. Bud was a pretty well-known Republican, but nonetheless he went with me to Washington to meet with Gephardt and his assistant. And it was his personal job to let them know he appreciated Gephardt's help. I may be dead wrong, but I bet you a buck Bud made a couple of appearances for Gephardt, who was very helpful to us.

"Somewhere along about that time, some guy wrote a smart ass news article about how Bud had taken the Cardinals job because everything was going against him," Davenport goes on. "His divorce, the new marriage, the company was in dire financial straits and so on. This guy said the only thing that could save the company would be an act of Congress. Bud was absolutely never daunted by that, and he gave me the kind of support as a partner to take it on. He really believed we could win. We did win—[with an act of Congress] that got PEBSCO going again."

The United States Conference of Mayors chose PEBSCO to establish their deferred compensation program. "In those days," says former executive director, John Gunther, "city governments didn't have much guidance in this field. They went out and contracted with whomever they wanted . . . . All of us had the idea that we ought to be helping them out. It was an ideal opportunity."

Roy Orr was president of the National Association of Counties (NACo) when NACo decided to establish a deferred compensation program for its member counties. Davenport met Orr when Orr was a commissioner in Dallas County. "Dave came into our offices and started talking about deferred compensation . . . . It got my attention, but it took awhile to sell the other commissioners because they weren't too interested in it when [they had] roads to patch and bridges to build . . . but Bud, as far as I'm concerned, pepped me up, because it gave instant credibility . . . . Bud wouldn't be associated with anything that wasn't first class. There were a thousand people out there selling deferred compensation, but I knew of his credibility and notoriety for being a straight shooter."

When NACo chose PEBSCO to administer their deferred compensation program, Richard Conder, then NACo's first vice president and today the majority leader of the North Carolina Senate, recalls, "We were debating between PEBSCO and another company. We elected to come back to Oklahoma City to learn a little bit more about PEBSCO . . . . Going out there I found PEBSCO had a real good track record, and they had a company with management and principles, with unquestioned integrity."

Orr adds, "In athletics, if you don't have your credibility, you lose your football players. If you don't have credibility in politics, you lose your constituents. One person can make a difference, and I think Bud Wilkinson made the difference between the NACo program being successful or just average."

PEBSCO, though it was a small company, was able to compete against industry giants, and began to take its place in the market. Nationwide Corporation became interested in PEBSCO and acquired the company in 1982. Peter Frenzer, currently president of Nationwide Life Insurance Company, says, "It was a new business, we thought it was an interesting business . . . and that the pension business was going to explode. As we got into it, we got more and more intrigued and convinced . . . we could provide not just the underwriting or the back office . . . but somehow get together and do the administration —streamline it.

The best way to do that was to buy it. PEBSCO was so successful it was going to drown itself in paper, and the people who were trying to administer it weren't used to managing paper flows . . . and we knew how to do it. It allowed us to make a real business out of it."

Frenzer adds, "Our major decision was a willingness to put up some money for a great idea. Dave Davenport was an idea guy. I visualized Bud as a venture capitalist . . . . I thought it was quite possible to sell a new concept if you can go with someone with a reputation like his. He was known and he had tremendous credibility throughout his whole career, so it was a big plus."

After the acquisition, Dad retired from his active role in PEBSCO, though he assisted in the transition. I became president of the company at that time, and eventually, all operations were moved from Oklahoma City to Columbus, Ohio, the home office of Nationwide. Today, PEBSCO generates almost $1 billion per year in cash contributions from more than 500,000 employees in 4500 cities and counties, as well as six state governments.

ᨠ

Without question, Dad was successful in business, and he took a considerable degree of pleasure in his business career. It was his last business activity, the presidency of the United States Gymnastics Federation, that provided him with one of the greatest satisfactions of his life. Under his leadership, the federation emerged from a sea of red ink and factionalism to become a streamlined, efficient, self-sufficient body that was finally a player in the international gymnastics arena. And when the Olympic gold medals came to Mary Lou Retton and the U.S. men in 1984, Dad was on top of the world. He loved amateur sports, and he felt privileged to help these outstanding young athletes reach their Olympic dreams.

Board member Bill Roetzhein was instrumental in bringing Dad into the world of gymnastics. "Gymnastics," he says, "had a history of infighting and pettiness. Everyone was trying to hold onto their own little segment of power and not working for the common good of winning Olympic medals and world championships. We needed someone who could ignite the gymnastic community and make them set [common] goals rather than gain individual power, so we could do well at the Los Angeles games, which were two or three years off."

A group of board members brainstormed about a possible president. "In those days," says Roetzhein, "the president had to be chosen from one of our constituent organizations, and it had to be the person named by that organization to the board, which was very limiting. In our brainstorming, we realized the next president couldn't be an insider, because each of those people had their little factions that supported them and people who strongly opposed them. We felt we had to bring in someone of stature, someone who would be respected by everyone, and so with that premise, we threw names on the table. Roger Council was executive director, and he mentioned Bud, whom he knew casually. We, of course, all knew Bud by reputation, and we came to the consensus that this would be the individual who could do it."

Roetzhein called Dad and asked him if he would be interested in serving and flew to St. Louis to brief him on the challenges facing gymnastics. Because the president had to come from the board of a constituent organization, Roetzhein and Dad scanned the list to see if Dad had an affiliation with any of the constituent groups. When they came to the YMCA, they had a match. Dad had led a very successful national fundraising drive for the Y. The man who was representing the Y on the board graciously stepped aside to allow Dad to take his place, and at the next board meeting, Dad, by unanimous vote, was elected president of the USGF.

In his new position, Dad brought his business savvy to the operations of the federation. He divided the job into manageable segments and tackled each in turn.

Dad dealt first with factionalism. "The approach he took," says Roetzhein, "was to sell the board on the idea that though they might not think Olympic medals affected their personal bailiwicks, they actually did. If we were world champions or Olympic champions, the press we would garner would help club owners, general gymnastics programs, Special Olympics—everybody. It was a trickle-down effect."

Next he turned his attention to the day-to-day operations of the federation. Mike Jacki, who soon became executive director, recalls, "After Bud had been in office a number of months, he realized it was going to be necessary to make some pretty broad-based changes. In his discussions with the executive committee, it was decided they would seek out a new executive director." It was a ticklish situation. "Roger Council, who was executive director at the time, was Kurt Thomas' coach and a wonderful person," says Jacki. "Roger had a doctorate in education and was very, very intelligent, but he was in an environment he just wasn't trained for."

Jacki, however, had been a gymnast at Iowa State and was working at the time for AMF in one of the divisions that manufactured gymnastics equipment. AMF, of course, had been one of the principal underwriters of the Lifetime Sports Foundation. "I got a phone call from Bud Wilkinson asking me to come to St. Louis to talk about being the executive director of the USGF. I was just about as excited to go there and talk to Bud Wilkinson as I was about the job itself."

During the interview, says Jacki, "He had a demeanor about him that brought a lot of enthusiasm out of the other person. Just something about his eyes and the way he looked at you, and he always had a smile. I remember asking myself as I was leaving, how he could possibly have gotten results out of football players? I always felt a football coach was a guy who says, 'Get in there and hit 'em,' and he was so incredibly compassionate and very personal."

When Jacki accepted the position, Dad called him and Council together for a meeting. "He made both of us very comfortable," says Jacki. "He said, 'Look, we're not kicking anybody out. This is just a change that needs to be made. Roger, you and I are going to work out something, but I want you to lend your support where it's needed.' He created a very nice working environment and it went very well. In fact, Roger was very relieved by the way the whole thing came out. He told me once he couldn't imagine anyone handling it better than Bud did. He dealt with some very sensitive issues and strong personalities, and it worked very, very well."

On the job, Jacki found Dad always in his corner. Jacki was given both the responsibility and authority to do what he was hired to do, and there was a strong supporter in the president's office. "He positioned himself perfectly and made my life not only tolerable during that next year, which was a complicated year, but really put us in a position where we were able to . . . restructure."

One of the earliest restructuring moves was to relocate the headquarters of the federation to Indianapolis. A grant from the Lilly Foundation eased the transition.

"We needed it," says Jacki. "We were in dire financial straits at the time, and they put us in nice office space at a very fair rent. There's no question that Bud's presence and the fact that he ... had taken the initiative in working out relationships with the Indianapolis people made a difference. When we got there, we were already good folks, all based on the relationships he had already created. They had great respect and admiration for him, and that made our lives a lot simpler."

Jacki would need Dad's support as he made his first staff appointment. "One of the first people I hired was a woman," says Jacki. "She was the first female event director, and I immediately got four or five calls from board members .... Bud and I talked about it, and at the board meeting, he was very pointed in saying, 'None of us is in a position to prejudge or make any determinations until we see this person's ability to perform. That's what we're going to base this [hiring] on.' Well, she ended up doing a great job, became assistant executive director and is now executive producer at ESPN.

"Bud and I were on the phone probably once or twice a week, plus a few extra meetings because Bud would come to some of the events. It was incredible how he made himself available."

Once the personnel issues were under control, Jacki and Dad turned to straightening out the financial mess. "First of all, we put together a business and operating plan and a management team that could run the whole thing," recalls Jacki. "By the end of the first year, we had a net income for the first time in four years. We made about $30,000, and in the second year we had a net income of a little over $1 million. We ran it like a business. We improved our membership programs, we went out and sold sponsorships, and we started doing all the other things we should have been doing. We put our debt away and continued to grow the business every year after that."

Dad also helped the USGF take its place on the world stage. "In 1983, he came to the World Championships in France and was there for the International Congress," says Jacki. "He became a good friend and confidant of Yuri Titov, who was president of the international federation. It was fabulous because Yuri was a three-time Olympic champion and secretary of the Soviet Olympic Committee . . . . In Russia, they held their coaches in very high regard, and from that time on, I was so amazed and impressed by Yuri's respect and admiration for Bud. At social functions, when Yuri saw Bud, he'd walk away from whoever he was with ... and shake Bud's hand and tell him how pleased he was to see him."

Social functions were important for cementing good relationships and cooperation within the international gymnastics world. According to Jacki, "Bud said, 'You've got to get them to like you and respect you. You can't keep jamming things down their throats, because they don't like us in the first place. We have to at least come to some common ground.' He and Donna were the perfect host and hostess at all our functions, because they were always so friendly and warm and open to these people. They remembered their names and their families and what their children were doing ... We made a new venture in international goodwill and Bud was very instrumental."

Dad paid for these gatherings and for all the travel expenses he and Donna incurred out of his own pocket, says Roetzhein. "I'm sure not too many people know that. He wanted the money to go to the athletes and for improvement in the program, so he accepted the responsibility of paying his own way."

At the Congress in 1984, the United States elected five members to International Federation committees, four more than had ever been elected before. "I don't think there's any question that Bud and Donna's presence ... and the way they handled these people gained a lot of respect and confidence from the international community," says Jacki.

For Dad, the 1984 Olympics were the crowning achievement. "The men's team gold medal would have happened even if the Russians hadn't boycotted," says Roetzhein. "It just happened we had an unusually fine group of athletes. One way you can tell you have world class athletes is that they invent new skills. If you look in the book from that year, there's the Gaylord 1, the Gaylord 2—there are moves named after athletes from that particular year. And if you look at the competitions leading toward the Olympics, you can see them building toward it, starting with Kurt Thomas."

An interesting side effect from the 1984 success was that the athletes left competitive gymnastics. "Normally," says Roetzhein, "when you're not so successful . . . you retain four athletes out of six or seven, and you add new people to those four. But they were so successful, [they moved on] into careers that were transformed more or less by their Olympic participation."

By 1985, Dad was slowing down a little bit, and multiple commitments were taking their toll. "I knew Bud wanted to stay involved," Jacki says, "but it was really hard for him because he had so many other things . . . He always made the meetings and the calls, and he was always there, but it was something you could tell was a bit of a conflict for him . . . I knew he was giving up other things."

It was time for him to leave the board, but his leaving would throw the organization back into its old ways of doing things—electing a president from the board. He had been able to accomplish what he had because of his more global perspective. He and Jacki were concerned about a return to factionalism. Dad's last act was to help orchestrate a by-laws change that would allow three members of the executive committee to be elected from outside the board, thus opening the office of president to a board member from the public/private sector.

"The next president was Mike Donahue," says Jacki. "He was director of sports marketing for McDonald's. Bud was involved in getting the McDonald's/USGF relationship put together in 1982 and made sure the relationship stayed intact . . . . When I mentioned his name, Bud thought he was a great choice. At the board meeting where we elected Mike, Bud was designated chairman emeritus and actually remained actively involved for a long, long time.

"I think some people had a hard time understanding that someone who didn't come from their sport would have Bud's genuine love and concern for this program and this group of athletes. There was no question that he did."

Donna concurs with Jacki's assessment. "Bud told me that he felt this was one of his finest contributions and one of the finest things he'd ever been involved in. He felt very, very gratified that he was able to get them on a sound financial footing and located in a community where they were appreciated and would be supported."

It was an especially sweet success in a life filled with successes.

# 11

## A Brief Return to Football

꙾

*"Dear Sir, I wish the town had kept you here . . ."*
—*Nemerov*

In the middle of Dad's business career, he unexpectedly returned to coaching. Over the years, there were many offers of coaching positions, but he turned them down, devoting himself to broadcasting, the Coach of the Year Clinics and his other business interests. At the time of his hiring by the St. Louis Football Cardinals, Dad was living in Oklahoma City and serving as chairman of the board of PEBSCO. In 1977, however, when the IRS issued its ruling regarding approvals of additional governmental supplemental pension programs, he suddenly had a great deal of time on his hands. Into the vacuum stepped Cardinals owner Bill Bidwill with an offer to coach the team. Floyd Warmann, a St. Louis businessman and friend of Dad's, was the messenger who set up the original meetings between Bidwill and Dad.

Warmann says, "I had a public relations firm in St. Louis with Willie Zalkin; Bob Hyland, who was vice president of CBS and general manager of KMOX radio; and his son and his brother . . . . Bill Hyland kind of brought the Cardinals into the PR firm. Bidwill ran into trouble with Coach Don Coryell. I knew he was looking for a coach and he was looking for a name. The press was running against him with Coryell leaving.

"Bidwill came to me and asked me if I had any ideas. So I thought for a day or so and there was only one person on my mind. I thought, 'Dare I ask him?' I saw Bud shortly after that. I said, 'Billy's looking for a coach, one that's respected and one that can pull the team together, someone who has great personality, great drive, and great motivational powers. There's nobody now in that state of chaos, and they've lost a coach they liked very much. There's nobody I could think of other than you.' "

Dad asked to think about it and said he would not ask for the job. Bidwill would have to come to him. Warmann conveyed the message.

"Bidwill just looked at me and said, 'He wouldn't come out of retirement, would he?' and said he'd like to talk to Bud very much."

Because neither Bidwill nor Dad wanted to be seen talking about the position, they met at a restaurant in Washington, D.C., along with Donna and Warmann. As the evening wore on, Warmann left, and Dad and Donna remained to converse with Bidwill.

Donna recalls, "Floyd arranged a meeting and the subject came up in more of a jocular way, except that Bud got really excited about it . . . . Bud felt Billy would call, and when we returned home, Billy did call. The deal itself did not take too long to do."

After the agreement was inked, Warmann says, "Bidwill brought Bud to town. Bob Hyland, who had the No. 1 radio station and who fed the network, was going crazy . . . and I didn't even tell his brother or anyone else anything except that I was helping Bill find some personnel. They put two and two together, and I told them I was sworn to secrecy and I couldn't talk to anybody.

"So Bidwill sneaked Bud and Donna into town," Warmann continues, "and Hyland was looking frantically, frantically. All this time, he'd been talking to Bidwill on the phone, and Bidwill kept whistling *Boomer Sooner*, but Hyland never caught it . . . . Of course, I wouldn't have caught it either. *Boomer Sooner* is not a popular song. Anyway, Bidwill was laughing about it . . . . He said, 'I'm going to lock you in your room tonight. I don't want you out of this hotel, and I don't want you telling Hyland. I want everyone to have an even break at this.' . . . He had my phone shut off."

ﾞﾑ

It had been fourteen years since Dad had organized a depth chart, run a drill or walked a sideline. Nevertheless, he was more prepared to return to coaching than many people thought. The Coach of the Year Clinics kept him in touch with evolutions in the game, as did watching so many teams from the broadcast booth. He took on the challenge of the Cardinals in 1978.

Doug Grow, a sportswriter for the *St. Louis Post-Dispatch* recalls hearing of Dad's new position. "Billy called all the media to come over to Trader Vic's. He was going to have a press conference to name the new coach. He was like a kid with a new toy . . . . Nobody could figure it out. It was a tremendously well-kept secret. Nobody could break the story . . . . Billy loved nothing more than putting one over on the media. It's funny, he gets more focused on that kind of stuff than he does on whether the team is in the playoffs or not. He was just thrilled because he had tricked us all.

"He was also particularly mad at the *Globe Democrat* because Rich Koster had been taking some brutal shots at Bidwill and the Cardinal organization . . . . Bidwill set up the press conference so it would be for an afternoon release—it would be for the *Post-Dispatch*. I got to come into the room in advance. There sits Bud Wilkinson, and I couldn't believe it. Billy says, 'Here's our new football coach.' I was just dumbfounded."

Grow wasn't the only one. The players were astonished, says Roger Wehrli, an all-pro defensive back who started with the Cardinals in 1969 and who by 1978 had endured several coaching changes.

"It was a complete surprise," says Wehrli. "We had run through a few different coaches and everyone really liked Coryell. He left in kind of an uproar with the ownership, with Mr. Bidwill. There were a lot of rumors about different people, and then when Bidwill announced that Bud had been named as head coach, it really took everybody by surprise. Usually all the rumors start about the coaches who are out of work . . . and then they start looking to college and pro coaches that have recently been let go or are between jobs. Of course, Bud wasn't in the rumor mill."

Some members of the media were very vocal about their lack of belief in Dad's ability to pilot the team. College football was one thing, but wasn't this guy too old and too soft for the pros? And he'd been away for so long. *Sports Illustrated* jeered, "Ladies and gentlemen, step right up and have a look. All the management asks is that you don't breathe too hard on the body." March 2, 1978, the day he came on board, was the moment, the magazine said, "the tomb was opened." There was tabloid-type speculation that he had accepted the position to impress Donna, to prove that he was still a young man who could hold his own in a young man's game, or that he was like some old war horse who couldn't stand being away from football.

Some players agreed with their media counterparts. One of the loudest voices was that of center Tom Banks. He told reporters, "Insanity prevails."

Dad dealt with these doubts in the only way he knew how—directly and face to face. He and Donna flew to Alabama to talk with Banks.

"I remember they were staying at the Hilton in Birmingham," says Banks. "We went to breakfast, and . . . he asked me quite candidly what he had gotten himself into."

Banks painted a dismal portrait of the Cardinal management team. "I said, 'Coach, I don't know who you've talked to, but this is a mess you're getting into . . . .' It's funny, we had just gotten through our meal and we were sitting around and the news came over the TV that Terry Metcalf had just signed with a Canadian team. I looked at Coach and said, 'That's the kind of thing you're getting into.' "

Metcalf had been the Cardinals' all-pro running back— their go-to guy, but Bidwill had allowed him to play out his option and refused to increase his compensation; he also had traded all-pro guard Conrad Dobler and wide receiver Ike Harris.

"I didn't want to put a damper on his enthusiasm," says Banks. "I wanted him to know that those are the kinds of things you had to deal with; I wanted him to understand where I was coming from."

Dad also spent a great deal of time talking with all-pro fullback Jim Otis. "When Bud moved to St. Louis," he says, "he called me up and just wanted to chew the fat a little . . . . I was real excited that we'd gotten a coach of his caliber and that he would call to talk to me. I was just so impressed . . . . Most coaches took a little time with you as you went to camp, but this was substantially ahead of camp.

"One thing I remember," Otis says, "is that we talked about the team and the organization. I think he'd heard from other people in town about . . . the way the ownership wanted to manage the team and everything. The one thing he said to me was, 'I think I can get this thing turned around.' I'd been around a while and I knew what Bidwill was all about, but you know, when I left Bud that day, I thought maybe he *could* do it. I knew under the present ownership it would be pretty hard . . . but I never remember Bud Wilkinson saying, thinking or indicating anything negative."

ôa.

Going in, then, Dad knew he had two major problems. The first was control. Though Dad was permitted to control things on the field, Bidwill stage managed all other operations, including the draft.

Roger Wehrli says, "As the guys talked, we were surprised he would come into a situation that over the years had been kind of a coaching graveyard . . . where the coaches would come in and try to build something, and especially the way Coryell left, with the big hubbub of wanting to control more of the draft choices and have a little more say as to the players he put on the field. He wanted more input so he could build a cohesive unit over a period of years. That's pretty much the reason he left. Bud was coming into a situation where the same pattern had been replayed three times since I'd been here.

"Look at most of the successful coaches," Wehrli points out. "Look at Shula, Bud Grant . . . . I think they had a lot of input into the draft and they pretty much ran the show, even though in some cases the owners were pretty visible . . . . When it comes to on-the-field decisions, the coach needs to have serious input . . . but Bidwill wants control. He wants to have the last say on everything."

All-pro Dan Dierdorf says, "In those days the Cardinal coach had no input into the draft at all. George Boone ran the draft and that was just the way it was. Don Coryell knew he had a potent offensive team, and if we were ever going to get over the hump, it had to be by improving the defense . . . . Unbelievably on draft day in 1977, George Boone selects Steve Pisarkiewicz, the quarterback . . . . With Jim Hart in the prime of his career, they draft Steve. Don Coryell went up like a bottle rocket. It was the beginning of the end of the Coryell regime. That's the way it was when Bud was there, too."

Says former Dallas Cowboys coach Tom Landry, "It was impossible for Gene Stallings when he went to coach at St. Louis and couldn't scout anybody or make a trade or make a choice of who they were going to pick. You can't win at football if you're sitting there and letting someone else do all the picking of the personnel."

Sportscaster Jack Buck adds another perspective. "Billy got a great deal of name value when he hired Bud, but then he put him in a bad spot because of the way the club was administered, with Bill at the top and George Boone in the middle. The coach had no input. It can't be that way. It simply can't. The coach has to have some degree of input. Bud just walked into this shell and was trapped from the beginning. I don't think he stood a chance from the day he came in there. I like Bill. I get along well with him. I think I understand him. I know he tries to be a nice person, and sometimes he just can't pull it off. That's not a criticism. That's just the way he is."

Not only did Bidwill's coaches have little or no say regarding personnel, but they also had to contend with the owner's penny pinching, and most serious, says Donna, they had to deal with "the issue of how people were being treated." Player morale was Dad's second major problem.

According to Dierdorf, "We had dislodged the Cowboys as division champs. We won the division in '74 and '75; we barely missed in 1976. All of a sudden . . . with three consecutive winning seasons, we just exploded. You take Terry Metcalf and you take Don Coryell and you take Dobler, and you subtract those three guys from the mix and you have great trouble . . . . Then Billy goes out and hires Bud. In a matter of a couple of months, we went . . . from being real contenders in the NFL to a team in total chaos. We were just in shambles."

As a unit, the team was obviously in trouble, but individual players were having their problems with management, as well.

Veteran quarterback Jim Hart tells of the times he tried to get Bidwill even to acknowledge his presence. "When I was younger and would pass him in the hall, I was respectful and would say, 'Good morning, Mr. Bidwill.' One morning I passed him and said, 'Good morning,' and he said, 'Is it?' The next time he'd grunt or just say nothing at all. When I got a little older and a little more brash, I'd try other methods. I'd say, 'Hi, Bill,' or even try 'Billy.' Still couldn't get anything from him. So I gave up trying to talk to him. I just thought I'd speak to him if he spoke to me, and go about my business. That was pretty much it."

Jim Otis had similar dealings with Bidwill. "I had led the league in rushing and I was trying to save face. I wanted to receive a much higher salary than what I was being offered .... I didn't want more money than anybody, I just wanted money that was equal to what other people were getting who were doing what I was doing. Of course, when you lead the league, that means no one else *is* doing what you're doing. All I wanted was to elevate my salary to a decent number."

The salary negotiations didn't go well, and Otis faced the fact he wasn't going to get the money he felt he deserved. "We got down to $2500, and I said, 'I'll tell you what. We'll make a deal, but you'll have to buy $2500 worth of t-shirts and hand them out to guys during the summer, and write Eastern Divisional Champs on them, so every kid on the team can have three t-shirts, and it would be something they could see all the time .... It would be like a springboard for us.' It was just kind of a face-saving idea, and it would have been great for the team. They wouldn't do it."

Hart and Bidwill tangled over similar low-ticket items. "I went to him one year in the early '70s because I was doing a lot of speaking engagements and the kids in the audience would want memorabilia—individual or team pictures or decals—things like that. I'd go to the public relations office and say, 'Could I get some pictures to take to the banquet tonight?' and they'd give me six. I'd say, 'You know there are going to be 300-400 people there; if you could give me maybe 150-200 for the kids.' They'd tell me they only kept a dozen on hand."

Hart approached Bidwill, who said he would authorize Hart to have a picture made to use for his own purposes, but he'd have to pay for prints himself. "Back then you couldn't get them reproduced for the money we were making. I wasn't going to go out there and buy 1,000 of them with my own money."

Later in the '70s Bidwill relented and had color photos made of the team. "True to his tightwad image, however," Hart says, "Hamiltonian Federal Savings and Loan and KMOX radio paid for them, and it didn't cost him a cent. Even then we could only get a few hundred apiece."

Team decals also led to bad blood between Hart and Bidwill. "There was a transparent decal," Hart says, "that was reserved for season ticket holders; it had the Cardinal helmet logo on it, and below the helmet it said Season Ticket Holder. I thought they were neat. My stepdad and mom lived in Chicago and used to come to the practices regularly when we were in Lake Forest. I got hold of one of those decals. My dad wanted one so badly, so I gave it to him and he put it in the back window of his car."

One day on the way to practice, Bidwill noticed the decal. Stopping one of the trainers, he asked who the car belonged to. On hearing it was Hart's dad, he instructed the trainer to tell Hart to remove the sticker from the window. They were only for season ticket holders.

"I told the trainer," Hart says, "to tell Bidwill to stick it. The trainer said he couldn't do that. I told him to get Bidwill to come to me and tell me to take it out of the window, and I'd tell him what to do with it."

Picayune squabbles like these were souring the team's morale as fast as Dad was trying to build it up. And Dad's attempts to bring a more businesslike approach to team operations also were looked on with considerable disfavor.

Doug Grow puts his finger on the major issues separating Bidwill and Dad. "It was two people who were just running down two separate tracks. You had Bud, who wanted to run a professional football organization . . . and you had Bill, who wanted to get his ass out of a tight spot. He had gone through that ugly stuff with Coryell . . . and he needed to reclaim his name and reclaim any credibility he had in St. Louis. He had the chance to grab a legend. He did, but he was using it for one purpose and Bud came in with a whole different set of circumstances.

"There are a couple of things that drive Billy," Grow says. "One is he's very wealthy, but I don't think he has the extraordinary wealth of the ownership of the Dallas Cowboys and people like that. He has to have an operation that shows some profit. Second, he has a tremendous sense of history with the National

Football League .... In St. Louis, he wanted to be a loved character, he wanted to be the loved sports owner, but St. Louis already had Gussie Busch ... and beyond that, Billy wasn't able to let go and make the financial commitments he needed to make to make the winning happen ... so he became this angry fellow. He just wouldn't let go of control."

Hart continues, "You kind of had the feeling Bud could have turned things around if he'd been given the chance, but at the same time you knew there was no way Bud was going to wrestle the team away from Bidwill. He's got no identity if you take the team away from him. He's not stupid. Nobody would talk to the man if he didn't have his team. It was frustrating knowing that Bud and his contingent could have really done some great things, but you knew he was whistling in the wind—it wasn't going to be done."

"There were two mistakes that were made," says Dierdorf. "One, I think Billy made a mistake in thinking that after fourteen years Bud could just step right into that situation .... I don't know if you can just flip the switch and go right back into it. Coaching is a full-time, lifetime profession.

"I'm not sure Bud could have taken over a smooth-running ship ... and it was too much to ask when you factor into the equation that it was a fragmented football team and an organization that really didn't cater to the needs of the head coach. I don't know how you could have come up with a worse formula for what Bud attempted to do in 1978 .... The second mistake was that Bud took the job .... I wished he hadn't. I felt for him."

&

The differences in approach between Dad and Bidwill made themselves felt almost immediately. As Donna recalls, "When he first really got involved in finding out what the situation was, to say he was surprised wouldn't really be accurate—that would be to put it mildly. He would come home and say, 'I don't believe this. This is a bad situation.' "

Yet, even with the recipe for disaster sitting in his lap, Dad thought his positive attitude could go a long way toward reconciling Bidwill with his players—that he could build a cohesive unit from the clubhouse to the field. He couldn't. He became just another coach Bidwill eventually chewed up and spat out.

With his overwhelmingly positive attitude, Dad tried to build bridges between the organization and the players. "Bud was such a team person," Donna says. "You've got to make people feel included and to feel like they have a vested interest in it. That's what we both set out to do . . . . Bud thought . . . as a reasonable man, he could go to Billy and lay things on the table and say, 'We have some problems here. Now how do we solve them?' "

"Bud thought he could talk to Billy," echoes Floyd Warmann, "and be like a father or a brother to Billy, because Billy was a very lonesome person. He thought he might play some kind of a role in Billy's life as more than just a coach—as a friend—but when Billy got into that football stadium, he was a different person than he was socially.

"I think Bud genuinely liked Billy. I think Billy cared for Bud, but when it got down to the stadium, there were deep divisions as to how things were going to be run."

⸙

If he couldn't create immediate rapport with the front office, Dad knew he could at least solidify his team, and he set about doing just that. Jan Otis, Jim's wife, found Dad to be very different from other coaches.

"When I first married Jim," she says, "what I knew about football you could put in your little finger . . . . I didn't have any idea who Bud Wilkinson was, but Jim was excited about him. The first time we had a wives' luncheon, he was there. Of course, all of us were sitting around with our mouths open. We couldn't believe that Bud had come to the thing and was talking to us. He came basically to introduce himself to the wives and to say that he was there if we needed him.

"And, of course, I can remember Donna going out with us . . . we'd go out—just a bunch of girls. There was a real neat closeness, just the way Bud got with his players . . . . Bud and I didn't see each other a lot, but I knew if I called him—and this is a wife, not a player—and said I needed something, there wouldn't be any, 'Well, I don't know about that.' There would have been, 'What do you need and when do you need it?' "

Many players have memories of team get-togethers Dad and Donna arranged. "He loved to have them," Tom Banks says. "Whether it be after a ball game or once during training camp he did a thing where everybody brought their families out, with beer and food and sitting around afterwards. Bud loved to sing. He would bellow it out."

And Dierdorf remembers, "No team anywhere ever had a better rookie show than what we had in St. Louis in Bud's first year. He insisted on participating because he was a rookie coach .... He got right up there in front of the whole team, and we couldn't keep him down. We said, 'Coach, you don't have to do this,' but he said, 'I want to get up there.'

"When he got up and sang 'Oklahoma,' and did the whole thing," Dierdorf laughs, "I was watching and saying, 'Here's a guy who loves life. Here's a guy who enjoys every breath he gets.' He was having a heck of a time. He got up there, with that 'wind sweeping down the plain,' and he had us all in tears laughing."

Banks remembers too. "The first time I was really around him in this type of environment, he got up and was standing on a chair and belted out 'Oklahoma.' I thought, 'This man's great.' That's lodged in my memory forever. I really enjoyed that part of it."

Dad's concern for the Cardinals extended not just to the team as a whole, but also to individual players and their families. That concern sometimes brought him right into Bidwill's sights.

Bob Pollard, who came to the Cardinals from the New Orleans Saints in the Dobler trade, got to St. Louis the same time Dad did.

"The trade was a really big downer for me until I found out Bud was going to be head coach .... I was excited about that and about the fact that he was a new coach, someone who was probably going to be fair and let me display my talents. But he was more than a coach. He was a person who cared for you, not just as a player, but as an individual. He wanted to see everybody succeed ... and he helped you wherever he could and always had something encouraging to say.

"But," Pollard goes on, "It didn't take me long to find out the type of team it was going to be .... It seemed like the management of the team did everything they possibly could to discourage the players. One of the things Bud did was take on management about the clubhouse facility that was in need of repair. They made a lot of promises to him when he came in that they would improve the club facilities for the players, but by the time he got to his second year, his final year, they hadn't done them."

Dad didn't back down. "He held them to the table on that," Pollard says. He didn't say, 'Well, I'm concerned, but I'm worried about my job. I don't want to be rough with the management.' He didn't do that. He believed in what was right. I think that was the biggest reason he and management began pulling farther and farther apart. They didn't live up to the promises they made to him about the players."

Pollard had an individual problem with the management that Dad also took on. "When I came to the Cardinals," Pollard says, "I had just gone through a divorce, had just built a new home, and I had money that was deferred for the season. After I completed my first year, I really needed the money I had deferred so I could pay the bills back home. I was under a heavy financial burden."

Pollard approached the organization and asked for the money he had deferred. "I would take it through a loan or whatever and pay them back when the deferment came up. They said no way. It really upset me, because that was supposed to have been arranged during my trade . . . . I sat down and talked to Bud about it because he knew I was down. It was like $14,000 that I needed. Bud listened to me and wrote out a check for $14,000, gave it to me and said, 'Here, you pay me back next season.' That saved my life. It saved my home and everything else I had at the time. Without him, I would have lost it. He did some things like that for other people, too . . . . He stood up for the players no matter what. He's the kind of person the players felt comfortable with . . . . Because of his age and character they felt comfortable in talking with him."

Paradoxically, Dad's identification with the players may, in fact, have contributed to some of the on-field problems the team encountered during his tenure. According to Dierdorf, "Bud was almost too nice a guy. I think he thought that because it was the NFL, these guys had achieved enough . . . that they would know what was best for them and how to do it and that they would do it properly.

"Athletically," Dierdorf says, "pro athletes are so far superior to everybody else that even without a dedication to the game and without tremendous motivation, they are still good enough to play in the NFL. You had to prod and cajole and browbeat and push and shove these people sometimes even more than a college kid. I think it took Bud a while to figure that out because you don't believe it. You don't believe guys who are getting paid to play don't remember their assignments or they don't bother to study their playbook .... I think it opened his eyes; I think it blind-sided him."

è

Not only was Dad different from Bidwill, but he was also different from Coryell, and the players had to adjust to a new style of coaching. Because Dad knew his players would need time to get used to him, he tried to make the transition as easy as possible. He kept coaches Jim Hanifan, Coryell's right hand man, and Harry Gilmer, and he made only a few changes in the playbook.

"When Bud came in," says Hart, "[fear of change] was part of the anxiety on our part. Usually, whenever you have a coaching change, a system will change drastically as well—numbering systems, play calling, whatever .... The first calming influence Bud imparted to us was that he was new to the pro game and that we had had a successful offensive scheme. He wasn't going to change what we'd been used to. He said it was much easier for him to change, being just one person, than it was for forty guys to change."

Next Dad added assistant coaches such as Tom Bettis, Pete Elliott, Freddie Glick, Rudy Feldman, and Jerry Thompson and retained scouts Bo Bolinger and Stan West. He installed the 3-4 defense used by the majority of teams in the league and whose prototype, the Oklahoma 5-2, he had invented.

Though he kept Coryell's playbook, Dad's style of coaching was completely his own. Fullback Steve Jones says, "Coryell was so enthusiastic, energetic, jumping up and down and yelling and screaming. Bud was so low key, and kept his poise about him. I liked his positive attitude and his businesslike approach to the game."

After Dad had his eyes opened to the realities of working with pro players, those who mistook his laid-back, gentlemanly demeanor as weakness were soon disabused of that idea. "He was the ultimate velvet hammer," says Jim Otis. "He treated people with a lot of respect, but if they didn't react, if they didn't know what they were supposed to do, they were gone. Players knew that after a while. I think a lot of players, especially at our level, when they first met Bud . . . weren't sure he was tough enough. Well, they found out just where he was coming from."

A few of the players didn't know where he was coming from when it came to his pre-game talks, however. Jones says, "Coryell would be so excited, and Bud would be quoting some philosopher or admiral or something."

"Every coach has their own style," says Roger Wehrli, "but his was to bring in something he had experienced over his many years in coaching—the diverse life he had had and could talk about."

That kind of inspirational talk was lost on some players. "I used to enjoy the speeches on Saturday night," says Jim Hart. "They weren't profound stories; they were stories that he shared of how these great people shared with him. It was history. I found it very, very interesting. So many of the younger guys went, 'Oh, here we go again.' It was difficult because they would look at me and try to get me to break up . . . I'm trying to play both sides. I don't want them to think I'm a company man—I need to be with the players—but I'm also terribly interested in what the coach is trying to say and I'm kind of pissed off that he's trying to get them to use their heads, and all they're doing is saying, 'What the hell is he talking about now?' There was something behind what he was trying to say, and they just didn't get it."

Dan Dierdorf, too, says Dad's talks sometimes fell on deaf ears. "He took such an intellectual approach to everything that he was talking on a different plane than where a lot of the guys were. Half the guys in the room didn't know what the heck he was talking about."

ⱥ

No matter how good or bad his relationship was with his team or the management, Dad's job was to win football games, and the beginning of his first season was a coach's worst dream come to life. The team's record over the previous five years had been 42-27, and before the Coryell situation blew up, the Cardinals previous 7-7 season had started out at 7-1. However, says Doug Grow, "What you have to do objectively is to point out that the Cardinals, clear back to their Chicago roots, traditionally have been a second division team. When Bud came in, however, the team had come off a couple of decent years. Yet, when you look at it, almost all their winning seasons were filled with games that were won in the last seconds."

It was the era of the Cardiac Cardinals, but as Grow points out, "All of those winning seasons, retrospectively, could have been losing seasons, too. They were doing it with mirrors for a while."

And by 1978, Metcalf was gone, Harris was gone, Dobler was gone. The team, according to *Time* magazine, had a "peculiarly brittle winning record, one inclined to snap around playoff time." Tight end J. V. Cain, a talented athlete from whom the Cardinals were expecting a great deal, was sidelined with a ruptured Achilles tendon. Though he was rehabilitating himself as rapidly as possible, he would not return to playing status until 1979. As Washington Redskins running back Mike Thomas put it, "When we played the Cardinals [in 1978], you had to prepare for Terry Metcalf, J.V. Cain, Ike Harris, Mel Gray, Jim Otis, Jim Hart, and their offensive line. Terry, J.V. and Ike are gone. No matter what their management says, that hurts."

The Cardinals began the season with eight straight losses. The defeats were stomach-wrenching, says Dierdorf. "When you're 0-8, it's equivalent to being a baseball team and being winless at the All-Star break—being 0-82 at the All-Star break."

In hindsight, the losing streak wasn't terribly surprising. "We were starting to get older," says Tom Banks. "Coach Coryell had caught us on the upswing. We were all kids when he first came in 1973 . . . and we were lucky that coach Coryell came in and brought that young and enthusiastic staff with him. Bud got most of us on the downside."

Additionally, the team was weak in a crucial position—tight end. Cain was unavailable and other ends went down with injuries, too.

"Bud made one glaring change," says Hart, "and that was putting the tight end in the backfield. Putting him in a fullback position and making the defense declare what was the strong side and what was the weak side. We could run from that formation, although it was tough.

"When the tight end declared which side he was going to, then automatically the defense had to declare what's strong and what's weak. We could tell by film or by the first series what the defensive scheme was going to be against that particular formation. It takes a pretty talented team to do that, especially from the tight end position. For that particular scheme, we didn't have the talent.

"For the most part," Hart goes on, "it gave us an advantage, but you needed a Kellen Winslow or a J.V. Cain, and of course one of the reasons Bud came up with it was he was looking to use Cain, who was going to be a Winslow type of end, with all kinds of versatility—big, strong, fast, good hands—what a combination."

Combined with the four defeats that ended the '77 season, the team had lost twelve in a row.

"It was a hell of a thing. We had a tough time," says Banks. "We had been used to a lot of success . . . It was very frustrating. Everybody hung together, and Coach was the stabilizing factor. He was also in good spirits."

"It was really to Bud's credit that there was no finger pointing in the media; there was no blaming anyone else," says Dierdorf. "I was proud of the fact that the team didn't resort to it. It's the easiest thing to do . . . Bud's influence held things together."

"What surprised me," adds Grow, "was Bud's incredible patience. The losing did not outwardly change his approach at all."

Inwardly, however, Dad was churning. "It was stressful," Donna says. "I, of course, was very concerned because it was stressful. Bud wasn't used to losing. Of course, you get all of the negative comments coming from people and you feel pressure from the organization itself. Then, of course, everybody in the press box—meaning Billy's people—could coach better than Bud. It was stressful, but somehow everyone hung together."

Obviously it was a stressful time for the quarterback, too, and Hart was grateful for Dad's calming presence. "I used to look forward to going to the sidelines because I knew that I was going to feel so much better. He just made me feel at ease. You get a little excited about what's happening out there, people not hanging onto the ball or whatever. He could set that aside and he'd say, 'Now, don't worry about a thing. Things will work out.' You just had the feeling he knew what he was talking about."

In view of the losing streak, the press went surprisingly easy on Dad. They seemed to know what the problems were and were slow to lay all the responsibility at the head coach's door. "What was amazing about losing all those games is two things," says Grow. "To most of us in the media, Bud was such a pleasant breath of fresh air, most of us stuck with him pretty well. I think even the fans did. The fans found him so charming and so refreshing that everybody was pulling for him. I think it also pointed out how difficult the whole job was."

The drought was broken in a game with the Eagles in Philadelphia, and during the second half of the season, the Cardinals won six of eight games, finishing the season 6-10. Dad broke down and cried at the Philadelphia win; the players awarded him the game ball. "One of the most pleasant things for me," says Dierdorf, "was being captain of the team. I gave Bud the game ball after the Philadelphia game. That was quite a moment."

"The turnaround [after Philadelphia]," says Grow, "was phenomenal. Remember, by this time, Metcalf, the guy who really opened up their whole offense, was gone. Bud would have loved a player like Metcalf. But here Bud came in with an almost .500 season with a team that was aging, a step slower, and had lost its best athlete—the guy who made it possible for everyone else on that team. Bud had done that."

But at a cost of great frustration. In his entire career Dad had had only one losing season, and he was mystified that he couldn't seem to make any headway with Bidwill. Late in the first season, he and Donna invited Grow and his wife to dinner, and he shared his feelings in detail.

"My guess is," says Grow, "that Bud had tried honesty, charm, graciousness and being a gentleman to try to create the environment he needed. [At that dinner] he just let everything go. He talked about how frustrated he was—and it was all off the record. He had a wonderful way of doing that. He gave you as much rope as he thought he could, and then he'd test you a little bit. He'd say, 'This is off the record.' Actually, on the record he was quite candid and good. But off the record, he would tell you a little bit and if you didn't burn him with that, he'd tell you a little bit more the next time."

What Grow learned in the off-the-record comments was that Dad was considering buying the team. "He just unloaded and talked about what an incredibly frustrating experience it had been and what a jolt and surprise it was not to make things work the way he thought they would when he came in. I don't think Bud came to town expecting to buy the team, but I think midway through the first season he thought the only way to make the thing work was to come up with an ownership group of his own.

"You would have never known on the outside how tormented he was on the inside," Grow says. "He was just crushed. Here he was wearing his gray suits and business ties and looking like a company executive, but beneath all that was the heart of an athlete and a competitor. When he saw he couldn't compete, it was just tearing his guts up."

֍

However, as was his style, Dad looked forward to the next year, with the addition of O.J. Anderson, Theotis Brown and Thomas Lott to the Cardinal lineup. He especially relished the prospect of working with a healthy J.V. Cain.

Then Fate dealt the cruelest card. Cain, who had rehabilitated his ankle and body to the point that he was in the best shape of his life, died suddenly on the practice field during summer camp. It was a horrible blow to the team, both personally and professionally.

"I was standing right next to him," says Jim Otis. "It was just a little curl by the tight end, and I was running a little swing, and I saw J.V. He dropped the pass. He came walking back to the huddle and all of a sudden his arms went out and he went straight back. I thought he was screwing around—making a big deal out of missing the pass. That was it. He was dead on the field."

"An awful, awful experience," says Hart. "I remember the play vividly—5-60-5 Stop. Normally the tight end is a primary receiver. You look to the tight end and check the prospects of the tight end and to either the strong side or the weak side, and I think I remember throwing it downfield . . . . But the play ended and we turned to walk back to the huddle and I heard this big thud. I turned to look and he violently went down, like someone shot him . . . . He never regained consciousness.

"Bud handled it just like you would have expected, with the calming influence he exhibited as a coach on the field during a heated game. Just in complete control."

According to newspaper accounts, Dad and the players prayed on the field as the paramedics and doctors worked in vain to revive Cain. Though autopsy results were inconclusive, it appeared Cain had succumbed to some sort of cardiac arrhythmia.

The next day, says Otis, Dad moved into high gear to make sure the team could be present for Cain's funeral. "Bud got involved with the St. Louis community right away. He knew people. After he was here one year, he knew more people than most people meet and know if they've been in a town for ten years.

"Within hours of J.V.'s death, he had arranged for several corporate jets to take us down to Houston for J.V. and his family . . . . We went down and paid our last respects, did the pall bearing, and were back in town later that afternoon. I think we practiced that night. He didn't do it because we were such important people. He did it because he thought it was awfully important for us to be at that funeral and to be with that family, but it was also important for us not to skip a step with regard to practice."

As he was an exceptional athlete, Cain's death brought not only emotional pain, but also the practical problem of how to replace his services on the field.

"Everyone in the locker room knew we desperately needed a tight end," says Dierdorf. "The Cardinals made no attempt to go out and get a quality tight end. We were doomed without one. We had no chance. It's like every day went by, and we were waiting for them to make a move to get a tight end and it didn't happen."

The team wanted to bring back Jackie Smith, who had not been invited to camp the previous year and had not been picked up elsewhere.

"Bud and I had a conversation." says Hart. "He said, 'This is what I'm thinking. I'm going to approach Bidwill and say that the best thing for us to do is to invite Jackie Smith back. He's not been picked up, he's still out there, and you and I know he's in the best shape of his life, waiting for someone to call. What better situation than this?' I said, 'That's the greatest thing that could be done.' Bidwill wouldn't do it—no ifs, ands or buts.

"That was the second slap—the tragedy being number one, but now you have an opportunity to pick up the slack and to rally around and to bring back Jackie, who was let go. And then, no."

It was a costly mistake, says Roger Wehrli. "Smith was available and Bidwill wouldn't pick him up. Then, like a week or two later, one of the main tight ends from the Dallas Cowboys went down with a broken leg, and Dallas picked up Jackie the next day. He helped them get to the Super Bowl that year. Think of the morale boost it would have been to the players and to the community to have had the owner bring Jackie back that year."

Before the 1979 season began, there was one more painful duty—the retirement of Jim Otis. He'd been injured the previous season and was suffering from knee trouble.

"I felt like I could probably go ahead and overcome the hurdle and do well, but you have to remember, that was my tenth year. Bud brought in a bunch of young guys . . . and we weren't going to make any drive for the playoffs or anything. I think he wanted to get those young guys in there, and I really didn't play much in the preseason. I could kind of see the writing on the wall."

If Jim understood, Jan Otis didn't. "Until the day I die, I'll never forget that retirement of Jim's," she says. "It was on a Sunday . . . . He called me on the phone and said, 'I'm going to announce my retirement.' I went ballistic. I said, 'Don't let them do that to you,' and he said, 'No, I'm going to retire.' I was real upset and I got off the phone. Then Donna called and she invited Jim and I to dinner.

"I, being Irish, said, 'Donna, I don't know if I want to come.' Donna knew me and she said, 'That's okay. Talk to Jim when he gets home and then you call us.'

"Jim said, 'C'mon. we're going to go.' "

So the Otises showed up for dinner, Jan fuming. "Apparently Donna had warned Bud that I would come in and give it to him with both barrels. Bud said, 'I can't believe Jan would do that.' "

But she did. After cocktails, the four sat down and Jan blasted away. "I proceeded to tell him how wrong I thought he was, how Jim was one of the most productive players, and how could he take a guy and use him all through camp and the preseason and then cut him? I said, 'You've used him for nothing but cannon fodder, and I'm not happy with this situation. He's very unhappy. This was everything to Jim and then you go and cut him after all this.' Bud sat there and listened to me and was very polite, never got angry. You could never see any anger on his face."

Jan then waited for Dad to respond. "He said, 'Okay, you've had your say; now it's my time.' He told me how he felt that this wasn't the Jim Otis we knew and the Jim Otis who had played the year before. He said, 'I don't want Jim going out of this game at the bottom after trying to play this year and not being able to produce. Furthermore, there are bench sitters and there are non-bench sitters. Your husband cannot sit the bench. He cannot perform. I felt this was best for Jim. I'm not sure I've convinced Jim of this, but I truly think it is.' As long as I live, I'll swear it *was* the best thing for Jim. That's the way Bud always was. Pro ball didn't make him less caring about those kids than college did. He was concerned about what was going on in their lives. If he had had more time and Billy hadn't been the owner, it might have been a whole different ball game."

Because Donna and Jan were friends, Jan was surprised Donna could keep the secret about Dad's plans for Jim. "The Friday night before it happened, us girls were out together. She never acted any differently, never let on to anybody about anything. I told her later, 'You never even gave me an inkling.' She said she wouldn't have dreamed of it. It wasn't her place."

⁂

Before the opening of the '79 season, Dad began to get some hints that the writing might be on the wall for him, too. One month prior to the opening game against Pittsburgh, he requested four tickets for the manager of the Missouri Athletic Club. A week before the game, when Dad asked Cardinals' vice president of operations, Joe Sullivan, about the tickets, he was told Bidwill hadn't yet made up his mind whether Dad could have them. Dad finally wrote out a personal check for the four tickets, but the check was returned because the Cardinals had decided to deny the head coach his ticket request.

In the preseason, the Cardinals played Kansas City for the Governor's Cup—the championship of the state of Missouri—and many of the players' wives had driven to the game. The players asked if some of the spouses could fly back. There were many vacant seats, because after the game, Dad had given the team the weekend off. As soon as the plane was airborne, Bidwill tore into Dad, screaming, "Where will it end? Now you want to take charge of travel arrangements, too!"

The 1979 season was nearly as nightmarish as the previous year. Cain was dead, and by the second week in October, there were season-ending injuries to Dan Dierdorf, John Zook and Tim Kearney. Mark Arneson was out of commission for a few weeks, as were Tom Banks, Terry Stieve and Mel Gray. The offensive line almost never played together as a complete unit. Then Jim Hart was injured, too.

By the last week in October, the won-lost record was 2-6, though the defense was allowing only nineteen points per game, and there were bright spots in the offensive play of Ottis Anderson and the kicking of Steve Little. The Cardinals stood last in their division, but their statistics were not that much different from the league leaders—and in fact at the midpoint of the season they had won two games more than they had won to that point the year before.

Nonetheless, says Dierdorf, "I think they should have put a giant X through 1979 . . . because the football team never got over J.V.'s death. He was an immensely popular player. He'd fought back from the Achilles tendon surgery and come back to the point where he was 100 percent—better than ever, and then he just dies on the football field right in front of us.

"I remember walking around the campus at 3:00 a.m. with a bunch of the other guys talking. Football requires such a tremendous focus where you just block out everything else that goes on around you. It's so demanding, and there's physical pain involved and a commitment to play the game .... When J.V. died, all of us lost our focus. We were walking around going, 'It isn't that important.' It hit us so hard because we all loved J.V. He was classy. When you're killed in an automobile accident or your plane goes down or you get sick, that's different. He died with his uniform on, playing the game, right in front of us. It was devastating."

Also during the first half of the season a major public relations donnybrook developed over Jim Hart's play-calling abilities. Joe Sullivan's public statements about the situation included, "I know this. We lost our first eight games last year. Hart called the plays. We won six out of our last eight. The plays were called for him." Dad, however, told the press the play-calling system had remained the same throughout all of 1978, saying, "We're not doing anything differently than we did a year ago. We signal in every play; if Jim has something he likes better, he can go with it. But I am responsible for every play that's called."

Sullivan also said, "Jim was a plus fifty percent passer when the plays were called for him, and the present way, he is minus fifty percent." In fact, Hart was at exactly fifty percent.

Rich Koster posed the question in his column, "Is [the play calling controversy] just a small disagreement over a small issue? Or is it symptomatic of the Big Red politic, which previously has on occasion burst into the open?"

Surely Dad and the management were in disagreement. Steve Pisarkiewicz, back-up quarterback, was Bidwill's choice to pilot the team; Dad favored Jim Hart. A major reason was that Pisarkiewicz had only ten percent vision in one eye, and Dad considered vision the most necessary weapon for a quarterback to have in his arsenal. He felt the vision problem rendered Pisarkiewicz incapable of playing in the NFL.

He and Billy went to the mat over the issue. "Billy called Bud in," says Hart, "and said he wanted Pisarkiewicz to play the rest of the season and Bud said no. Billy said, 'I want to see what he can do.' Bud said, 'I can save you time and energy. I know what he can do. He can't do anything, and I'm not going to play him.'"

After the thirteenth game of the season, Bidwill dumped Dad. At the team meeting, Dad told the team ,"I'm no longer the coach," and left the dressing room. Fifteen minutes later, various members of the team came to his office and presented a strike plan. If he was no longer the coach, they did not intend to play the next game. Dad was stunned, and explained that the repercussions to their careers would be so enormous he couldn't allow them to take such an action. "You're smarter than that," he said, and after another two-hour team meeting, the players abandoned the idea.

No doubt hurt and chagrined, Dad kept his emotions to himself. At the press conference to announce his firing, he said, "The owner of anything has the right to run it the way he wants to run it." And months later, when reporters were still hounding him to answer Bidwill in kind, he refrained, saying only, "It was just one of those things." He did say he felt the Cardinals were only a few players short of being contenders and that patience and a good draft process were required to build a winning tradition, but that was about as fiery as he got, at least publicly, about his abrupt departure from the team. Donna remembers, "What he said was he had always respected pro football players, but respected them even more after working with them because of their total dedication to their profession. I don't think he really ever had any regrets about the whole experience."

Hart says, "The thing that always bothered me about Bud's dismissal was that I worried he had defended me to the point where it cost him his job. He said, 'Nah, don't worry about that. He was going to fire me anyway.' But I'll always think about that. If I hadn't been part of the equation, maybe it wouldn't have happened."

Banks recalls the aftermath. "The worst time was when they dropped the ax on Bud. I remember we went to Chicago to play the last game of the season . . . . We got the hell beat out of us. We had a party at Jim Hart's house and everybody signed the game ball and we gave it to Coach afterwards just to tell him how much we appreciated all of his efforts.

"We all knew how much he had banged his head against a stone wall and tried to make things different. I remember him coming out to Jim's house where we all felt like we could say to him that we appreciated his efforts. I feel good about that. Hell, it don't matter how things happen on the field, if somebody is giving it all they've got and doing things to make it better, that's what you remember."

That's what Dad remembered, too.

&

Following the Cardinal adventure, Dad returned to his business interests, the USGF and broadcasting. It was during this period of his broadcast career that Bill Flemming noticed Dad was starting to tire. The trajectory that had shot upward since his youth was reversing direction, and the final opponent was the one he could not vanquish.

# Epilogue

ﾒ

*"There hath passed away a glory from the earth . . ."*
—*Wordsworth*

The aging process can be difficult and sad. In Dad's case, it became so. Beset first by congestive heart failure in 1986, he was further weakened by a series of strokes that robbed him of his sight and impaired some aspects of his memory.

Even as his strength drained, his zest for living and his adventuresome spirit seemed to grow. He was still concerned with always doing his best, and his gentlemanly demeanor stayed with him until his final days. As I think of his activities during the latter stages of his life, several pictures crowd my memory.

In September of 1991, a huge testimonial dinner was held in Dad's honor in Oklahoma, with more than 500 people in attendance. Curt Gowdy served as master of ceremonies; Chris Schenkel and Jim Simpson were guest speakers, as were many of Dad's former All-American players.

Lee Allan Smith headed the Bud Wilkinson Tribute Committee. "I was very close to Billy Vessels, Eddie Crowder, Buddy Leake and Dick Ellis," he says. "We talked about how overdue this was and ... why hadn't it ever occurred? There were a lot of former players and players that came after him that urged us to do it. That evening brought Bud's players and fans back in touch .... They got to talk to him; they got to talk to each other."

The evening's program called for Dad to respond after the series of remembrances and toasts was completed. "He hadn't spoken publicly for a long time," says Donna. "He was concerned that he would not be able to do it up to his own standards. So he practiced. He always practiced before he spoke, but now he practiced even harder—in fact, right up until we left to go to the dinner."

Pat and I stayed with him as he sat backstage, conserving his energy. But when he approached the lectern, though he was frail and his voice not as robust as it once had been, the message was vintage Bud. He spoke about the will to prepare—the will he had shown so strongly in getting ready for that evening.

The next day, Dad was honored at halftime at the Oklahoma football stadium. The sell-out crowd gave him a standing ovation, and he graciously raised his hat in a salute of thanks.

Smith concludes, "Right after it happened, not only did people talk about how terrible it was Bud's recognition hadn't occurred before, but people like Jim Weatherall and several others called and said, 'I want to thank you and tell you how great this was and how meaningful it was.' "

For Dad, too.

و

About a month after the tribute, Dad finally admitted his eyesight had deteriorated to the point he required a driver. He couldn't park properly, and his car had taken a beating on both sides and the fenders.

Dad's friend Floyd Warmann approached Jack Flach, a retired political editor and columnist for the St. Louis *Globe Democrat*, asking Flach if he could help out with the driving. Flach agreed, if it was to be only for a couple of hours a day.

Flach says, "Bud had his own routes. We didn't vary from one street to the other. He reminded me of a very disciplined football coach, where this is the way it's been and this is the way it's going to be. Instead of going to the drive-up window of the neighborhood Boatmen's Bank, it had to be the downtown Boatmen's Bank. He went up and down about twenty steps at that bank. He was going to do it, and he was going to do it by himself .... He didn't want anyone holding on to him or anything.

"Politics was my living," Flach continues. "My hobby was sports. It seemed as though sports was Bud's work and his hobby was politics. I'd start talking about the old Oklahoma football teams, and he'd start talking politics. He'd want my views on this, and I'd want his views on that. Neither of us could carry on a conversation in one line for more than two or three minutes because he'd get into my field and I'd try to get into his."

ða

In October 1992, Dad suffered a stroke that seriously impaired his memory and obliterated his eyesight. Flach says, "The morning of the stroke when Donna called me and I picked him up, he was wavering walking down the steps of his home. I asked him if he was feeling all right, and he said, 'Oh, yes, I just didn't sleep too well last night.' When we got to the car, I noticed he couldn't see the door handle. I took him back inside. Donna told me she was fearful he might have suffered a minor stroke .... There was just a night and day difference in him.

"After this stroke, he went downhill so fast," Flach remembers. "He wouldn't go into the store or the bank. He'd sit in the car and sleep or close his eyes. There was no interest anymore."

Nonetheless, Dad's lifelong positive attitude remained intact. "His philosophy remained the same," says Flach. "He'd say, 'It always could be worse.' I made a practice of occasionally mentioning when I saw a newspaper article about somebody in bad shape and not going to live much longer, and he'd say, 'That's what I mean, Jack. I could always be worse than I am now.' "

I, too, noticed a change in Dad. During visits or telephone calls, it became apparent to me that he was losing his grasp on events around him. He couldn't remember what football game he was listening to, whether he had taken his medicine or to whose home he and Donna were going for dinner.

ða

ॐ

For many years, Dad and Donna traveled to Europe. Because his health had failed so dramatically and there probably would be no more chances for such trips, in the summer of 1993, my wife, Rita, and I joined Dad and Donna on a trip to the south of France, one of Dad's favorite places on earth, and then on to Paris. He had great difficulty navigating stairways and steps, but his debility could not impair his enjoyment. He savored the cheeses and wines, and reveled even in the size of the napkins at the Tour d'Argent, where we all had a spectacular meal together. He told me how much he regretted not being able to see the sights he loved, but said he had been there so many times, he could sense what was happening, and he was happy.

Though Dad was patient and courteous, he still had a great deal of resolve, and when he thought he was right, he insisted on having his way. During an exhausting nine-hour drive to Paris, he was quiet and peaceful, sleeping occasionally. When we arrived in Paris, we debated about finding a taxi to lead us to the hotel so we wouldn't get lost. We were confident we could find the way, but after it became apparent we didn't know where we were, Dad demanded we find a taxi. He must have reiterated this request at least twenty times within a fifteen-minute period, which obviously frustrated the rest of us, who were tired after the strenuous drive. We finally found a taxi, and discovered Dad was right. We never would have found the hotel on our own. After we arrived at the hotel, he returned to his quiet demeanor.

Though there were moments like this throughout the trip, most of the time Dad maintained his enthusiastic sparkle, sharing with us the beauty of the places he loved.

ॐ

In January, 1994, Dad underwent a heart procedure to open a valve and improve his breathing. A month later he fell down a flight of stairs at home and dislocated his shoulder. Pat visited with him and returned saying he didn't think he would ever see our father alive again.

I visited Dad the next week and was with him for six of his last eight days—a time when I frequently shed tears in private.

When I first walked into the house, a nurse's voice greeted me. The effect was strange. It was the first time in my life Dad had not met me either at the door or in the living room.

The first thing I noticed when I entered Dad and Donna's room was his open mouth. His breathing was labored; throughout the evening he was disoriented, slurring his words and confusing me with Pat.

The next morning I met Jim Timmerberg, who coordinated Dad's care after Dad was released from the hospital. "When I interviewed for the job," he says, "Bud was still in the hospital. When he came home I don't think anyone knew he was dying except the doctor. I knew shortly after I came on . . . . He had wanted to come home. Home was important to him.

"I was struck," Timmerberg says, "by how polite and kind he was . . . . I didn't detect any of the normal sort of animosity toward caregivers that sometimes happens when people can't take care of themselves. I told him one time that our roles were reversed now, and I was the coach. He smiled and said, 'Yes, that's true,' and he was more than willing to do things the way I asked him to.

"He could be firm, though. He and I got into it only once. He let me know in no uncertain terms there was no way I was going to do what I thought I was going to do. I think I started to repeat it, and he said, 'I don't want to talk about it.' I continued to say it, and I thought he was going to come out of that bed and get me."

"He was really a player," Timmerberg concludes. "He started out as a player and he ended up as a player—a team player right up to the end. And even though he had a full complement of nurses, he pushed himself to his personal limits."

I was so grateful for Timmerberg and the other nurses who filled Dad's last days with such empathy, sensitivity and kindness. It allowed the rest of us just to be his family and not to worry about medical details. He couldn't have been in better hands.

ᘒ⧫

If anyone ever doubted Dad's toughness and resolve in life, those qualities were reconfirmed by the manner in which he handled his death. When I returned to St. Louis after a two-day absence, there was a noticeable difference in his appearance. His eyes were only half open. He couldn't speak. His breathing was irregular.

On Wednesday evening, February 9, 1994, after getting into my pajamas, I came into Dad's room to kiss him goodnight. Donna and I asked the nurse to notify us if there was any change in Dad's breathing. Suddenly his breath became softer and slower. I asked, "Is this it?" The nurse nodded.

Donna and I stayed next to Dad's bed and continued to talk to him, stroke him and hold him. Donna asked the nurse to call Neville Grant, Dad's doctor and friend, who came immediately.

During the last fifteen minutes of his life, I stood next to Dad's bed, looking at him, my thoughts racing. I reflected on all he had done for so many people. I thought about the sheer magnitude of his life. I remembered his kindness, patience, gentleness, selflessness, and his fatherly love—all combined with the toughness, determination, competitiveness and love for life that made him what he was. I was so proud he was my father.

He continued to breathe more slowly and much more peacefully. Donna lay next to him, cradling him until he took his last breath.

ঌ

Among Dad's effects was an undated letter from a member of one of the Sooner teams who had wanted to be a great football player, but who had never achieved glory on the gridiron. He was graduating and going first to the Marine Corps and then to law school, and he obviously wanted to share some feelings with Dad. The letter read in part:

*The great truths which I was able to observe through watching your conduct are the most valuable things [that] will leave the university with me.*

*You have showed us how to be gentlemen at all times . . . . To conduct myself as a man in the face of any adversity, any temptation, and especially in the face of the easy way out . . . has been the greatest lesson I have learned . . . . This lesson will go with me wherever I may be sent in life. I hope that someday I, too, will be able to maintain such an example as to help others discover the true meaning of life.*

*May you always meet with good fortune, sir, and may you continue leading others as you have led me . . . . You will always have my gratitude, my respect and admiration, and my sincere friendship.*

For Dad, there could be no greater tribute.

# Index